(PARTICIPATORY) ACTION RESEARCH

PRINCIPLES, APPROACHES AND APPLICATIONS

RESEARCH METHODOLOGY AND DATA ANALYSIS

Additional books in this series can be found on Nova's website under the Series tab.

Additional e-books in this series can be found on Nova's website under the eBooks tab.

RESEARCH METHODOLOGY AND DATA ANALYSIS

(PARTICIPATORY) ACTION RESEARCH

PRINCIPLES, APPROACHES AND APPLICATIONS

JOSEPH CALDER

AND

JACOB FOLETTA

EDITORS

nova
science publishers
New York

NOTICE TO THE READER

Library of Congress Cataloging-in-Publication Data

ISBN: 978-1-53613-041-6

Published by Nova Science Publishers, Inc. † *New York*

CONTENTS

Preface   vii

Chapter 1   Exploring the Benefits of Reform Mathematics:
                 Goals in Becoming Mathematically Literate   1
                 Laura Ann Hayden

Chapter 2   Literature Circles as Tools for Student
                 Dialogue and Empowerment   57
                 Ryan Flessner

Chapter 3   Action Research: The Researcher's Role
                 and Engagement in K-20 STEM Education   89
                 Andrea C. Burrows, Meghan Lockwood,
                 Christina Belardo and Edward Janak

Chapter 4   Teaching Participatory Action Research:
                 The Search for Pedagogical Insights   125
                 Lawrence Susskind, Dayna Cunningham
                 and Isadora Araujo Cruxên

Chapter 5   Using Action Research and an Imported
                 Conceptual Framework to Study the Individual
                 Dimension of Curriculum Relevance   151
                 Francisco Sousa

Chapter 6   Transforming University Teaching: Participatory
                  Action Research to Promote Disruptive Practices   **177**
                  Elia Fernández-Díaz, Carlos Rodríguez-Hoyos
                  and Adelina Calvo

Chapter 7   Action Research to Improve Higher Education   **197**
                  Alecsandra Ventura

Chapter 8   Teacher-Centred Action Research in a Remote
                  Participatory Environment: A Reflection on a
                  Case of Chemistry Curriculum Innovation in a
                  Swiss Vocational School   **215**
                  Ivano Laudonia and Ingo Eilks

Chapter 9   From Group Development to Intervention:
                  Applying Participatory Action Research in Italy   **233**
                  Nadia Rania, Alessandra Brameri,
                  Laura Migliorini and Emanuela Gandolfo

Chapter 10   The Application of Participatory Action Research
                  to Enhance the Health Care of the
                  Wood-Carving Community   **251**
                  Susanha Yimyam and Avorn Opatpatanakit

Index   **285**

PREFACE

In this book, authors present current research on the implementation of reform mathematics in order to identify, explore, and evaluate five specific goals. Students were presented with problem solving activities that correlated with real-world situations. During this process, students tracked their confidence and growth as mathematicians. Next, the ways in which students learn to effectively engage in natural discussions related to the literature they are reading are examined. Barriers to the implementation of literature circles in the classroom are discussed, and ideas for successful execution are highlighted. Action research (AR) leaders' roles are explored through two studies, with the frame constituting of K-20 science, technology, engineering, and mathematics (STEM) education and how participant engagement leads to AR project insight. The authors provide suggestions for future AR leaders. This compilation goes on to discuss how teaching Participatory Action Research (PAR) in MIT's Department of Urban Studies and Planning has led to focus on the responsibilities of action researchers and their obligations to the communities and places in which they work; and the importance of building the capacity of community members so that they can take control of the research being done about, with, and for them. The authors explore the way in which Curriculum Studies have addressed relevance and by proposing a framework for the study of curriculum relevance in general, which was adapted from literature on Science Education. The proposal considers three dimensions of relevance: societal, vocational, and individual. A chapter is included which fully addresses the analysis of one of the cases developed in the authors' previous work, in which students have to reconstruct their memories about the experiences they had during compulsory education in order to compare them with the experiences they have during the practicum. The authors share their concerns about the process of accompaniment, the process of student participation in the design and assessment of the subjects, and the search for situated and transformative learning in a university context. The use of action research in higher education is proposed, especially in programs that use practical approaches such as residency programs in healthcare. The text discusses similar themes such as andragogy, meaningful learning, active learning, and systemic thinking. Additionally, a teacher-driven approach for changes in teaching chemical bonding was chosen, inspired by the PAR model suggested by Eilks and Ralle. The authors determine that remote networking of a teacher action researcher with a PAR-driven community of practitioners and academic educational researchers helped strengthen the process of research and development and contributed to strengthen the teacher's continuous professional development. Subsequently, an application of participatory action research (PAR) conducted in Italy is illustrated. In describing the structure of action research, it can first be asserted that it is not a linear methodology of research but instead a cyclical process that proceeds through greater levels of complexity. In conclusion, the book aims to determine the relationship between the principles, approaches and applications of participatory action research (PAR) by using a case study of wood-carving workers. The authors maintain that although this project was successful in increasing health awareness of the workers and the community, long-term impact and sustainability of networking and activities need to be examined.

Chapter 1 - This study represents one educator's teacher research project that evaluated the benefits of reform mathematics in a multi-age $3^{rd}/4^{th}$ grade classroom. With the implementation of reform mathematics, five specific goals (NCTM, 1989) were identified, explored, and evaluated through this research. In order to connect the mathematical skills they were learning in the classroom to the society in which they live, students were presented with problem solving activities that correlated with real-world situations. During this process, students tracked their confidence and growth as mathematicians. This study provides insight into the benefits of implementing reform mathematics in an elementary classroom and how NCTM's five essential mathematical goals were met in the process.

Chapter 2 - Studying the implementation of literature circles in his fourth grade classroom, Flessner examines the ways in which his students learn to effectively engage in natural discussions related to the literature they are reading. Barriers to the implementation of literature circles in the classroom are discussed, and ideas for successful execution are highlighted. Engaging students as co-researchers, Flessner utilizes literature circles as a way for his students to take control of their learning. This empowerment leads to the co-construction of a tool to evaluate the effectiveness of the literature circle process. Limitations to teacher research, generally, and to this study, specifically, are discussed at the end of the chapter along with the study's significance and suggestions for further research. The chapter's Epilogue highlights the author's journey in the fifteen years since the completion of this study. Additional readings are offered for readers who wish to further pursue the topic(s) of literature circles and/or teacher research.

Chapter 3 - This chapter explores the action research (AR) leaders' roles through two studies. The frame is K-20 science, technology, engineering, and mathematics (STEM) education and integration and how participant engagement leads to AR project insight. Specifically, the authors set the stage with the evolution of science education and then use an informal Girl Scout water quality project and a college level science and art integration project as means of analyzing what worked and what is needed in K-20 science education AR projects. The authors end the chapter with a focus on AR leaders and offer suggestions to consider. The authors recognize and value that citizen science, or inclusion of non-professionals in scientific research, as well as unusual stakeholders can increase scientific knowledge and involve communities in solutions to problems. The authors investigated science education through AR projects that touch on the three dimensions of the Next Generation Science Standards (NGSS) and the progression of new ideas. As a methodology, AR was embraced, and the stakeholders' roles were explored. Results show that the AR leaders' roles should include participating completely in an AR project, embracing conflict as a normal part of the process, accentuating stakeholder voice, promoting process engagement, and actively looking for barriers to the AR process. These are vital factors for contextual understanding. Implications include increased AR impact through action items for K-20 AR leaders and stakeholders, which could impact the success of a science focused AR project.

Chapter 4 - Most graduate social science departments and professional degree programs require their students to study both qualitative and quantitative research methods. This binary focus typically glosses over questions such as who defines the subject matter and scope of the research and who owns or controls research findings. In this chapter, the authors discuss how teaching Participatory Action Research (PAR) in MIT's Department of Urban Studies and Planning has pushed us to focus on (1) the responsibilities of action researchers and their obligations to the communities and places in which they work; and (2) the importance of building the capacity of community members so that they can take control of the research being done about, with, and for them. While various manuals have suggested the best ways of doing this kind of work in practice, very little attention has been given to how to teach PAR methods to graduate students and research partners. The authors offer six considerations that they consider central to PAR pedagogy and, in the remainder of the chapter, describe how each of these considerations has informed the intellectual framework and pedagogical strategies at the heart of their teaching. One of the big surprises for us has been the extent to which a half-semester PAR module can radically alter the way professional degree candidates think about the rest of their course work and future careers. The authors conclude with an invitation to their academic colleagues who teach quantitative and qualitative research methods, but do not include any discussion of PAR-oriented issues and approaches in their courses.

Chapter 5 - Curriculum relevance has not been presented as a priority topic in Curriculum Studies. Nevertheless, some researchers within this field have addressed that same topic in ways that suggest that there is much work to be done in its conceptualization. Interestingly, potential contributions to such conceptualization can be found in other fields, within the wider field of Education. For example, some research on both Mathematics Education and Science Education has addressed issues of content relevance in these specific contexts. The conceptual frameworks that directed the studies can be considered in the context of Curriculum Studies in general, although the above-mentioned researchers do not usually call for such generalization. Accordingly, the chapter starts out by examining how Curriculum Studies have addressed relevance and by proposing a framework for the study of curriculum relevance in general, which was adapted from literature on Science Education. The proposal considers three dimensions of relevance: societal, vocational, and individual. Then the text narrows the focus to the individual dimension and presents some notes related to its meaning. The chapter proceeds with a discussion on the importance of action research in the study of the individual dimension of curriculum relevance. Finally, an action research project, which was focused on students' acknowledgement of curriculum relevance, is presented. The project took place in the Azores Islands, Portugal, and was carried out by a team that included researchers from the only university located in the region, as well as teachers of elementary schools from that same region. The problem that prompted the emergence of the project was some teachers' complaints about some students' alleged lack of interest for the school and the curriculum. Action research allowed the team to deepen the participants' understanding of the problem, which, in turn, facilitated the design of instructional strategies that took the students' views of curriculum relevance into consideration. Data reveal a tendency towards both future relevance and extrinsic aspects of relevance. Nevertheless, the outcomes of the project include evidence of improvements in the students' acknowledgment of both present relevance and intrinsic aspects of relevance.

Chapter 6 - The work presented in this chapter forms part of an innovation project in Higher Education focused on Lesson Study (LS). Through a process of action-research the authors have succeeded in generating actions to transform their teaching practice and reflect on the knowledge that has emerged during the course of the actions they devised. In addition to describing the process of action-research the authors have designed, this chapter fully addresses the analysis of one of the cases developed in their work, in which students have to reconstruct their memories about the experiences they had during compulsory education in order to compare them with the experiences they have during the practicum. Likewise, the authors have been able to share their concerns about the process of accompaniment, the process of student participation in the design and assessment of the subjects and the search for situated and transformative learning in a university context, among other issues. Finally, based on the review of critical incidents that have concerned us the authors have proposed improvements they consider appropriate in order to continue the next cycle of action-research.

Chapter 7 - Action research in higher education can improve students' critical thinking and promotes innovation. However, many teachers do not know the method or do not know how to use it to make teaching and learning more effective. This paper proposes the use of action research in higher education, especially in programs that use practical approaches such as residency programs in health care. With a clear and results-oriented approach, the text presents the educational advantages of action research and the challenges to overcome. It also proposes an innovative model of learning assessment based on integrating theory and practice. For this, the paper uses the two juxtaposed and interdependent cycles of action research, the first cycle focused on problem-solving and the second describing the research process. Within this context, the text discusses similar themes such as andragogy, meaningful learning, active learning, and systemic thinking.

Chapter 8 - In 2002, Eilks and Ralle suggested a specific model of how to apply participatory action research (PAR) for domain specific educational research and innovation. The model was described for the field of science education and was used in numerous projects and cases for evidence-based innovation of the science curriculum and its related media and pedagogy. The model bases on a close cooperation of a group of teachers with science educators from the university under involvement of graduate student teachers and PhD students in science education. However, it is not always possible to create a suitable environment on-site for such a research model if the practice field is remote to other potentially interested teachers and far away from a feasible academic institution fitting the research and innovation interest. This chapter describes such a case. It deals with research-based innovation of the pedagogy of chemistry teaching in vocational education in southern Switzerland. A teacher-driven approach for changes in teaching chemical bonding was chosen, inspired by the PAR model suggested by Eilks and Ralle. A remote access of the individual teacher researcher was established via email and Skype with an already existing PAR network of secondary chemistry teachers in the west of Germany. The network is coordinated and supported by an academic group experienced in PAR from northern Germany, namely from the University of Bremen. The chapter discusses the project and reflects on how the remote networking of the teacher action researcher with a PAR-driven community of practitioners and academic educational researchers helped strengthening the process of research and development and contributed to strengthen the teacher's continuous professional development.

Chapter 9 - Since its origins, participatory action research has been characterized as a methodology that is able to promote change within the real world of everyday life. Participatory action research, as Lewin understood it, is not academic research but instead is oriented toward modifying the "field" and the context through its knowledge; it is a co-generative process through which professional researchers and interested members of a local organization, community, or specially created organization collaborate to research, understand and resolve problems of mutual interest. Participatory action research is a social process in which professional knowledge, process skills, research skills and democratic values are the basis for co-created knowledge and social change. This methodology tries to transcend the difference between theory and practice in an attempt to activate a circular process between knowledge and the transformation of reality. In describing the structure of action research, it can first be asserted that it is not a linear methodology of research but instead a cyclical process that proceeds through greater levels of complexity and recursivity. The aim of this chapter is to illustrate an application of participatory action research (PAR) conducted in Italy. The authors illustrate the three phases of a PAR project realized in fourteen small municipalities in a suburban area located in the hinterland of a medium-sized city in northwestern Italy to promote a change in students' feelings, perceptions and knowledge of well-being and, in particular, their relations regarding the use of new technologies.

Chapter 10 - The Khun-Kong community is famous for its woodcarving production, which contributes significantly to the local economy. However, the work conditions and environment may be harmful and detrimental to the workers' health. This developmental research study, 'Enhancing the Health of the Wood-Carving Community,' used community collaboration to engage with various sectors and groups. Action research is considered one of the most important strategies in confronting health problems and promoting community health. The purpose of this study was to build the self-care capacity among wood-carving workers and their community. The study was divided into two phases: a community and health impact assessment phase; and an implementation phase. Both qualitative and quantitative methods were used in Phase One (community and health impact assessment) to investigate the work conditions and the environments that may impact the health of wood-carving workers and their community. Community-based participatory research was used in Phase Two (community implementation phase) to develop a network of woodcarving workers to promote self-care, to enhance the capability for self-care among peer leaders of wood-carving workers, as well as to develop a self-care guidebook and media tools for a health promotion campaign. This chapter focuses on Phase Two to draw linkages between the principles, approaches and applications of community-based participatory action research through this case study on health promotion among wood-carving workers. Participatory learning was used for peer leader training. Community participation aided the development a self-care network for a health promotion campaign as well as a self-care guidebook and media materials. The self-care network consisted of the research team, a community committee, and trained peer leaders. Quantitative data were analyzed using frequency, percentage and a t-test, whereas qualitative data were analyzed using content analysis. During *Phase Two* one guidebook and three types of media instruments, namely posters, VCD, and radio spots, were developed. These materials were examined by a group of workers for appropriateness for both content and presentation and were found to be satisfactory. After receiving training, peer leaders' knowledge and awareness of work-related health problems and preventive self-care increased significantly. Their skills and confidence in risk assessment and self-care instruction also improved. The self-care network identified new ways of thinking, problem solving, and sustainable self-care. Self-reliance was perceived as an important aspect of health care. Finally, workers' health status, perception of health risk and health behaviors also improved. In the community, skills in problem identification and problem solving were learned. Although this project was successful in increasing health awareness of the workers and the community, the long-term impact and sustainability of networking and activities need to be examined. Furthermore, co-operation with other relevant institutions or professions are suggested to produce and use the guidebook and media materials with other woodcarving workers to improve work conditions and the environment.

In: (Participatory) Action Research   ISBN: 978-1-53613-041-6
Editors: J. Calder and J. Foletta   © 2018 Nova Science Publishers, Inc.

Chapter 1

EXPLORING THE BENEFITS OF REFORM MATHEMATICS: GOALS IN BECOMING MATHEMATICALLY LITERATE

Laura Ann Hayden[*]

Indianapolis Public Schools/Butler University Laboratory School
Indianapolis, Indiana, US

ABSTRACT

This study represents one educator's teacher research project that evaluated the benefits of reform mathematics in a multi-age $3^{rd}/4^{th}$ grade classroom. With the implementation of reform mathematics, five specific goals (NCTM, 1989) were identified, explored, and evaluated through this research. In order to connect the mathematical skills they were learning in the classroom to the society in which they live, students were presented with problem solving activities that correlated with real-world situations. During this process, students tracked their confidence and growth as mathematicians. This study provides insight into the benefits of

---

[*] Corresponding Author Email: HaydenL@myips.org. Phone: 847-363-5017.

implementing reform mathematics in an elementary classroom and how NCTM's five essential mathematical goals were met in the process.

Keywords: reform mathematics, mathematical literacy, teacher research

INTRODUCTION

"Miss Hayden, I love math. Can we just do it all day?" suggested Cornelia[1], an enthusiastic 4th grade student in my 3rd/4th grade classroom. These are the words and excitement all teachers want to hear coming from their students. In that moment, I saw myself within the ecstatic, overjoyed, and eager to learn 10-year old little girl. Cornelia was a student who was new to our school, and I was intrigued by her new found joy and interest in mathematics. She reminded me of a similar moment I experienced on my journey in growing as an educator when I discovered my love of math.

At the completion of my undergraduate education, I was young, eager, and determined to find any teaching job that would begin my career as an educator. After accepting my first teaching position as a 4th grade teacher in an urban school district, I was prepared to learn from veteran educators. Relying on the educators at my school, I quickly conformed to the culture of my school. This culture promoted an essentialist teaching philosophy where it was believed that "an effective core curriculum in the early grades – the chief practical need of American elementary education – must necessarily take a *somewhat* traditional flavor" (Hirsh, 2009, p. 56). As a new teacher, I didn't allow myself to have the experience to develop or voice my opinion, which had a major influence on my teaching throughout my first year as an educator. Between my first and second year of teaching I took advantage of various professional development opportunities that my school, district, and community held and was intrigued by the various practices that were being introduced and implemented in schools in my

---

[1] Names of all students and other individuals in this project are pseudonyms to protect the confidentiality of those engaged in this research project.

community; specifically, *reform mathematics*[2] (Hiebert, J., Carpenter, T.P., Fennema, E., Fuson, K.C., Wearne, D., Murrary, H., Oliver, A., & Human, P., 1997; McDonald, 2014; National Council of Teachers of Mathematics (NCTM), 1989; Schoenfeld, 2004). I wanted to shift my instruction by including key elements of reform mathematics into my teaching. Some of these key elements include: project work, group and individual assignments, discussions between all members of the classroom community, various mathematical methods, and exposition by me, the teacher (NCTM, 1989).

Being open to having "a change in attitude and beliefs as well as in practice and expectations" (Hiebert, et al., 1997, p. xiv), I began to implement aspects of reform mathematics into my classroom. As I deepened my understanding of reform mathematics and developed as a teacher, I saw my passion for learning, discovering, and teaching math increase simply by changing the way I was thinking about how mathematics education should be explored in the classroom. Through this journey, I began to find my voice as an educator through believing and supporting the idea of reform mathematics. I found myself being more confident as a teacher in my mathematics instruction, and my students showed confidence as mathematical thinkers. I also saw a change in attitude when it was time for our math block. Students were making deeper connections as well as furthering their ability to talk as mathematicians, which allowed me to learn from and develop the concept of reform mathematics. Discovering a belief in a philosophy that was different from practices at the school where I taught prevented me from fully exploring and implementing teaching techniques aligned with reform mathematics. After three years of teaching, I took a position at a school that not only supported the idea of exploring reform mathematics but also allowed me to teach in a more progressive student-centered way (Dewey, 1938; Harold, 1972; & Hartung, 1939). I knew that the change in school and district would allow me the opportunity to continue implementing and developing

---

[2] Reform mathematics is foundational to this study and will be further explored in the literature review.

techniques and strategies that would support my desire in creating a reform mathematics classroom. As I reflect on my journey of embracing reform mathematics, I am left wondering if my students experience a similar discovery. Some students' school settings have given them exposure to reform mathematics curricula. In comparison, some students come from a more traditional background like Cornelia and myself. Through this study, I wanted to explore the benefits of integrating reform mathematics and/or what barriers my students encountered on their own journey of becoming mathematicians.

QUESTION

As my understanding and research of reform mathematics developed, I continued to implement the concept into my 3rd/4th grade multi-age classroom. Through this I was intrigued to learn that in 1989, the National Council of Teachers of Mathematics developed goals to "insure that all students [had] an opportunity to become mathematically literate" (p. 5). For the purpose of this research, I began to document how - through reform mathematics - my students were meeting the five mathematical goals created for students: (1) students learn to value mathematics, (2) students become confident in their ability to do mathematics, (3) student become mathematical problem solvers, (4) students learn to communicate mathematically, and (5) students learn to reason mathematically (NCTM, 1989, p. 5). This led me to ask the question: *What are benefits to the implementation of reform mathematics in my 3rd/4th grade classroom?*

CONTEXT

District Demographics

This study took place in Indianapolis Public Schools (IPS), an urban district in the United States. The district serves approximately 30,000 students (Indianapolis Department of Education, 2016). According to the demographics listed on the Indiana Department of Education's website (2015), the district is comprised of 48.9% African American students, 25.1% Hispanic students, 20.6% Caucasian students, 4.6% Multiracial students, 0.6% Asian students, 0.1% Native Hawaiian or Other Pacific Islander, and less than 0.1% American Indian students. The Department of Education (2015) also reports 68.1% students qualify for free meals, 2.6% qualify for reduced-priced meals, and 29.3% pay for their meals.

In order to meet the diverse needs of IPS students, the district developed a magnet school program that allows parents to have a choice in where they send their children to school. The magnet schools within IPS appeal to families who are looking to enroll their children in a school with a specialized curriculum, innovative theme, and unique teaching techniques. Although any family can apply to the magnet schools, they are known to have lengthy waitlists.

School Demographics

The Indianapolis Public Schools/Butler University Laboratory School[3] (Lab School), the school where this study took place, was in its fifth year as one of the nine magnet elementary schools in IPS. The Indiana Department of Education's (IDOE) data from the 2015-2016 school year reported that the Lab School had 432 students with 60.6% White students, 25% Black students, 6.7% Multiracial students, 6.3% Hispanic students, 0.9% Asian students, and 0.5% American Indiana students. The Department of Education (2015) also reports 23.8% students qualify for free meals, 3.9% qualify for reduced-priced meals, and 72.2% pay for their meals. With students having a choice in deciding to attend the Lab School,

---

[3] The Lab School has a close partnership with Butler University. Due to this partnership the school and university collaborate through professional development, curriculum writing, and supporting staff members' exploration of the school's unique philosophy.

it is important to note that 94% of the students lived within IPS boundaries, and six percent of the students lived outside of the school district.

Classroom Demographics

The classroom in which this study took place reflected similar demographics to the school. Of the 22 students, 50% were male and 50% were female. The Lab School utilizes a multi-age classroom structure where "some grade-specific teaching may occur because of State-mandated curricula and testing but cross-grade teaching is the norm, based on the teacher's judgment of the developmental level of each child" (Lloyd, 1999, p. 189). Therefore, the classroom being studied had both 3rd and 4th graders as participants. Within this classroom context, 17 students were 3rd graders while 5 students were 4th graders. Although students had the opportunity to opt out of the study, 100% of the students in my class chose to participate. All students who participated in the study are referred to by pseudonyms.

Reggio-Inspired Learning

Within this district, school, and classroom profile, the Lab School is inspired by the Reggio Emilia philosophy (Edwards, Gandini, & Forman 1993, Cadwell, 2003). Although there are many qualities that make the Lab School a Reggio-inspired school, not all will be discussed in this study. The Lab School supports the ideas that all students are capable of constructing their own learning. Students are encouraged to work together and collaborate in order to support learning in the classroom. Through working in pairs or small groups, students develop their own ways of expressing themselves through one of their "Hundred Languages" (Edwards, Gandini, & Forman, 2011, p. 3) (i.e., communicative, artistic, symbolic, cognitive). Through various representations of student learning occurring the classroom, the Reggio philosophy encourages educators to be mindful of the students' thinking.

As teachers, it is expected that we allow students to explore ideas, work on projects, and guide students through both open-ended discovery and problem solving (Cadwell, 2003). The Reggio philosophy encourages teachers to be researchers and learn along with the students. Analyzing students' thinking and learning through *documentation*[4] (Cadwell, 1997, 2003, & Wien, 2011) provides teachers at the Lab School a way to be reflective about how the learning of the students is progressing. Teachers are able to guide their instruction by observing students' interests, asking questions, and generating conversation within the classroom.

Many visitors initially notice the classroom environments at the Lab School. "Every corner of every space has an identity and a purpose, is rich in potential to engage and to communicate, and is valued and cared for by children and adults" (Cadwell, 1997, p. 5). Within the Reggio-inspired philosophy, the environment in which students learn is viewed as the *third teacher*[5] (Cadwell, 2003; Fraser, 2006; Tarini & White, 1998) where students are able to make their own discoveries.

It is important to note that the Reggio theory and Reggio-inspired practice have more commonly been seen and researched within early childhood classrooms. As the Lab School evolved from a K/1 school to a K-5 school, we discovered that the concept of implementing Reggio-inspired practices into all classrooms (i.e., the intermediate classrooms) also needed to evolve. Gandini (1993) suggests that the Reggio model "consists of reflection on theory, practice, and further careful reflection…that is continuously renewed and re-adjusted." Therefore, the concept of Reggio-inspired practices may look different at the Lab School than at other schools that identify as a Reggio-inspired school since we are discovering and adjusting to what all our students need, not just those in early childhood classrooms.

Much research and development has gone into the Lab School creating Reggio-inspired learning environment. The Lab School's philosophy and

---

[4] Documentation is a way educators make the learning that is happening in the classroom visible in order to show students' thoughts and feelings of a specific concept.

[5] Within a Reggio-inspired classroom, the teacher pays close attention to how the environment should be set up in order to promote student exploration.

reform mathematics align with one another in the belief that learning is a naturally active process for students as they discover patterns, make inferences from observations, and question their curiosities (NRC, 1989, p. 43). The research and development of both philosophies, Reggio-inspired learning and reform mathematics, are foundational to this study and provide an opportunity for me to contribute to the research base already in print.

LITERATURE REVIEW

Discussions about the "call for reform in teaching and learning mathematics" (NCTM, 1989, p. 1) have been going on since the late 1800s. The history of how reform mathematics was developed will be discussed since there have been multiple efforts over the years to change how math instruction should be revised to support students' learning in different ways. As the years progressed, so did the need and vision for reform in school mathematics. The journey of how reform mathematics evolved will be reviewed in order to provide background on the efforts educators and students have made thus far in changing mathematics within schools.

Late 1800s – Early 1900s

In the 1890's student enrollment was very low in comparison to today, especially at the high school level. This was due to students only being exposed to the very basics in elementary school and high school being very rigorous. There was a large gap in the curriculum in regards to mathematics education resulting in students not valuing mathematics and not being prepared to enter society with the necessary foundational skills.

With an interest in developing and expanding education for students in the 1890's, educators, from many subject areas, came together and wrote the *Committee of Ten Report* in 1893. This committee of educators discussed a variety of items including best methods of instruction for students and how students should be assessed. Although geared towards intermediate education, it provided a foundation in discussing mathematics education and how it should be integrated within schools. The report suggested that a mathematics curriculum be introduced beginning at the intermediate grades in order to prepare students for secondary school. The report, "had great influence on the organization and teaching of the subjects considered, and it set up discussions that resulted in the appointment of other committees to formulate programs more suited to new conditions" (Briggs, 1931, p. 140). Although the report began the discussion of reform mathematics, it wasn't until the 1900's that scholars specifically interested in mathematics began a more deliberate exploration into how math should be taught.

David Eugene Smith, an established mathematics professor at Columbia University, proposed that educators should work together and think about the philosophy, history, and pedagogy of mathematics (Donoghue, 2003). In doing so, Smith inspired the committee of faculty members of Columbia's Teacher College to work together to bridge the gap between mathematics specialists and regular classroom teachers. *The Teaching of Elementary Mathematics* (Smith, 1900) was created and was the first textbook for educators that included content and teaching methods to be used in schools.

Through this work, it became obvious that pedagogical ideals needed to be explored further. E.H. Moore, president of the American Mathematics Society (AMS) and a mathematician at the University of Chicago, played an important role in developing mathematical pedagogy at all levels through what he called the *laboratory method* (Roberts, 2001, p. 691). Moore believed that a curriculum should depend "on the needs and strengths of the students" (Roberts, 2001, p. 691). This idea aligned well with the well-known theories and writings of John Dewey (1938) who also participated "in the laboratory school connected to the University of Chicago" (p. 7). The overlap between the work of Moore and Dewey served as a stepping-stone in developing reform mathematics in the early 1900's. With Moore's background in mathematics and Dewey's well known educational philosophy of progressivism (Dewey, 1938) they were able to test the ideas of "teaching and learning of mathematics in what became known as the Dewey Laboratory School" (Ratner, 1992, p. 105). Moore suggested that mathematics in the elementary classroom should include guided discovery where the teacher worked as a collaborator and students worked independently or in small groups (Donoghue, 2003, p. 168) based "on the needs and strengths of the students" (Roberts, 2001, p. 691). The view that Moore and Dewey both supported was often referred to as the laboratory method. The method of mathematics education quickly divided the community into supporters and skeptics who not only questioned the teaching of mathematics but education in general.

By 1915, Dewey published *Democracy and Education* in which he shared that the purpose of education should be to "help each individual to develop personal initiative and adaptability so that his or her continuing reassessment of the meaning of experience would lead to growth" (Donoghue, 2003, p. 183). This sparked discussion with educators with different views on the purpose of education and resulted in the development of the *Cardinal Principles of Secondary Education* (National Education Association of the United States) that was issued in 1918. The report identified health, command of fundamental processes, worthy home membership, vocation, citizenship, worthy use of leisure, and ethical character as the main purposes of education. In response to the report, the mathematics education community continued discussing their own ideas and began examining how math was being taught in schools. William Heard Kilpatrick, a leader of the progressive education movement, chaired a committee that identified reasons for inquiry within mathematics education. Due to the committee being primarily educators and not mathematicians, it was quickly criticized resulting in lack of credibility.

Development of National Council of Teachers of Mathematics (NCTM)

Throughout the country, there "were strong local and regional associations and able spokesmen [*sic*] among their ranks, [however], the profession needed a unified voice to defend against educational interlopers" (Donoghue, 2003, p. 186). In order to unite educators and defend mathematics education, 127 mathematics teachers formed the National Council of Teachers of Mathematics (NCTM) in 1920. C.M. Austin, the first president of NCTM gathered teachers from around the country to create an organization that would present constructive programs designed by teachers rather than reformers (Austin, 1921). As the leading voice in mathematics education, NCTM discussed what, when, and how mathematics should be taught to students. NCTM worked as the professional leaders and began developing a math curriculum in order for it to be more prevalent in schools.

New Math, 1957

With the launch of Sputnik in 1957, "the general pubic [began] to see the immediate need for stronger mathematics and science programs in schools" (Payne, 2003, p. 562). At this point, the School Mathematics Study Group (SMSG) (Payne, 2003) began making experimental units that eventually became known as "New Math." The idea of New Math proved to be challenging for students, but it also allowed more opportunity for students to make sense of the math due to the inclusion of social issues and its focus on students making meaning.

SMSG continued to work on improving mathematics education and promoting its benefits; however, incongruence between the content and students' backgrounds was soon noted. Many educators didn't feel comfortable or prepared to implement New Math due to the radical change from math as computational to an emphasis on meaning making. Students and parents also lacked the background necessary to think about math in any other way than computational. Because of this, opinions were quickly voiced and change was demanded.

Due to the push-back in embracing New Math, the idea quickly faded, and educators took on a *back-to-basics* (Schoenfeld, 2004) mentality.

"Back to basics meant textbooks that had no smell of new math" (Payne, 2003, p. 590) and was simply practice in arithmetic. Joseph N. Payne (2003), a former professor of mathematics education at the University of Michigan, believed that this lead to "the worst decade in history for mathematics education" (Payne, 2003, p. 591). With the efforts and progress made in reform mathematics by multiple educators after Sputnik, "the curriculum returned to what it had been before" (Schoenfeld, 2004, p. 258) in focusing on skills and procedures.

Agenda for Action, 1980

During the 1980's, there was a realization in conversations surrounding the need for a change in mathematics education. Many students across the nation were showing minimal ability to problem solve and weren't developing their mathematical knowledge base beyond mastering core procedures. The National Assessment of Educational Progress (NAEP) examined patterns of activity in math classrooms in the late 1980's and discovered that "many students view mathematics as mainly memorizing rules rather than as a creative activity" (Research Advisory Committee of the National Council of Teachers of Mathematics, 1988, p.5). This sparked NCTM's initiative in creating a clearer focus on the future of mathematics and *Agenda for Action* (NCTM, 1980) was created.

> The *Agenda* expressed a vision that was endorsed by numerous groups, given relatively wide circulation, and used to guide NCTM publications and actions from 1980 until the 1989 release of the first *Standards* document, *Curriculum and Evaluation Standards for School Mathematics*. (Fey & Graeber, 2003, p. 553)

One of the primary goals for NCTM when publishing *An Agenda for Action* was to have students develop their problem-solving skills

(Schoenfeld, 2004). Therefore, "goals for mathematics instruction had to be much broader than mere content mastery. Students needed to learn to think mathematically as well as to master the relevant mathematical content" (Schoenfeld, 2004, p. 263).

A Nation at Risk, 1983

A Nation at Risk (National Commission on Excellence in Education) reported in 1983 that "the educational foundations of our society are presently being eroded by a rising tide of mediocrity that threatens our very future as a Nation." With the push for a change within the system, mathematics educators thought about the changes that could be made with curriculum, structure of schools, and education of teachers (National Research Council (NRC), 1989, p. 3). Changes that were discussed focused on the exposure to more math for students and teachers. It was thought that if more teachers were educated or provided more support in the teaching of mathematics, students would be exposed to more and be able to develop a deeper meaning of mathematics. *A Nation at Risk* (1983) stated that a goal was "to develop the talents of all to their fullest" (p. 5) potential. The report noted that this goal could be obtained if there was follow through with the recommendations. While developing the recommendations, the committee held the belief that if students had the desire to be a life-long learner they would be prepared with the skills necessary be involved citizens within their society. It was suggested that the context be expanded, the rigor of the standards and expectations be increased, more time was to be devoted to mathematics in the classroom, the preparation of teachers should be improved, and there should be more leadership support within schools. The recommendations started a different kind of activity within schools due to the new focus of what citizens were now being told was a valuable part of students' education.

Curriculum and Evaluation Standards for School Mathematics, 1989

> All industrialized countries have experienced a shift from an industrial to an information society, a shift that has transformed both the aspects of mathematics that need to be transmitted to students and the concepts and procedures they must master if they are to be self-fulfilled, productive citizens in the next century. (NCTM, 1989, p. 3)

Throughout history, there have been multiple reasons for educators to gather; the change in society had played a major role in when these gatherings occurred. With NCTM established, math educators continued to gather because they wanted to ensure all students received a quality education, they needed to make goals for students to become mathematically literate, and they wanted to promote change. Therefore, NCTM's Board of Directors put together a group of educators called the Commission on Standards for School Mathematics and asked them to develop a vision of what it means for students to be mathematically literate (NCTM, 1989).

Twenty-four members of NCTM collaborated and produced the *Curriculum and Evaluation Standards for School Mathematics* (NCTM, 1989), also known as the *Standards.* This text was a resource many schools used to pull themes from when building their math curriculum. In order for students to explore the *Standards,* goals for students were created to support their development which included: (1) that they learn to value mathematics, (2) that they become confident in their ability to do mathematics, (3) that they become mathematical problem solvers, (4) that they learn to communicate mathematically, and (5) that they learn to reason mathematically (NCTM, 1989, p. 5). The goals that NCTM established were based off of the idea that math for students should be about learning processes where discoveries are made, not memorized.

With the vagueness of the *Standards* and student goals, educators either embraced or challenged how students' mathematical achievement should be assessed; some schools focused more on student portfolios or projects while others administered multiple-choice tests. Following *A Nation at Risk,* the *Standards* intrigued educators as a possible solution to reform mathematics; however, the *Standards* weren't designed to be a national curriculum. By 1993, textbook publishers created reform texts that slowly became popular, but there was still no data gathered stating that reform mathematics curricula were successful. Schoenfeld (1994) states that the implementation of a reform mathematics curriculum made many educators nervous due to the lack of proof that the curriculum was, or could be, successful. The lack of proof was due to a small amount of students being exposed to reform mathematics and those same students not having enough time to continue being immersed into a classroom where reform mathematics was being incorporated. With no consistency in implementation, students and teachers struggled to maintain the desire to continue working on integrating reform mathematics into the classroom.

The underlying factor in making reform mathematics successful is finding a balance of incorporating more projects, qualitative assessments, discussions within the classroom, being exposed to a variety of methods, and clarification about conjectures from the teacher (NCTM, 1989). In order to implement these factors in the classroom, it comes down to how knowledgeable, flexile, and optimistic the teacher is about reform mathematics. "This means knowing the mathematics well, having a sense of when to let students explore and when to tell them what they need to know, and knowing how to nudge them in productive directions" (Schoenfeld, 1994, p. 272). Teachers and parents struggled to wrap their mind around the new way math was being taught due to their background in traditional education and concerns were raised. Schoenfeld (1994) believes that there is a middle ground between reform and traditionalists; this is one reason why there has been so much back and forth in the field of mathematics education.

Principles and Standards for School Mathematics, 2000

At the turn of the millennium, the world was experiencing dramatic changes that, once again, influenced mathematics education. "The need to understand and be able to use mathematics in everyday life and in the workplace [had] never been greater" (NCTM, 2000, p. 4). Citizens with a conceptual understanding of mathematics had considerably more opportunities and options in developing their future in reference to their workplace and technical community. The *Principles and Standards for School Mathematics* (2000) were created by NCTM to address the changes within society. At this point, not all students were provided the same opportunities and support to learn significant mathematical skills. With adequate resources for educators to grow as professionals, the incorporation of technology into mathematics education, engaging mathematical tasks, student exploration about their own conjectures, and promotion of student conversations, it was believed that students would be provide a high-quality and engaging mathematics education.

Principles to Action, 2014

With NCTM's efforts aligned with reform mathematics through the publication of *Agenda for Action* (1980), *Curriculum and Evaluation Standards for School Mathematics* (1989), and *Principles and Standards for School Mathematics* (2000), the development of the Common Core State Standards presented the committee with a new topic to discuss. In order "to ensure that all students learn to become mathematic thinkers and are prepared for any academic career or professional path they choose," (NCTM, 2014, p. vii) *Principles to Action: Ensuring Mathematical Success for All* (2014) was published. *Principles to Action* focused on how teachers, school leaders, and other stakeholders could implement change within their schools by describing the conditions, structures, and policies that must be in place for all schools to effectively reform their mathematics curriculum. Reviewing the realities of mathematics education today, NCTM believes:

> The widespread adoption of the Common Core State Standards for Mathematics presents an unprecedented opportunity for systematic improvement in mathematics education in the United States. The Common Core State Standards offer a foundation for the development of more rigorous, focused, and coherent mathematics curricula, instruction, and assessments that promote conceptual understandings and reasoning as well as skill fluency. This foundation will help to ensure that all students are ready for college and the workplace when they graduate from high school and that they are prepared to take their place as productive, full participants in society. (NCTM, 2014, p. 4)

In educating teachers, school leaders, and stakeholders about the ideas discussed in *Principles to Action*, reform mathematics can once again be a change for mathematics education. After a decade of more prominent experienced teachers and research evidence, reform mathematics is becoming more well known to educators and showing more growth as educators research the benefits of this practice into their classrooms.

NCTM strongly encourages teachers, coaches, specialists, administrators, and educational leaders throughout schools and districts to research their practice. Unless this is done, "beliefs will remain unproductive and obstacles will continue to thwart progress until we collectively and collaboratively confront them and take the action required for solving and overcoming these challenges" (NCTM, 2014, p. 109). Taking action through researching reform mathematics within the classroom is a step toward gathering further evidence and developing resources for other educators that are skeptical. As we have learned through the journey of implementing reform mathematics, teachers' voices are important in promoting reform mathematics. The growth in educator support has allowed for NCTM to push through the obstacles of the past and look ahead to the future as resources for reform mathematics are being developed. This research project is my attempt to contribute to this professional dialogue.

RESEARCH DESIGN

I identify myself as the researcher in this study as a *constructivist* (Creswell, 2003). Constructivism focuses heavily on the researcher building a deeper understanding of what is being researched. As the researcher, my focus was to build an understanding of how implementing reform mathematics in my classroom impacted my students' journeys in becoming mathematicians. In order to do this, I had "to rely as much as possible on the participants' views of the situation being studied" (Creswell, 2003) as well as keep my question broad so I could construct my own meaning. I expected that I would discover multiple meanings due to having multiple participants with different backgrounds. I also knew that my own theory would develop throughout the research process.

According to Crotty (1998), it is assumed that as a constructivist, meaning is constructed through interactions with the world. This idea aligns with the reform mathematics belief that "learning [is] an active process rather than one of memorization and practice," (Schoenfeld, 2004, p. 266). Thus, the characteristics of a constructivist's framework align with the philosophical foundation of this study, reform mathematics. The ways in which I view myself as a researcher and the way students show their learning in a mathematics classroom were, therefore, in sync with one another throughout the study.

Teacher Research

This study can be viewed as *teacher research* (Cochran-Smith & Lytle, 1993, Anderson, Herr, & Nihlen, 2007) as I was the teacher and the researcher gathering data about teaching, learning, and schooling from within my current classroom context. Teacher research allows classroom-based educators to be involved in the research process and deepen their understandings in order to improve their teaching. In this study, I examined how teaching reform mathematics strengthened students', as well as my own, understandings, development, and learning. This study also assisted me in recognizing how reform mathematics is a foundational component of our school's math curriculum.

In developing my question, I wanted to be intimately involved in the research in order to strategically improve my classroom practices. Teacher research urges "teachers to identify their own question, document their own observations, analyze and interpret data in light of their current theories, and share their results primarily with other teachers," (Cochran-Smith & Lytle, p. 9, 1993). This concept supported my vision of researching as a practicing teacher as well as becoming a leader for other teachers who plan to implement reform mathematics practices into their own classroom. Conducting this teacher research allowed me to grow as a teacher and reflect on theories in which I already believe strongly.

Conducting teacher research within the Lab School aligns with one of our school's Reggio-inspired fundamental beliefs of *teacher as researcher* (Cadwell, 1997, 2003). As a teacher researcher, I documented students' mathematical learning processes throughout the year and allowed students to become researchers as well. Through my and my students' reflections and documentation we were better able to understand the thinking that was happening in the classroom, evaluate our own work, and exchange ideas with others (Cadwell, 2003). The process of documenting students' learning acted as a provocation and reflective tool, which allowed me to track how my students were meeting the five mathematical goals through reform mathematics and how I was changing as a teacher of mathematics.

Qualitative Approach

The research that was conducted utilized a *qualitative approach* (Creswell, 2003, Anderson, Herr, & Nihlen, 2007). Observations, narratives, conversations, interviews with students, and a host of classroom artifacts were conducted/ collected throughout the study. As a constructivist, I believe that multiple meanings can be made which lead me to lean towards an open-ended approach in order to allow deeper analysis and the possibility for new questions to arise. I am aware that qualitative research requires more in-depth analysis and clean answers may not be discovered. Anderson, Herr, and Nihlen (2007) outline characteristics for qualitative research in which the following apply to this study:

1. The research conducted was in a natural setting.
2. I, as the researcher, was responsible for the collection of data.
3. The research utilized qualitative methods.
4. The sampling logic is purposeful and relevant to the research question as it shifts.
5. Grounded theory is utilized in order to allow the data to lead to finding a theory rather than going into the research with a set theory.
6. The design of the research emerged over time through the research process.
7. The study is written as a narrative rather than a scientific report.
8. Tentative applications are made because realities are multiple and different, and the findings are dependent on the interactions between self and participants.

As a qualitative study, this research doesn't rely on concrete measurements but rather descriptions from observations, open-ended interviews, conversations, and the many forms of documentation collected through the examination of classroom artifacts (Anderson, Herr, and Nihlen, 2007; Hubbard & Power, 2003). My goal for this study was to gather insight on students' thoughts and feelings as mathematicians that would shine light on their perspectives of being in a reform mathematics classroom. Reflection has been an important part in my understanding and growth as an educator and was an essential aspect within this study as well.

Data Collection

Prior to starting my thesis work, I kept a journal that included thoughts and actions related to lessons, students, and interactions I had with colleagues throughout the day. This allowed me to identify what intrigued me as an educator and what points of tension I continued to feel and question. Connelly & Clandinin (1988) suggest that in developing a question to research, one must "read carefully to see if you can pick up any threads or themes, things that seem to recur" (p. 37) within your journal. This is how I discovered my recurring entries about the math happening in my classroom. Through this discovery I continued to keep my teacher journal but also began collecting various data sources that included documentation of student talk, whole group conversations, interviews, student reflections, and student work that would support my research of reform mathematics.

Teacher Journal

My teacher journal initially provided me a safe place to document things that I was noticing in my classroom but turned into a place where my research concept unfolded. Writing in my teacher journal regularly provided descriptions of action, children, events, and reactions that I had before, during, and after specific teaching moments (Connelly & Clandinin, 1988, p. 36).

Student Talk

Within this study, *student talk* (MacLean & Mohr, 1999, p.37) was a source of data collection that provided the most insight on students' thoughts and understandings. I initially began taking notes in my research journal about what students were saying; eventually, though, I decided that audiotaping student conversations would allow me to revisit and analyze their thinking more deeply. In addition, this allowed me to reflect on their words and follow up with students if I needed further information on their thoughts.

Student Reflection

Students were asked to reflect on themselves as mathematicians for this study. This reflection had students think about what was happening in their own work as well as their peers' work and required students to write about what they thought was happening (MacLean & Mohr, 1999, p. 43). Students' final reflections required students to fill out a *Math Block Reflection* (see Appendix A) where students answered open-ended questions in response to viewing their math work. The written comments by students about their own work proved to be a data source that lead me as the researcher to question more about students' thinking. This process made me realize that conducting interviews with a few students would be beneficial in order to clarify their ideas about reform mathematics.

Whole Group Conversations

In the classroom we have always had whole group conversations about students' thinking. Therefore, this procedure wasn't new to the students. Through audio recording the conversations, I was able to fully capture what all participants had to say (myself included). I was able to see a change in how they were discussing their mathematical thoughts. Because of the quality of the discussions, I found it beneficial to transcribe each conversation. This process also encouraged students to think carefully about what they were saying as they knew they were being recorded. I didn't want students' fear of being audiotaped to hinder their ability to share their thoughts, so I audiotaped our conversations regularly. The regularity of these recordings, and the discussions that occurred as a result of the recordings, allowed students to become more comfortable with the process.

Interviews

Throughout this study I was able to interview 11 students one-on-one which allowed them to share openly about their opinions of mathematics. Even though I was their teacher, I encouraged students to be honest with their opinions. We discussed prior to the interviews that sharing both positive and negative emotions in relation to math would help make me be a better teacher for them and for students with whom I work in the future. Students were aware they were being interviewed and audiotaped. The situation offered them the opportunity to reflect and share additional insights on their short answer responses from their *Math Block Reflection*.

Student Work/Artifacts

Students' math notebooks and math work were collected as sources of data in order to determine the growth of each student as a mathematician throughout the year. Students' notebooks and work were used for me as the researcher to evaluate my teaching and assess students' understanding and growth. In addition, students analyzed these classroom artifacts in order to share their feelings and reflect on ways they grew as mathematicians.

Methods for Data Analysis

In collecting pages of teacher journal entries, student reflections, multiple audio recordings, various transcriptions, and student work, the data accumulated rapidly. As a researcher I needed to develop a system that would keep the data that was collected organized in order to share my findings later. Anderson, Herr, & Nihlen (2007) suggest that creating a coding system would enable me to see categories within the data which would make the data more manageable (p. 216). Therefore, I came up with various ways to manage the data and keep it organized.

Coding

I began by *coding* (Falk, 2005) the data that I had collected into themes. The first step in organizing my data involved assigning colors to the mathematical goals that I wanted to see within the data that was collected. After reading through my teacher journal, transcriptions, student reflections, and student work I was able to highlight where themes related to the mathematical goals were emerging. I was able to identify all five mathematical goals including: students learn to value mathematics, students become confident in their ability to do mathematics, student become mathematical problem solvers, students learn to communicate mathematically, and students learn to reason mathematically (NCTM, 1989). Not only was I able to identify where the chosen themes emerged, I was able to identify other themes that I wasn't expecting to discover.

Triangulation

In collecting a wide variety of data sources, *triangulating* (Hubbard & Power, 1993, p. 124) the data allowed me to "compare different kinds of data on [my] question from a variety of sources" (MacLean & Mohr, 1999, p. 62). With initial findings in individual data sources it was important that these findings were supported by other data sources as well. Through triangulation, I was able to validate my findings and see the impact through several data sources.

Critical Friends

Due to this research being part of a master's degree program, I had a cohort of peers who served as critical friends through the research process. My critical friends helped me develop a focus, organize a framework, and guided me through collecting my data (MacLean & Mohr, 1999). Together, we discussed and identified patterns from the data that were collected. They also assisted in validating my own findings after I went through the process of analyzing the data.

Member Checking

Through this study, I constantly made sure to check in with the students to verify that I was representing their thoughts and ideas accurately (Falk, 2005). In most cases, students were able to return with deeper insights that were beneficial to the research. In a sense, the students became co-researchers and were able to reflect on their own work - as well as the work of others - and showed interest in researching their own work regularly (MacLean & Mohr, 1999).

FINDINGS

Due to my question about the benefits of reform mathematics being so broad, I was able to gain insight on different aspects of reform mathematics. As I reflected as a teacher and collected data from my students, I noticed that many of my findings connected to the goals NCTM (1989) established for young mathematicians:

1. students learn to value mathematics
2. students become confident in their ability to do mathematics
3. student become mathematical problem solvers
4. students learn to communicate mathematically
5. students learn to reason mathematically

These goals set up how I went about analyzing and discovering my findings within this research. By gaining background knowledge about the evolution of NCTM and their efforts in promoting reform mathematics, these goals have been foundational in developing students and teachers as mathematicians.

Goal #1: Students Learn to Value Mathematics

As students explore mathematics, their understanding and value of mathematical concepts is imperative in their development. The first goal is for students to learn to value mathematics "so they can appreciate the role of mathematics in the development of the contemporary society and explore relationships" (NCTM, 1989, p. 5). I posed the question "Is math important? Why? Why Not?" to my class to gain insight into whether or not students valued mathematics.

At the beginning of our whole class conversation students were asked to vote on the question "Is Math Important?" which resulted in all students believing that math was important. When the students all agreed that mathematical skills were important, I immediately asked them "Why?" The class responded and agreed that math is important because you need it to get a college degree and you use it every day.

Miss Hayden: Why is math important?
Shawn: You need math to get a good college degree.

Miss Hayden: Okay, can you tell me what you mean by that?

Shawn: Like, if you want to get into college and get a good job you need to know math because you will need math at the job you end up doing.

Miss Hayden: What job do you hope to end up doing?

Shawn: I want to be an accountant.

Miss Hayden: So, what ways would you use math in being an accountant?

Shawn: Well, I would need to know how to add, subtract, multiply and divide every day to do all my work for people. (Transcription, 4/4/16)

In Shawn' example of why he thinks mathematics is important he related the importance to him as a skill that he would need in the future to be successful at his desired job. Shawn's idea aligns with NCTM's idea that "students learn to become mathematical thinkers and are prepared for any academic career or profession that they choose," (NCTM, 2014, p. vii). Other students then thought about what their future jobs would be and how math is incorporated into many jobs. This added to our class conversation as Jeff realized that "math is basically something you use every day" (Transcription, 4/4/16).

At this point in our conversation, students were asked to turn and talk to a fellow mathematician about where they use math. Students shared out that when they eat food, make food, go to the store, run a store, use coupons or get deals, vote, or deal with money that they are using their math skills. It was interesting to me that the examples my students shared all related to problem solving questions we had done in class throughout the year:

- Miss Ruffolo was baking cupcakes; each batch had (*6, 9, 12*) cupcakes in it. She made (*2, 5, 10*) batches of cupcakes, how many did she make? (Lesson Plan, 9/9/15)
- Joe Hogsett received 36,201 votes more than Chuck Brewer in the 2015 Indianapolis Mayoral Election. How many votes did Chuck Brewer receive if Joe Hogsett had a total of 92,521 votes? (Lesson Plan, 11/4/15)

- The "Just be Beautiful: Hair & Nail Salon" was offering manicures and hair accessories. They offered (*3, 9, 10*) different colors of nail polish. Each manicure was (*$5, $12, $15.50*). How many manicures did they have to do to earn (*$200, $500, $350*)? (Lesson Plan, 3/8/16)

These are questions and topics that we explored in-depth as a class through projects. As the teacher, I was purposefully making connections between the mathematical skills under study and where they might see these skills outside of school. If students are asking the question, "*When are we going to use this?*" then they aren't seeing value in the mathematics being discussed in the classroom. It should be our goal as educators to provide students with examples of where they would use mathematical skills in society. In doing so, students will no longer have to ask the question, "*When am I going to use this?*" Instead, students will begin to find the value of mathematics independently.

Goal #2: Students Become Confident in their Ability to do Math

In order for students to become independent mathematicians who explore the values of mathematics on their own, students "need to view themselves as capable of using their growing mathematical power to make sense of new problem situations in the world around them" (NCTM, 1989, p. 6). The second mathematical goal suggested by NCTM notes that students should become confident in their ability to do math. In my classroom, we call ourselves mathematicians, and students truly believe that they are mathematicians because we "explore math" (Jeff, Transcription 4/4/16) concepts in various ways.

At the beginning of the year, we established routines within the classroom. General routines were established, and routines for the various content areas were also created. We discussed what a mathematician is and what a mathematician does in order to be successful. As a class we discovered that a mathematician:

- does lots of math *all* the time (i.e., not only during the daily math block)
- takes tests to demonstrate understanding
- sometimes use addition, subtraction, multiplication, and division when solving problems
- experiments with strategies
- comes up with strategies to share with fellow mathematicians
- shows all mathematical thinking (Classroom Anchor Chart, 8/5/15)

Throughout the year, we referred back to the anchor chart and revised our idea of how we can be successful mathematicians. The definition and expectations of a mathematician have allowed all students to see that "everybody is a mathematician" (NCTM, 1989, p. 6) and provided them with the confidence to do math, experiment with strategies they want to try, and come up with their own. Haystead and Marzano (2009) believe that students who understand the expectations will perform at higher levels compared to students in classrooms where expectations are unclear.

Students reflected independently as they looked back through their math journals and completed their *Math Block Reflection* (see Appendix A). Students were asked, *"How do you feel about math?"* and all responded with some type of positive feeling such as they felt good, happy, they like it, or thought it was fun. I interviewed a few students whose responses I wanted to know more about:

> Miss Hayden: How do you feel about math?
> Cornelia: I love it!
> Miss Hayden: Have you always loved math?
> Cornelia: No, I started loving it this year…
> Miss Hayden: That is so great! What made you change your mind about math and allowed you to enjoy it?
> Cornelia: The projects that we do. The first project where we built the neighborhood…
> Miss Hayden: The Real Estate Project?

Cornelia: Yes, I liked it because we got to be creative in building our own neighborhood but we also did math with really challenging numbers. (Transcription, 3/18/16)

Cornelia continued to teach me about her journey as a mathematician. I believe that her journey is something that stands out so much because she just enrolled at the Lab School this year. Because Cornelia was a student who has never been part of a reform mathematics classroom before, I have seen the most growth in her as well as other students who were new to the Lab School and the concept of reform mathematics. As I reflected on this day of interviewing students, I wrote:

I feel that my students have come a long way, especially the students that are new to the Lab School. Many of them expressed that at their old schools they found math really intimidating partly due to the "big" books that they worked through. They expressed that they were scared to be "wrong" and had the pressure of always being "right." (Teacher Journal, 3/18/16)

I noticed that this pressure could quickly diminish any confidence students have with themselves as mathematicians. This concept of always being "right" would serve as students' only way to feel confident in themselves and doesn't provide support for struggling mathematicians.

They expressed that they now like being challenged through projects and various number sets because, to them, being a successful mathematician isn't about getting the "right" answer. Instead, how they solve problems and communicate what they are thinking is what really allows them to grow. (Teacher Journal Continued, 3/18/16).

Thinking of the struggling mathematicians in my classroom, I thought that they may have expressed a lack of confidence in their mathematical ability, but their responses on their *Math Block Reflection* were more reflective than students who could be viewed as strong mathematicians. One student shared that "When I see math, I feel happy," and another shared, "I really like math, it's pretty much the thing I look forward to in school" (Student Math Block Reflection Responses, 3/16/16). This allowed me to see that they were seeing growth within themselves and trusting their own mathematical thinking even as struggling mathematicians.

Goal #3: Students Become Mathematical Problem Solvers

One area where my students feel the most confident within their mathematical ability is when they solve problems. Problem solving is an important component of reform mathematics that is incorporated daily into our classroom. The concept of problem solving was introduced through NCTM's, *An Agenda for Action* (1980) and has remained a cornerstone component of reform mathematics.

> To develop such abilities, students need to work on problems that may take hours, days, and even weeks to solve. Although some may be relatively simple exercise to be accomplished independently, other should involve small groups or an entire class working cooperatively. (NCTM, 1989, p. 6)

Within the classroom, students have expressed their love of problem solving and how, at the Lab School where reform mathematics is being implemented, problem solving is a component that they enjoy.

> Miss Hayden: This being your first year at the Lab School, how do you compare math at your old school to here?
> Janet: Here (referring to the Lab School) we do something better!
> Miss Hayden: What makes it better?
> Janet: Well, we get to do problem solving and go over our work. I mean, we have to sometimes do problems independently but we aren't alone. We don't always have to do it alone and at least we go over it. And, sometimes you even pull us to the side to try and help us through our work if we are struggling.
> Miss Hayden: Tell me more about that.

Janet: I like doing some of it on my own but sometimes I get stuck and need to talk it out. (Transcription 3/18/16)

When students were asked *what do you do well in math?* Students shared "I think I am good at solving problems," "I like to solve problems," and "As a mathematician I feel that I really understand math, I can understand a problem that is given to me and solve it efficiently" (Student Math Block Reflection Responses, 3/16/16). Not only have students expressed their joy in the general concept of solving problems, but they enjoy the aspect of choosing their own number set when attempting to solve problems.

> Miss Hayden: What is your favorite thing about our math block?
> Calvin: Problem Solving
> Miss Hayden: Why is problem solving your favorite?
> Calvin: It is independent and fun to do.
> Miss Hayden: What makes it fun?
> Calvin: When we get to pick our own number sets it is a challenge, and I like doing challenging problems. (Transcription 3/18/16)

Providing students with number sets has allowed students to work on being confident as mathematicians. Many students choose a number set that they feel is just right for them prior to challenging themselves with a harder one in order to master a strategy (see Figure 1).

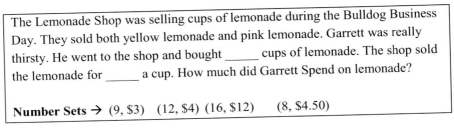

The Lemonade Shop was selling cups of lemonade during the Bulldog Business Day. They sold both yellow lemonade and pink lemonade. Garrett was really thirsty. He went to the shop and bought _____ cups of lemonade. The shop sold the lemonade for _____ a cup. How much did Garrett Spend on lemonade?

Number Sets → (9, $3)   (12, $4) (16, $12)   (8, $4.50)

Figure 1. Student Problem Solving 3/15/16.

Within our classroom, if we are not doing a daily problem solving task, students are working on a project in which they have a variety of problems to solve. We began a geography unit project where students explored locations of their favorite places, determined distances, compared distances, converted mileage, used elapsed time to created daily itineraries, and budgeted out a trip.

> We began our geography unit today and the kids are loving it. They generated so many mathematical questions in relation to planning a trip. Their excitement really has sparked a desire to continue with this project and see where they take it. (Teacher Journal 4/18/16)

After this reflection, a few days of letting students explore, and allowing myself to find what direction they were taking the project, I asked students to share their thoughts about the project. When asked, *what was the purpose of this unit?* Students shared that they learned about distances, time, and how they will need to have these skills later in life when planning a trip. One student suggested that we take this project and explore how much it would cost if were to go on a class trip the Indianapolis Children's Museum. Through projects such as this, students develop their own problems to solve, teachers provide open-ended learning possibilities, and opportunities to explore and find the value of having a variety of mathematical skills are given.

The problem solving component of reform mathematics has allowed students the opportunity to meet all five goals NCTM suggests will foster a mathematically literate student. Within purposeful and authentic problem solving problems that students can relate to, students can find the value of learning a specific mathematical skill and where they will need to use the skill in society. Students have become more confident in their mathematical abilities through problem solving. Students have realized that there is more than one way to solve problems and there isn't a "right" or "wrong" way to approach a problem. Through problem solving, students are expected to show their thinking and reasoning in order to demonstrate their conceptual understandings. With the ample amount of mathematical connections and the many possibilities of including problem solving into a math block, reform mathematics offers all children the opportunity to develop into mathematically literate students.

Goal #4: Students Learn to Communicate Mathematically

Problem solving has allowed students to demonstrate their mathematical understanding through the opportunity to explore various strategies when solving a problem. Schoenfeld (2004) recognized that in a reform mathematics classroom, "competent problem solvers persevered. They were...able to communicate the results of their mathematical work effectively, both orally and [in writing]" (p. 263). Communicating orally and in writing is a struggle for students, especially if they haven't been exposed to various ways of communicating their thinking. Reform mathematics supports students' ability to explore and discover their own strategies. Students learn from one another how to communicate their thinking by talking out their processes.

In order for students to be mathematically literate, they need to have the "opportunity to read, write, and discuss ideas in which the use of the language of mathematics becomes natural" (NCTM, 1989, p. 6). Not only did students work on this goal during problem solving, but students felt that sharing with the class served a purpose while making discoveries. Students who had never been in a reform mathematics classroom struggled with this goal initially. In most cases, they were never asked to explain their thinking or the process that lead them to solving a problem but, rather, were asked what they got as their answer.

Having students examine their own work provided me with insight on how they thought they had grown throughout the year as they communicated their mathematical thinking. I went through each student's notebook and identified a problem solving question from the beginning of the year. In order to see students' growth through oral and written communication, I gave students the same problem that they had previously solved. At this point in my data collection, students were unaware of how they had previously solved the problem. After completing the problem solving for the second time, I returned their original problem solving and had them compare their work.

Students noticed that as mathematicians they were picking number sets that worked for them at the time of their development and they were getting the right answer. Although these noticing are important to recognize and celebrate, their critiques of their beginning of the year work shared more insight on their understanding of what it means to be a mathematician who can communicate her/his thinking. They shared that their work wasn't organized, was inefficient, and left the reader confused with what was being represented as their thinking and answer.

Miss Hayden: What is something that you notice about yourself as a mathematician?

Lucy: I didn't really challenge myself before.

Miss Hayden: What do you mean by that?

Lucy: Like, uh, I picked the easiest numbers when I knew it right away.

Miss Hayden: Okay. Dani, what did you notice about yourself as a mathematician?

Dani: I noticed that I wasn't neat so you couldn't see what I was trying to do.

Miss Hayden: Why would that be important?

Dani: Well, if somebody goes over my work they could understand what math I was trying to write down.

Miss Hayden: Jeremiah, what did you notice about yourself as a mathematician?

Jeremiah: At the beginning of the year I didn't write a sentence, just a number.

Miss Hayden: Oh, interesting. Do you mean that you didn't write a word sentence to share what you thought the answer was?

Jeremiah: Yes, I do that now.

Miss Hayden: What else did you notice about yourselves as mathematicians or the strategies you used?

Janet: I didn't always use an efficient strategy.

Shawn: Neither did I. I used random strategies.

Miss Hayden: Can you tell me more about that?

Nessie: I was trying to do a strategy that I didn't understand.

Miss Hayden: Was that helpful when you were trying to solve the problem?

Nessie: No, I probably should have used a strategy I knew but I know more now.

(Class Conversation, 3/15/16)

These discoveries were made by multiple students through a whole class conversation as we examined one student's notebook. As we examined students' notebooks through the year and how they solved the problems that I had chosen for them, they realized that they were still getting the correct answers but they were also organizing their thinking, challenging themselves with harder number sets, sometimes coming up with two efficient strategies, answering the question in context, and allowing fellow mathematicians to follow what they were thinking and how they got their answers.

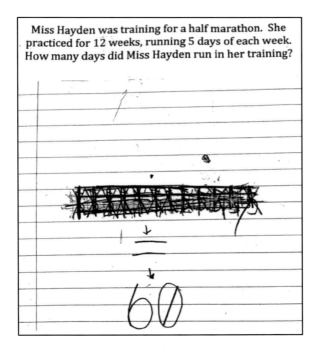

Figure 2. Lee's Problem Solving from the Beginning of the Year.

With so many discoveries made by students, it was important for me as their teacher to reflect on their individual journeys to determine if the goal of learning to communicate mathematically was being met. Lee was a student who was new to the school and struggled at the beginning of the year to communicate what he was thinking (see Figure 2). Through conversations with him, he expressed confidence in getting the correct answer, but when I pushed him to tell me about how he got there he struggled to communicate what he was doing.

Figure 2 shows Lee's beginning of the year problem-solving sample where he wasn't able to communicate how he landed on the answer of 60. Through his crossed out work, I noticed that he counted by 5 twelve times but what concerned me the most was that he didn't see the value in the process that he went through to get that answer.

Knowing that this was the goal that would prevent Lee from becoming mathematically literate, I wanted to make sure that he knew that his work is just as important as his answer. Through whole class shares, Lee was able to develop his understanding of how to communicate his mathematical thinking (see Figure 3).

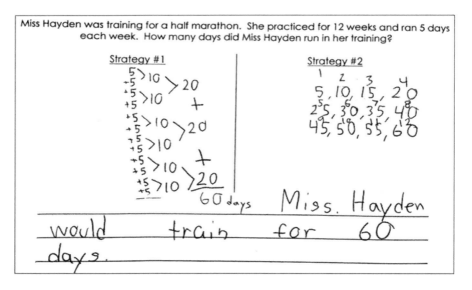

Figure 3. Lee's Problem Solving from the Middle of the Year.

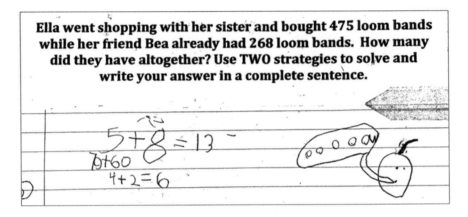

Figure 4. Calvin's Problem Solving from the Beginning of the Year.

Lee stated in his reflection of his own mathematical work at the beginning of the year that he "didn't do much work" and it was "sloppy." This reflection was reflective of what many of the students in the classroom noticed about their work. Many of them seemed to be disappointed in themselves; however, they seemed to be holding themselves to higher standards, which allowed them to truly see how much they had grown as individual mathematicians.

Another one of my students, Calvin, also struggled with the concept of being able to communicate what he was thinking. In talking with him at the beginning of the year, I could tell that he had really great thinking but couldn't verbally articulate what he was thinking as he solved his problem. His typical response when I asked him how he solved a problem or how he got to his answer was "I don't know, I just knew." Calvin's beginning of the year problem (Figure 4) shows a mathematician who is attempting to communicate what his thinking is; however, it is evident that he struggles to write down what he knows. At that point in the year, it was important to expose Calvin to learning mathematical terms in order to communicate his thinking.

Calvin is one student who has shown the most growth in regards to this goal. Many students in the classroom could state that they have grown as mathematicians through understanding various strategies and communicating their thinking, but Calvin is a mathematician that at the beginning of the year didn't understand what "showing your thinking/work" meant. Comparing Calvin's problem solving from the beginning of the year (Figure 4) to his work at the end of the year (see Figure 5) demonstrates his growth in being able to communicate his thinking. The relationship between Calvin's Beginning of the Year problem and his second strategy for his Middle of the Year problem showed that he can communicate his understanding of place value (something that he had struggled with at the beginning of the year). Calvin's second strategy also shows that he understands that when the digits 4 and 2 are in the hundreds place that they represent 400 and 200 instead of 4 and 2. However, reviewing the strategies that Calvin came up with at the Middle of the Year shows that he is still doing mental math through each strategy. After breaking down 475 and 268 into expanded form and adding the place values together, he added the resulting sums of 600, 130, and 13 mentally. Adding addition signs between 600, 130, and 13 would help him better communicate this step in the process.

Similarly, in his first strategy, Calvin shows an understanding of the traditional algorithm. While he regroups from the ones to the tens place, he does not show that he also regroups from the tens to the hundreds – even though he got the correct answer. Carefully communicating *all* that he is doing is something that Calvin needs to continue working on. Although there are still improvements to be made, it is important that the progress that he has made (e.g., multiple strategies, regrouping, expanded form, communicating most steps) is recognized.

Not only did Calvin grow in communicating his mathematical thinking, but he grew through recognizing who he is as a mathematician. Calvin wrote on his Math Block Reflection (see Figure 6) that showing his work is something that he struggles with, but he also feels that he has grown in that aspect of being a mathematician as well. This reflection shows that although it's a struggle for him, he hasn't lost confidence in his ability to overcome the struggle.

Calvin also shared his discoveries about himself as a mathematician through a whole class conversation we had:

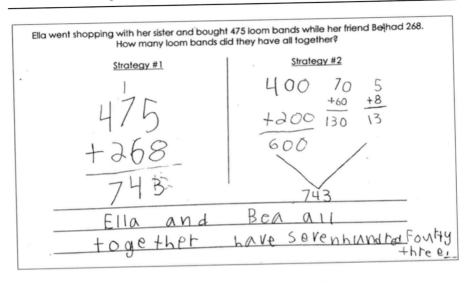

Figure 5. Calvin's Problem Solving from the Middle of the Year.

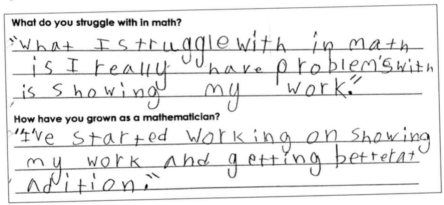

Figure 6. Calvin's Math Block Reflection 3/15/16.

Miss Hayden: Calvin, what did you notice about yourself?

Calvin: Well, I have learned how to show my work.

Miss Hayden: Okay, how have you learned how to do that?

Calvin: During share [whole class discussions].

Miss Hayden: How has share helped you show your work?

Calvin: I can see how other people figured it out, like what strategy they used.

(Transcription, 3/18/16)

Many students shared their appreciation for the share time that we set aside as a part of our reform mathematics classroom. This time allowed "students to communicate their ideas, they learn to clarify, refine, and consolidate their thinking" (NCTM. 1989, p. 6) as they shared with their classmates. Marley stated that, "When we share, I get feedback from other people when they ask me questions, and it helps me think about what I need to work on" (Transcription, 3/18/16). As this quote shows, share time allowed students to support one another as they reached the goals of becoming mathematically literate.

Goal #5: Students Learn to Reason Mathematically

As noted above, share time allowed students to offer their findings, strategies, and conjectures about mathematics to their peers. Holding students accountable during share challenged their thinking and reasoning skills while also providing students the ability to dig more deeply. Through NCTM's (1989) goals, "a demonstration of good reasoning should be rewarded even more than students' ability to find correct answers" (p. 6). I saw my students meeting this goal through problem solving as they used direct modeling, counting on, or derived facts (Carpenter, T.P., Fennema, E., Franke, M.L., Levi, L., & Empson, S.B., 2015) to represent their thinking. In order to foster reasoning within our math block, students were able to decide how to approach a problem. As their teacher, I encouraged my students to use different ways to represent their thinking, and they knew that I didn't expect all students to approach a problem the same way. "Since no specific pathway has been suggested or is implied, and students could use several different approaches to enter and solve the task (e.g., guess and check, make a table, etc.)" (NCTM, 2014, p. 20). Therefore, students had more of an opportunity to make connections as they reasoned through how they would solve a problem.

For example, students were given the problem: Miss Ruffolo is baking cupcakes. Each batch has 12 cupcakes in it. She makes 3 batches. How many cupcakes does she have in all? (See Figures 7 & 8). The following students approached the problem differently due to the way they were reasoning through the problem, but the way they communicated their reasoning for solving the problem is reflective of their growth as young mathematicians as well as how they are constructing strategies that are meaningful to them.[6]

Evangeline explained her strategies to the class and confidently supported her strategies as other mathematicians in the room asked how she solved the problem. She shared that she thought about one batch of cupcakes at a time. She noted that batch one had 12 cupcakes, adding batch two would make 24 cupcakes, and then adding the final batch of cupcakes would give her 36. With some mental math happening as Evangeline solved the problem, she orally communicated her reasoning for setting up a ratio table to solve the problem. Her second strategy may not be viewed as the most efficient strategy, but it correlates with the first strategy as she represents one batch of cupcakes at a time.

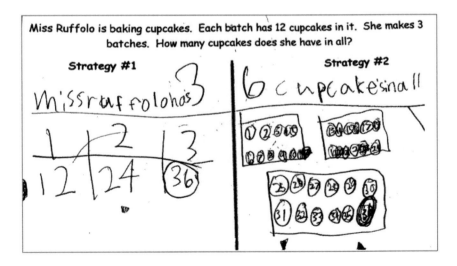

Figure 7. Evangeline's Problem Solving from 9/24/15.

---

[6] See Carpenter, et al. (2015) for a description of the various strategies students use when problem solving in mathematics.

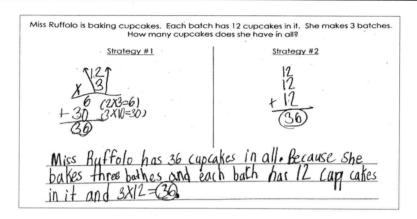

Figure 8. Nessie's Problem Solving from 9/24/15.

Due to Nessie solving the problem using a more traditional approach, I conferred with her about her thinking. While explaining her 1st strategy, she added an arrow and wrote (2 x 3 = 6) and then another arrow and wrote (3 x 10 = 30). As Nessie was explaining her reasoning, I became concerned that she had just memorized a strategy that another mathematician used within the classroom when finding a product. So, I challenged her to share her reasoning behind her 2nd strategy. It seemed easier for her to explain her second strategy. She noted that there were 3 batches of cupcakes, so she wrote 12 three times because there were 12 cupcakes in each batch. This conversation with Nessie made me realize the importance of conceptually understanding strategies that students are using to solve problems. Therefore, I gave her more credit towards her second strategy than her first since she was able to conceptually walk through her thinking. Nessie reflected on the problems that she did (see Figure 9), and I believe she sees the importance of understanding what the problem is asking her prior to determining how to approach a problem.

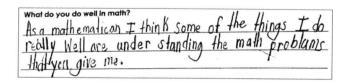

Figure 9. Nessi's Math Block Reflection 3/15/16.

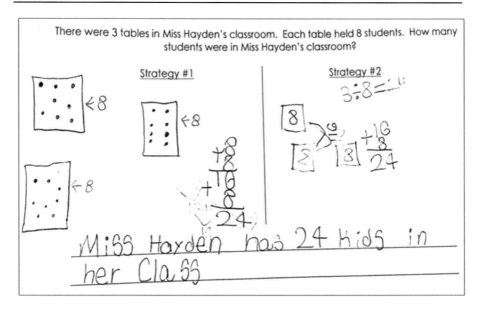

Figure 10. Jeff's Problem Solving 10/1/16.

In order to be an effective teacher, it's important to "understand how contexts, culture, conditions, and language can be used to create mathematical tasks that draw on students' prior knowledge and experiences" (NCTM. 2014, p. 17). In doing this, more students understand the problem and reason through how to solve it. Providing students, like Jeff (see Figure 10), the opportunity to attempt a problem that relates to their environments allows them to reason through how to solve the problem conceptually.

Jeff's first strategy and written answer provide insight into his understanding of the problem. Through my assessment, I noted that he was able to understand the question and visually conceptualize what was being asked. Comparing Jeff's first and second strategy, I noticed that he was able to determine a way that he could be more efficient with his second strategy as he transitioned from dots to whole numbers when representing 8 students at each table. Since he was able to visually see and recognize what the numbers in the problem represented, we talked about the reasoning behind the number sentence that he wrote: $3 \div 8 = 24$. When I asked if he thought about the problem as having 3 tables that he split into 8 students, he responded that he had 3 tables of 8 students. At this point it was clear that Jeff understood how to solve the problem and just needed assistance with how to communicate what he was thinking when he used a numeric representation.

In comparing students' mathematical work with their reflections I saw that Ethan described his struggles to understand what the problem means (Ethan's Math Block Reflection, 3/16/16). At the beginning of the year, this was definitely something with which Ethan struggled (see Figure 11).

Ethan was a student I worked with throughout the year. I consistently asked him to read the problem aloud prior to determining a solution. In reading the problem aloud and talking through what the context was, Ethan began to understand the idea of conceptually understanding the problem before simply looking for numbers within the problem and seeing how they relate to one another. Ethan wrote, "I did a box with fours and a box with twos." This showed that there was no connection with the math being done or the context of the problem. In comparing where Ethan was at the beginning of the year to the middle of the year (see Figure 12), it is obvious that growth was made in communicating his thinking and reasoning about what the problem was asking.

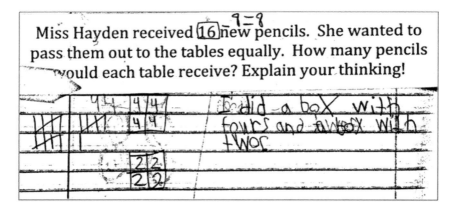

Figure 11. Ethan's Problem Solving from the Beginning of the Year.

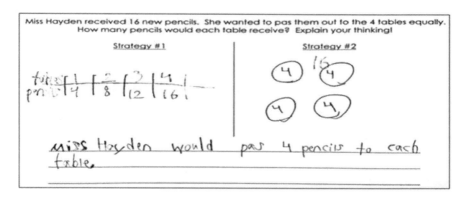

Figure 12. Ethan's Problem Solving from the Middle of the Year.

Becoming Mathematically Literate

"The intent of these goals is that students will become mathematically literate" (NCTM, 1989, p. 6). The five goals examined above hold students accountable in developing an understanding, reasoning, and dialogue about mathematics. In many ways, students are able to simultaneously work on multiple goals as they develop as mathematicians. As students are developing their skills in becoming problem solvers, they reason through the mathematical problem and discover ways to communicate their thinking as mathematicians. By connecting problem solving activities to the societies in which children live, students are able to value the skills discussed in the classroom as important concepts that they will need on a daily basis. As students work toward the suggested goals, they become more confident in their abilities to develop their own mathematical thinking and they view themselves as mathematicians.

CONCLUSION

I began this teacher research project in order to understand and document the journey my students take in becoming literate mathematicians. Through building my knowledge base of how reform mathematics has developed throughout history, I was able to identify five critical goals that I believe students should strive to achieve as mathematicians. These goals have become foundational within my classroom, and I feel that a reform mathematics curriculum best supports students' development as mathematicians as they work toward achieving these goals. NCTM (2014) believes that "effective teaching of mathematics establishes clear goals for the mathematics that students are learning, situates goals with the learning progression, and uses the goals to guide instructional decisions" (p. 10). With these goals set for students as a foundation to their learning process in becoming mathematicians, they will build a deeper conceptual understanding of mathematical skills that they value, become confident in their ability to be mathematical problem solvers, and communicate their reasoning as mathematicians.

Within my journey as an educator, I have discovered that reform mathematics not only supports my students as mathematical thinkers, it also supports me as a mathematics educator. My belief in the purpose of teaching mathematics within my classroom has evolved as I hold my students accountable for striving to meet the goals set by NCTM rather than memorizing routines related to basic skills. I believe that the goals that were set by NCTM can be achieved by students as long as teachers understand the importance of them, incorporate ways students can achieve the goals within the classroom, and hold students to the expectation of striving to meet each goal. "The opportunity for all students to experience these components of mathematical training is at the heart of our vision of a quality mathematics program," (NCTM, 1989, p. 5). This also requires that educators be educated (or educate themselves) on how to begin implementing these goals within the classroom.

Implications

As a mathematics educator, I believe that it is valuable to strive and meet the mathematically literate goals and become a mathematician prior to expecting the same from my students. I believe that in order to become an effective mathematics educator, you need to start your own journey in becoming mathematically literate and be open to viewing math differently than maybe you did as a young mathematician. Having experienced a similar journey as many of my students provided me the opportunity to relate to their development as mathematicians. Through becoming mathematically literate, I was able to establish clear mathematical goals, select a progression of relevant activities, and develop problems that align with the goals. I am now able to better support my students in becoming mathematically literate due to understanding their development as mathematicians.

In making a commitment to actively incorporate reform mathematics into my classroom and focusing on the five goals in becoming mathematically literate, I believe that "words become actions and the actions lead to more productive beliefs, new norms of instructional practice, and the implementation of the essential supporting elements will overcome the obstacles that currently prevent school mathematics from ensuring mathematical success for all students" (NCTM, 2014, p. 117). Striving to be a leader within my school's community of teachers, I need to share my students' mathematical journeys. To continue to improve mathematics instruction for our young mathematicians, all teachers must start implementing reform mathematics gradually by setting goals for students, document their mathematical journey, and engage in mathematical conversations regularly (inside and outside of the classroom).

Part of my school's Reggio-inspired philosophy supports the idea of documenting students' work as a way of communicating and representing student thinking. Although documentation serves many purposes, the main purpose aligned with this study would be that documentation creates "an archive that traces the history of the school and the pleasure in the process of learning experienced by many children and their teachers" (Gandini as cited in Cadwell, 2003, p. 5). The documentation within this thesis provides evidence of students' processes of developing as mathematicians who are striving to be mathematically literate. Not only does this concept of documentation align with my school's unique philosophy of education, it also aligns with the expectations of how to effectively implement reform mathematics into a classroom. "Effective teaching of mathematics uses evidence of student thinking to assess progress toward mathematical understanding and to adjust instruction continually in ways that support and extend learning" (NCTM, 2014, p. 53). I highly encourage educators to begin documenting students' thinking while allowing the students to be part of the process. Students will be able to see their growth and challenge themselves as learners. Through collecting and documenting evidence of my students' thinking in the classroom, I am able to add to the conversation about how to effectively implement reform mathematics and the benefits of incorporating this philosophy.

As discovered throughout the history of reform mathematics, the struggle many educators faced as they began to implement this philosophy into the classroom was the lack of proof that was available to show it was successful. Schoenfeld (2004), stated that "the reform curricula would fail because they cannot yet produce real proof, or real standards" (p. 270). In continuing to document my students' mathematical journeys, data will be collected, used as evidence, and will become proof of a reform mathematics curricula being successful in developing mathematically literate students. Another way to build proof is to have educators join the journey in implementing reform mathematics into a variety of classrooms. If more educators implement this philosophy, there is more opportunity for the collection of evidence in order to track growth and support students as they become mathematicians.

Future Research

Knowing that this is only one study researched by one teacher, it isn't generalizable. In order for educators to find proof in the benefits of reform mathematics, more educators would need to research the implementation of reform mathematics into their classroom and document their findings. With ample amounts of educators collaborating about reform mathematics, a larger sample of diverse students, teachers, and schools will be included and the field can begin to generalize across these studies.

In order for educators to implement reform mathematics in their classrooms, a foundation of what a reform mathematics curriculum looks like could be a beneficial resource. Educators that have already begun implementing reform mathematics need to come together and share how their curriculum was developed with reform mathematics as the foundation. Through the research that was conducted in my classroom, I have developed new wonderings about reform mathematics that I would like to explore based off of my findings. Working in a school that is still developing its curriculum, I would like to explore how to take the teaching and learning going on in the classroom and develop a curriculum that would offer support to educators who want to implement reform mathematics into their classrooms. It would be interesting to focus on creating a curriculum that is focused on using the goals that were used within this study as foundational expectations for students' development as mathematicians. As educators implement reform mathematics, they must begin to document students' thinking, capture the progression of their lessons, and construct outlines of the curricula they are building.

To go along with researching the development of a reform mathematics curriculum in a Reggio-inspired school, I would like to also continue to explore how problem solving activities can best support students' development as mathematicians. Within this study, my students reflected on individual problem solving from the beginning of the year and compared it to their mathematical work in the middle of the year. Through this data collection activity, I was impressed with how reflective students were about their mathematical growth and ability. Because of the level of excitement from students about their self-reflections, I would like to develop a way for students to track their progress as growing mathematicians. Whether pre and post problem solving problem assessment at the beginning and end of each unit or a monthly math notebook reflection, students need to regularly reflect on their progress and determine if they are meeting the goals in order to become mathematically literate. Educators need to inject purposeful reflection into their problem solving as they implement it as a primary component of their math blocks.

Final Thoughts

As an educator, I believe that researching my instruction and student development is part of my responsibility in supporting my students in becoming successful members of society. Teachers who document their research have provided other teachers the ability to explore and experiment within their own classrooms. This provides other educators an opportunity to add to the conversation and share additional findings that will in turn develop the profession and authenticate teacher research. Recognizing NCTM's efforts in researching the profession of mathematics education has provided me a foundation and platform to continue researching how to improve my instruction and support my students through their mathematical journey.

> …professionals who are responsible for students' mathematical learning are never satisfied with their accomplishments and are always working to increase the impact that they have on their students' mathematics learning… . As professionals, mathematics teachers recognize that their own learning is never finished and continually seek to improve and enhance their mathematical knowledge for teaching, their knowledge of mathematical pedagogy, and their knowledge of students as learners of mathematics. (NCTM, 2014, p. 99)

I believe that an effective teacher is constantly doing research within the classroom, preparing documentation of work being done by teacher and students, and sharing the responsibility of being a researcher with the students (Cadwell, 2003). As the history of reform mathematics demonstrates, society is known to change and this impacts students' education. It is our responsibility as educators to continue researching best practices to meet the needs of students as society changes. Teacher research allows educators to effectively evaluate their instruction while providing students an opportunity to receive an education that will make them successful contributors within their societies.

APPENDIX

Math Block Reflection   **Mathematician:** _____

After looking at how far you have come as a mathematician from the beginning of the year, reflection on yourself as a mathematician.

How do you feel about math?

_____

_____

_____

What do you do well in math?

_____

_____

_____

What do you struggle with in math?

_____

_____

_____

How have you grown as a mathematician?

_____

_____

_____

What do you need from me as your teacher to support you as a mathematician?

_____

_____

_____

REFERENCES

Anderson, G.L., Herr, K., & Nihlen, A.S. (EDS.). (2007). *Studying your own school: An educator's guide to practitioner action research.* Thousand Oaks, CA: Corwin Press.

Austin, C.M. (1921). The National Council of Teachers of Mathematics. *The mathematics teacher, 14*(1), 1-4.

Briggs, T. H. (1931). *The Committee of Ten. Junior-Senior High School Clearing House,* 6(3), 134–141. Retrieved from http://www.jstor.org/stable/30173638

Cadwell, L.B. (2003). *Bringing learning to life: The Reggio approach to early childhood education.* New York, NY: Teachers College Press.

Carpenter, T.P., Fennema, E., Franke, M.L., Levi, L., & Empson, S.B. (2015). *Children's mathematics: Cognitively guided instruction.* Portsmouth, NH: Heinemann.

Cochran-Smith, M., & Donnell, K. (2006). Practitioner inquiry: Blurring the boundaries of research and practice. In J. L. Green, G. Camilli, P.B. Elmore (Eds.) *Handbook of complementary methods in education research* (pp. 503-518) Mahwah, NJ: Lawrence Erlbaum Associates.

Connelly, F.M. & Clandinin D.J. (1988). *Teachers as curriculum planners: Narratives of experience.* New York: NY: Teachers College Press.

Creswell, J.W. (2005) *Educational research: Planning, conducting, and evaluating quantitative and qualitative research.* Upper Saddle River, NJ: Merrill.

Crotty, M. 1998. *The foundations of social research: Meaning and perspective in the research process.* Thousands Oaks, CA: Sage Publications.

Gandini, L. (1993). Fundamentals of the Reggio approach to early childhood education. *Young Children, 49*(1), 4-8.

Dewey, J. (1915). *Democracy and education: An introduction to the philosophy of education.* New York, NY: The MacMillan Company.

Dewey, J. (1938). *Experience and education.* New York, NY: Simon & Schuster.

Donoghue, E.F. (2003). The emergence of a profession: Mathematics education in the United States 1890-1920. In G.M.A. Stanic & J. Kilpatrick (Eds.), *A history of school mathematics* (pp. 159-194). Reston, VA: National Council of Teachers of Mathematics, Inc.

Edwards, C., Gandini, L., & Forman, G. (Eds.). (2011). *The hundred languages of children: The Reggio Emilia experience in transformation.* Santa Barbara, CA: Praeger.

Falk, B., & Blumenreich, M. (2005). *The power of questions: A guide to teacher and student research.* Portsmouth, NH: Heinemann.

Fey, J.T. & Graeber, A.O. (2003). From the new math to the agenda for action. In G.M.A. Stanic & J. Kilpatrick (Eds.), *A history of school mathematics* (pp. 159-194). Reston, VA: National Council of Teachers of Mathematics, Inc.

Fraser, S. (2006). *Authentic childhood: Experiencing Reggio Emilia in the classroom.* Toronto: Nelson.

Harold, B. (1972). Beyond student-centered teaching, *Change, 4*(8), 48-53.

Hartung, M.L. (1939). Mathematics in progressive education. *The Mathematics Teacher, 32*(6), 265-269.

Haystead, M.W. & Marzano, R.J. (2009). *Meta-analytic synthesis of studies conducted at Marzano Research Laboratory on instructional strategies.* Englewood, CO: Marzano Research Laboratory.

Hiebert, J., Carpenter, T.P., Fennema, E., Fuson, K.C., Wearne, D., Murray, H., Oliver, A., Human, P. (1997). *Making sense: Teaching and learning mathematics with understanding.* Portsmouth, NH: Heinemann.

Hirsh, E.D. (2009). *The making of Americans: Democracy and our schools.* Grand Rapids, MI: Yale University Press.

Hubbard, R.S., & Power, B.M. (2003). *The art of classroom inquiry: A handbook for teacher researchers.* Portsmouth, NH: Heinemann.

Indiana Department of Education. (2016, January). *School demographics.* Indianapolis, IN: Author. Retrieved from http://www.doe.in.gov/.

Lloyd, L. (1999). Multi-age classes and high ability students. *Review of Educational Research, 69*(2), 187–212.

MacLean, M.S. & Mohr, M.M. (1999). *Teacher researchers at work.* Berkley, CA: National Writing Project.

McDonald, J.P. (2014). *American school reform: What works, what fails, and why.* Chicago, IL: The University of Chicago Press.

National Commission on Excellence in Education (1983). *A nation at risk: The imperative for education reform.* Washington D.C.: U.S. Government Printing Office.

National Council of Teachers of Mathematics (1980). *An agenda for research action in mathematics education: Beginning the discussion.* Reston, VA: National Council of Teachers of Mathematics, Inc.

National Council of Teachers of Mathematics (1989). *Curriculum and evaluation standards for school mathematics.* Reston, VA: National Council of Teachers of Mathematics, Inc.

National Council of Teachers of Mathematics (2000). *Principles and standards for school mathematics.* Reston, VA: National Council of Teachers of Mathematics, Inc.

National Council of Teachers of Mathematics (2014). *Principles to actions: Ensuring mathematical success for all.* Reston, VA: National Council of Teachers of Mathematics, Inc.

National Education Association of the United States. (1918). *Cardinal principles of secondary education: A report of the commission on the reorganization of secondary education, appointed by the National Education Association.* Washington: Government Printing Office.

National Research Council. (1989). *Everybody counts: A report to the nation on the future of mathematical education.* Washington, DC: National Academy Press.

Payne, J.N., (2003). The new math and its aftermath, grades K-8. In G.M.A. Stanic & J. Kilpatrick (Eds.), *A history of school mathematics* (pp. 559-598). Reston, VA: National Council of Teachers of Mathematics, Inc.

Roberts, D. L. (2001). E. H. Moore's early twentieth-century program for reform in mathematics education. *The American Mathematical Monthly, 108*(8), 689–696.

Ratner, S. (1992). John Dewey, E.H. Moore, and the philosophy of mathematics education in the twentieth century. *Journal of Mathematical Behaviors, 11*(1), 105-116.

Schoenfeld, A.H. (2004). The math wars. *Educational Policy, 18*(1), 253-286.

Smith, D.E. (1900). *The teaching of elementary mathematics.* New York, NY: The Macmillan Company.

Tarini, E., & White, L. (1998). Looking in the mirror: A reflection of Reggio practice in Winnetka. In C. Edwards, L. Gandini, & G. Forman (Eds.), *The hundred languages of children: The Reggio Emilia approach – advanced reflections* (pp. 375-404). Westport, CT: Ablex Publishing.

Wien, C.A. (2011). Learning to document in Reggio-inspired education. *Early Childhood Research & Practice,* 13(2).

ABOUT THE AUTHOR

Laura Ann Hayden is a 3rd and 4th grade teacher at the Indianapolis Public Schools/Butler University Laboratory School in Indianapolis, IN (United States). Through receiving her Masters in Effective Teaching and Leadership at Butler University, she researched the benefits of implementing reform mathematics into her classroom.

In: (Participatory) Action Research
Editors: J. Calder and J. Foletta

ISBN: 978-1-53613-041-6
© 2018 Nova Science Publishers, Inc.

Chapter 2

LITERATURE CIRCLES AS TOOLS FOR STUDENT DIALOGUE AND EMPOWERMENT

Ryan Flessner[*]

Butler University, College of Education, Indianapolis, IN, US

ABSTRACT

Studying the implementation of literature circles in his fourth grade classroom, Flessner examines the ways in which his students learn to effectively engage in natural discussions related to the literature they are reading. Barriers to the implementation of literature circles in the classroom are discussed, and ideas for successful execution are highlighted. Engaging students as co-researchers, Flessner utilizes literature circles as a way for his students to take control of their learning. This empowerment leads to the co-construction of a tool to evaluate the effectiveness of the literature circle process. Limitations to teacher research, generally, and to this study, specifically, are discussed at the end of the chapter along with the study's significance and suggestions for further research. The chapter's Epilogue highlights the author's journey in the fifteen years since the completion of this study. Additional readings

---

[*] Email: rflessne@butler.edu. Phone: 317.940.8397.

are offered for readers who wish to further pursue the topic(s) of literature circles and/or teacher research.

INTRODUCTION

For many years, teachers have attempted to vary the delivery of reading instruction at the intermediate level.[1] Historically, authors have highlighted a plethora of approaches including Reader's Workshop (Atwell, 1998; Calkins, 2001), Guided Reading (Fountas & Pinnell, 1996), and Reader's Theatre (Short, Harste, & Burke, 1996). Teachers use these methods—as well as many other practices—in order to diversify their reading instruction and to meet the needs of the variety of learners within their classrooms.

Since the mid-1980s, the term *literature circles* has been used more and more frequently when referring to the teaching of reading. Kathy Short's 1986 doctoral dissertation at Indiana University was the first piece of writing to use the term *literature circles* (Daniels, 1994). Short (1986) coined the term in order to describe:

> …small groups [designed] to get children participating in open-ended discussions about a shared story. Instead of centering on a predetermined set of questions [, students] were focused on exploring and discovering meaning together. (1986, p. 309)

Adult discussion groups based on common reading material have been in existence for quite some time. Yet, the use of these same types of interactions around a common text in intermediate grade classrooms has just started to increase in the past few decades. Research pertaining to literature circles often notes that literature circles are used to promote student choice and control over what they read and how they make

---

[1] For the purposes of this piece, the term *intermediate* refers to students in grades 4-6. In the United States, these grade levels typically correlate with children whose ages range from 9-12 years.

meaning from chosen texts (Brabham & Villaume, 2000; Burns, 1998; Noll, 1994; Pierce, 1990; Samway et al., 1991; Scott, 1994).

Because of their potential to empower students and increase dialogue to support student learning, I decided to begin using literature circles in my fourth grade classroom. Once I began this implementation, I was surprised to find that students struggled to have natural conversations when discussing their common texts. I read the research on literature circles carefully, modeled different techniques for discussion, and asked for regular student feedback. Though my students showed evidence that they had understood the strategy lessons (Harvey & Goudvis, 2000), were able to identify the elements of the story (Calkins, 2001), and knew how to make appropriate connections, inferences, and predictions (Harvey & Goudvis, 2000), their conversations were monotonous, predictable, and robotic.

Therefore, in this study, I asked students to identify and implement the elements of a quality discussion. In doing so, I concentrated on the elements of student choice and control. I employed the concept of student control by asking students to identify the necessary elements of a quality discussion. Student choice was utilized as the children analyzed their own dialogue and began to implement strategies to improve their conversations that they, themselves, had devised.

RESEARCH QUESTIONS

Through my research, I attempted to answer the following questions:

- According to fourth graders, what are the common elements of a quality discussion?
- After analyzing their own discussions, how do fourth graders identify and implement strategies for effective dialogue?

It was important that this study addressed each of these questions. First of all, students needed to be able to comprehend the purposes of literature circles. If natural dialogue was found to be unobtainable, the process of literature circles would have been ineffective. I hoped that by recognizing the elements of a quality discussion, students would begin to internalize the process in order to participate in more productive literature circles— literature circles that encouraged more thoughtful dialogue, that allowed students greater understanding of the texts they were reading, that allowed them to relate the books to their own lives and experiences.

Therefore, the second question was crucial to this project. In order to evaluate their own learning, students had to be given the opportunity to assess the literature circles of which they were a part. The purpose of this portion of the project was for students to dissect their own conversations in order to identify positive elements of their conversations as well as aspects that needed attention. The success of the literature circles would need to be judged by the students' ability to define standards of quality and the students' effectiveness at implementing these standards.

In addition, I examined my own practices in order to assist the students through the various phases of the study. Short and her colleagues (1999 update) state that, "Through careful observation of our [behaviors] we are likely to uncover the hidden roles we play and we can become more reflective as teachers" (p. 377). Throughout the process, I needed to reflect with the students in order to alleviate or alter practices that hinder effective literature circles.

REVIEW OF LITERATURE[2]

The writings of several educational theorists have been influential to the design and implementation of literature circles in intermediate classrooms. Most notable are the writings of Jerome Bruner, Lev Vygotsky, and John Dewey. The concept of *scaffolding* as introduced by

---

[2] In the Epilogue, I note that 15 years has passed since this study took place. In order to sustain the integrity of the piece as it was originally conceived, I have not updated my references within the text of the chapter. However, I have provided references to more current literature on this topic in the "Additional Readings" section at the end of the chapter.

Bruner (1961) is evident in literature circles as teachers use temporary support structures to help students learn to take control of their own discussions. Vygotsky's (1978) *zone of proximal development* [i.e., "What the child is able to do in collaboration today he [*sic*] will be able to do independently tomorrow" (Vygotsky as cited in Rieber & Carton, 1987, p. 211)] presents itself in the form of teacher modeling and other activities that promote the eventual move to student control (Daniels, 1994). John Dewey (1916) promoted learning by doing, student decision making and responsibility, and teachers as guides or coaches. All of these principles are employed as teachers implement literature circles. All of these ideas will be explored further in the following sections.

Literature circles are also one way in which teachers can provided a more balanced approach to the teaching of reading (Watson, 1990). In place of traditional basal reading programs, proponents of literature-based programs highlight the necessity of interactions with unabridged texts that lead to enjoyment and interpretation of literature (Peterson & Eeds, 1990). However, the move from basal readers (which often present shortened or abridged versions of stories or books) to full-length texts is not the only change taking place. Instruction must change along with the materials. The balanced literacy movement and its proponents incorporate relevant curriculum, promote cooperative learning opportunities, and address issues of diversity (Atwell, 1998).

Furthermore, a certain type of environment is necessary when attempting to carry out this style of instruction. Studies have identified a host of philosophical stances championed by teachers who have successfully implemented literature circles. These classrooms provide a secure and comfortable setting, promote ownership through student choice and control, expect varied constructions of meaning, encourage collaborative learning, and applaud risk taking (Scott, 1994; Watson, 1990).

A prevalent theme in studies of classrooms employing literature circles was a need for students to play a more active role in their own reading instruction (Noll, 1994; Scott, 1994). Many educators agree that, "For reading to become a lifelong habit and a deeply owned skill, it has to be voluntary, anchored in feelings of pleasure and power" (Daniels, 1994, p. 19). Literature circles provide this sense of ownership. In addition, other purposes for literature circles include creating cooperative, responsible, pleasurable classroom, strengthening literacy and conversational skills, and encouraging students to read in order to construct personal meaning (Burns, 1998; Scott, 1994).

With all of these benefits of literature circles, Brabham and Villaume (2000) remind us that we must keep our purpose in mind to avoid narrowing or losing sight of the focus for literature circles. These purposes are evident through several features of literature circles. Common characteristics include social interaction, groups of mixed ability, substantial time to read and discuss during the school day, and an assortment of reading materials. Discussions highlight comprehension, reading processes, discussion of literary elements, content other than the direct focus of the book, personal stories, and an unpredictable order (Burns, 1998; Daniels, 1994; Hanssen, 1990).

Based on these purposes and features, literature circles have a wide array of effects on the classroom and the participants. In typical situations, students become more confident, engaged, and knowledgeable (Samway et al., 1991). They view themselves as readers and understand themselves and others better as they explore personal situations, express opinions, disagree, problem solve, and discuss sensitive issues (Peralta-Nash & Dutch, 2000; Samway et al., 1991).

METHODOLOGY

In order to create a complete picture of literature circles, various methods of data collection were utilized. The first opportunity for data collection was student journals. The assumptions and perceptions of students were analyzed through their writing. Secondly, a class discussion was held to highlight or challenge these assumptions and perceptions and to articulate the concepts of effective dialogue. Students began to demonstrate their understanding of this concept while they built on previous knowledge and attempted to challenge some of their own misperceptions. The next step in the data collection process included the recording and analyzing of actual literature circles. The students analyzed their own discussions and began to construct a plethora of ideas for creating more natural discussions.

Participants and Settings

I teach fourth graders at the University School[3], a small, independent school located on the Upper West Side of New York City. As families are responsible for yearly tuition in excess of $20,000, students at the University School come, primarily, from upper class families within New York City. Of the twelve students in my classroom, four students are given additional reading and writing support during the week. There are two African American students, one Latino student, and one student of Middle Eastern decent in my classroom. The other eight students are of Caucasian descent.

Data Collection

Phase One: Student Assumptions and Perceptions of Literature Circles

The first set of data collected (in mid-December and throughout the beginning of February) focused on students' perceptions and assumptions of literature circles. This data was collected by reviewing students' writing journals. Several journal entries were evaluated. Earlier in the year, students responded to their work in literature circles on three occasions.

---

[3] For reasons of confidentiality, all school and student names are pseudonyms.

These entries were used in order to evaluate the perceptions of the students as they were introduced to literature circles. Other journal entries were analyzed, as well. One addressed the idea of effective dialogue. Another addressed the changes that students were witnessing throughout the project. A final entry asked for general feelings of the students' literature circle experiences. This journal entry was used as a comparison piece for early entries written by each student.

Phase Two: Defining Effective Dialogue

The second phase of data collection (which took place in mid-January) focused on defining the elements of effective dialogue. A teacher-led discussion was recorded in student and teacher journals in order to allow students to create their own standards for excellence. Based on this discussion, students began to identify strategies that they could employ in literature circles. In addition, further evidence that was helpful for this portion of data collection was identified by searching through student assignments from prior rounds of literature circles.

Phase Three: Literature Circle Analysis

A third and final phase of data collection (which took place throughout the month of January and the beginning of February) surrounded the analysis of actual literature circles. The class and I recorded a variety of literature circles. Students were asked to examine these recordings. In doing so, students were able to identify successful (as well as ineffective) discussion techniques and the benefits these elements had on their discussions. Writing from students' journals, transcribed portions of the conversations, and my own reflections through a teacher journal were used as data sources for the analytical process.

Throughout this analysis, students were required to consistently reflect on their participation in literature circles. They were frequently reminded of the educational purposes and curricular goals of literature circles, but they were also expected to create natural conversations that promoted student choice and control.

Data Analysis

By analyzing student journals, I began to find patterns of student understandings and perceptions of (or misconceptions that interfered with) quality dialogue. These patterns were the building blocks for a class discussion about the significance of literature circle implementation. Through analysis of the data from this conversation, the students and I created a list of characteristics indicative of successful literature circles. Once these characteristics had been identified, students were able to participate in self-analysis of their own literature circle conversations. Using student and teacher analysis of several literature circles, I became more able to show the progression toward more independent, natural conversations.

FINDINGS

Throughout the study, new and exciting information began to develop. Each phase of the process brought about surprising insights from the children that helped them become more active members of the evaluative process. Furthermore, the students were open, honest, and extremely willing to participate. In doing so, they were empowered to assist me as I examined my own teaching practices.

The following review of the findings will look at each phase of the data collection process. The first section will explore student assumptions and perceptions of literature circles. Second, I review the process in which we – the students and I – engaged in the process of defining effective dialogue. Finally, I capture the main findings from our collaborative literature circle analysis.

Phase One: Student Assumptions and Perceptions of Literature Circles

Reviewing students' journal entries from the previous round of literature circles proved to be a fruitful activity. Though I regularly check through the students' writing journals, this rereading helped to focus my attention on very specific information. I read through a new lens: that of a researcher rather than simply as the classroom teacher.

In October, the students completed their first round of literature circles. As this was their introduction to the concept, I felt it was important to use role sheets (Daniels, 1994) in order to familiarize students with the concept of a literary discussion. While I strive to allow for student creativity, I fear that my instruction may seem disorganized. For this reason, I decided to utilize the role sheet method to introduce literature circles to my fourth graders. Literature circles allowed for student choice, control, and creativity while providing a structured environment in which a new concept could be introduced.

At the start of the process, I taught one role at a time (e.g., Discussion Director, Illuminator, Connector, etc.). To begin, I modeled the process for the students. We then read a book together, completed the role sheets, and discussed the types of questions we had formulated through the use of these sheets. I then asked student volunteers to model how the role sheets worked in combination. Students then tried these roles independently with one another.

The students' journals helped me gain insight into the understandings and/or confusions occurring during this initial introduction. In October, reviewing the journals helped me discover what I needed to re-teach. In December, these entries helped me review the history of my students' experiences with literature circles and allowed me to construct lessons that would lead to the evaluative process the students and I would undertake. What I found was that students were able to make preliminary judgments of their conversations before the formal evaluative process began.

Several elements from the students' journals were helpful. First, I asked them to write about why we were doing literature circles. Their answers varied in many ways and helped me to evaluate their understanding of the purpose of using this pedagogical tool. Several students highlighted the social aspects of literature circles. Tommy commented that, "...we do literature circles so we can learn and listen to our friends" (Journal Entry, Oct. 17). Starr agreed by writing "I think we do this to help our reading skills and to learn to listen to each other...this isn't a one man act" (Journal Entry, Oct. 17). Leonard reflected, "[In] literature circles...we get to learn and teach ourselves. We are in groups to learn from what we read and to learn from other kids" (Journal Entry, Oct. 17).

Other students commented on aspects related to study skills. Jake stated that, "Literature circles will get us better organized" (Journal Entry, Oct. 29). Callie felt that, "Literature circles give us some responsibility" (Journal Entry, Oct. 17).

Yet another group of students commented on the academic side of literature circles. Riley reflected on one of the roles (Literary Luminary) by stating "We do a literature circle to be able to understand sentences better" (Journal Entry, Oct. 17). According to J. J., "We do literature circles because it helps us with our vocabulary and spelling" (Journal Entry, Oct. 17). Loren saw an even further advantage to literature circles. She wrote, "Why do we do literature circles? Because it's more fun than doing worksheets" (Journal Entry, Oct. 17, 2001).

After identifying the students' perceptions of the purposes of literature circles, I began to look for initial responses to the concept. I wanted to know how the students were feeling. I was looking for evidence of interest, empowerment, or concern. There responses were, once again, varied and helpful.

Many students stated that literature circles would help them become more comfortable with their classmates. For example, Annabelle felt that, "Most of the people in my group I don't know, and I want to know them" (Journal Entry, Oct. 29). However, some students were not so excited about the prospect of working in a group. Andrew confided, "I actually myself would rather read by myself than with a group because I can read faster than a lot of people" (Journal Entry, Oct. 17). As the sessions progressed, the group unanimously agreed that literature circles were a positive experience. Those students who had initial concerns became more comfortable with the format, and began to see the advantages to discussing literature with their peers. As the introduction to the process of literature circles was completed and the first books were chosen, Andrew mentioned, "I am really excited about this…because I think from what I've done it will be cool" (Journal Entry, Oct. 29). Riley waxed poetic as he wrote of the introduction to literature circles. He said, "…it was sort of like a puzzle that we had to put together… . We put together the outlining of the puzzle… and it's helping me understand books" (Journal Entry, Oct. 17).

Another interesting set of data came from the children's responses to the role sheet format. Several students thought the role sheets were helpful. Callie wrote, "The reason we have [role sheets] in the first place is so we don't get completely lost" (Journal Entry, Nov. 6). Other students saw the benefits of role sheets, but also realized that they needed to use them sparingly. Myles acknowledged:

> …you write down questions on your role sheet they you practice them so you can get rid of them before the literature circle. If you use the role sheets it's not a discussion, it's just people asking each other questions. (Journal Entry, Nov. 6)

Zoe agreed by commenting, "Soon I think that the groups will be able to leave the role sheets behind and just have a regular discussion" (Journal Entry, Nov. 6, 2001). J. J. made an insightful remark when he noted, "Once we practice we can use our heads instead of our sheets" (Journal Entry, Nov. 6).

Others had a more negative response to role sheets. Riley felt that, "In literature circles the point is to know what to say… . The sheets distract you a lot more so you can't concentrate as much as you want" (Journal Entry, Nov. 8). Loren also felt that role sheets were somewhat of a hindrance. She argued:

> I think that getting rid of role sheets might help us with our discussion. We might feel that we can take more parts in the discussion

and not just stay in our own space. Some kids may be able to do more in the discussion but maybe, other kids take all the parts then they might think they don't have to do anything in literature circles. (Journal Entry, Nov. 6)

All of these comments helped me dissect my own teaching practices. As a result, after the first round of literature circles, I asked the children to leave the role sheets behind. However, I also asked them to remember the various roles as they began to construct questions for the upcoming round of literature circles. In addition, a review of my own journal entries helped to reassess the amount of time I was providing between literature circles. One student, Tommy, mentioned that, "I think Mr. Flessner could let us have a little more time. But it's okay he has a busy schedule" (Journal Entry, Oct. 18). A thoughtful young man, Tommy helped me focus my attention on what children need to read, understand and prepare for literature circles. During the second round of literature circles, I asked students to complete a variety of assignments as they read. Literature circles became just one piece of my reading instruction. Rather than meeting every day to discuss their books, students were asked to prepare for literature circles only once a week. Because of this change, students seemed more prepared, more capable of seeing the big picture, and more willing to listen to their classmates, discuss their ideas, and use their opinions to engage in friendly debates.

Throughout the second and third rounds of literature circles, the students became more comfortable with the format as well as the evaluative techniques that were introduced (these will be described in greater detail later in the chapter). Their enthusiasm and excitement became contagious as the project continued. Later journal entries showed their growth and wisdom. When asked to reflect on their literature circle experiences, the students were happy to oblige. Zoe stated, "I...learned that I made some mistakes and it's not the end of the world" (Journal Entry, Jan. 24). Annabelle became aware of the responsibility I was transferring to the students through the use of literature circles. She wrote, "I feel it is our responsibility to make these literature circles wonderful....

It is nice to have the ability to do this" (Journal Entry, Jan. 24). Further comments from the students will be explored in the next two sections.

Phase Two: Defining Effective Dialogue

In literature circles, effective dialogue is the key to student choice and control. If students are capable of contributing to quality discussions, there is little need for teacher interference. The teacher can take a step back, allow the students to learn from exploring issues together, and become more of a resource than the arbiter of knowledge.

As I reflected on the first round of literature circles in our classroom, one concern that arose was the children's inability to create a natural discussion. Even the students noticed that their conversations were missing something. Jake observed, "We will know when we are doing real literature circles when our conversations start flowing and there are not big pauses in our conversation" (Journal Entry, Nov. 6). This study was designed to help alleviate the issue of unnatural conversations. The crux of the study was for students to identify the elements of effective dialogue, create a useful format for this information, and to evaluate their own literature circles.

Through group journal entries and a class discussion, the children created a checklist with which literature circles could be evaluated. Though I was hesitant to create a checklist fearing it would "lead to role sheets in disguise" (Teacher Journal, Nov. 17), the students convinced me by arguing that a checklist is different than a grade. In words that surpassed my expectations for nine- and ten-year-olds, they argued that grades were used to give a final assessment, but a checklist was a way to help create guidelines for them to follow. The checklist would be used as a guide while preparing for literature circles and as a way to assess what the groups were doing well and what improvements could be made after literature circles were reviewed.

Therefore, a checklist was created. After brainstorming in groups, looking for commonality between groups, and a little bartering, the class displayed what it deemed the qualities of an effective literature circle. What was interesting after looking at the compiled list was that student had done a wonderful job of listing the social aspects of literature circles (e.g., listen to others, avoid arguing, show your personal best, etc.), but had neglected to include the academic aspects of literature circles (identify and discuss plot, setting, literary devices, etc.). As I mentioned this, their pencils began to move feverishly. The following day, the class had completed its requirements for the literature circle checklist. Some fine-tuning was necessary, but after several conversations and minor revisions, the checklist was finalized.

The students had grouped the checklist criteria under four headings: Getting Ready, Group Behavior, Discussion Structure, and When Speaking (a copy of the checklist has been included as an Appendix to this chapter). Once the checklist was developed, the students were ready to begin evaluating themselves and their discussions.

Phase Three: Literature Circle Analysis

To begin, students watched videotapes of three literature circles that had been filmed in December (during the second round of literature circles). Using the checklists, the students were asked to evaluate the videotapes. Because the checklist was quite extensive, the class was divided into four groups, each group responsible for one section of the checklist. After viewing the first videotape, the students sat silently, stunned. I asked the children what they were thinking, and they started to giggle. This was disappointing as we had specifically discussed the fact that the sheets were not to judge but to support one another. Unfortunately, some students' initial instinct was to exert their power. Jake, for instance, commented, "Whenever I am watching a videotape of a literature circle I feel like I am the teacher and I get to grade kids on what they do" (Journal Entry, Jan. 24). On the other hand, uneasiness was experienced by others. "It is very hard to evaluate your friends because you don't want to say they're bad, but you don't want to lie when you are evaluating because it's to help them improve on literature circles" confided Callie (Journal Entry, Jan. 24). It was important at this point to remind students that the checklists were not to "grade" their peers but, rather, to look for strengths and areas of need. Throughout the evaluative process, the students needed to be reminded of this fact.

Another dilemma encountered was the lack of evidence the children were using as they evaluated their peers. Comments such as 'yes' and 'no' were common responses on the checklists. When asked to substantiate their claims, many were unable to do so. As we proceeded with our evaluations, the students continued to work on improving the evidence they were supplying to substantiate the claims on their evaluations.

For the next month, the students and I evaluated other videotapes and live literature circles. The children became more confident in their abilities to evaluate. By reviewing their checklists, the videotaped literature circles, and their journal entries (which included comments on the process of evaluating literature circles), I was able to judge the effectiveness of this study.

Early checklists contain little proof to substantiate evaluative claims made by the children. Students often gave opinions as to whether or not the groups were fulfilling the requirements of effective dialogue, but could not back up their claims with evidence. For example, a comment recorded regularly was, "One time they wandered off the topic." Another frequent judgment was, "Everyone answered one of the questions." These comments had potential to be helpful to the group; however, without pinpointing exact discussion points, the comments lacked evidence to support the group in continuing to improve their literature circles.

After each videotape, I asked students to volunteer to read their findings. We discussed the evaluators' comments, what they had found that was helpful, and what further evidence could have been added to assist the group as they attempted to improve their discussions. At the beginning of this process, few students raised their hands to volunteer their comments. Students understood what was supposed to be happening. Yet, they were unsure as to what was acceptable. Therefore, I changed my tactic. I began to collect evaluations as soon as the videotapes were turned off and the students had had a chance to complete their comments. In the moment, I selected and read comments from students who had successfully justified their evaluations of their peers. This allowed students to hear what an effective evaluation sounded like, and they became more comfortable offering constructive feedback to one another.

By the end of the study, students were running out of room on the sheets. Their comments were often difficult to read because arrows were used to find open space on the paper to finish sentences. I was often asked to give the students extra time to complete evaluations, and some students even took their evaluations to recess so they could squeeze in final comments.

This process impacted literature circles in many ways. Most importantly, because students had taken on the role of the evaluator, they became more familiar with what was expected in a literature circle. They knew what criteria were used to evaluate the circles; they knew what was regularly missing in the discussions; and they understood the importance of attending to as many of the criteria as possible. Students noticed early on that few of the groups were "looking for examples of creative writing" (one of the criteria under "Getting Ready"). After several comments on this weakness, each group made an extra effort to prove that they could be successful in this area. Tommy was very proud to note that Leonard had discussed a simile during a discussion of *The Search for Delicious* (Babbitt, 1969). He even cited the specific sentence Leonard had noted, "It slipped right through his hands like a small fish" (Literature Circle Evaluation, Feb. 1). When I asked for volunteers to comment on the literature circle, Tommy's hand shot up in the air. This type of volunteerism was prominent by the end of the study.

Journal entries also showed the students' growth in ability and confidence. In her journal Starr wrote "I learned more about literature circles after creating the checklist because after we made the checklist I could really pick out the things I needed to improve and the things I should keep up" (Journal Entry, Jan. 24). Furthermore, Annabelle felt that, "...We should have more videotapes because people can't catch their own mistakes unless you look over your past literature circles" (Journal Entry,

Jan. 24). Throughout the process, students seemed to become more comfortable with the evaluative process. They began to realize that literature circles were not just another assignment. They were learning experiences. Myles summarized by writing, "By evaluating literature circles I as able to see what I needed to improve on. You could also learn what you did right, so you always do that and you know it's right" (Journal Entry, Jan. 24).

DISCUSSION OF THE FINDINGS

As stated at the beginning of this chapter, I designed this study to answer to main questions:

- According to fourth graders, what are the common elements of a quality discussion?
- After analyzing their own discussions, how do fourth graders identify and implement strategies for effective dialogue?

I feel the evidence shows that both of these questions have been answered.

First of all, fourth graders were able to identify the elements of a quality discussion through the creation of the checklist. Obviously, it was imperative that students had the opportunity to become familiar with the techniques necessary for quality literature circles. However, after introductory lessons (and with practice), students were able to identify the criteria necessary for the checklist. When reminded that they were focusing on the social side of literature circles while omitting the academic portions, they easily switched gears to include this information.

Furthermore, what was most striking about this process was that students were able to identify instructional approaches that were hindering the process of a quality discussion. For some, the requirement to utilize role sheets needed to be removed. For others, time was a concern. After reviewing these responses, I was able to make changes in the format to accommodate these needs.

As for the second research question, students grew into the responsibility of evaluating their discussions and applying their findings. Students took the responsibilities of evaluating extremely seriously. After addressing the issue of power and judgment, the students were able to use constructive responses to the criteria to assist their classmates on their journeys to effective dialogue. The checklist, ultimately, became a tool for formative assessment. Most importantly, this tool was not solely my responsibility. Students assisted in its creation and utilization.

Through this process, the children immediately noticed successes and challenges inherent in the implementation of literature circles. By attending to these strengths and needs, students began to build deeper understandings of the content and the process of literature circles.

LIMITATIONS

Several components of this study may be considered limiting. First of all, the demographics of the students and the class size may not align with those in most schools. Individual educators should use their own particular lenses as well as knowledge of their own students as they read this study and apply its findings to their own practices.

Secondly, the research takes place on a small scale. Additional time, money, and other resources would be required to recreate this study on a larger scale. As the study progressed, time became the most precious resource as well as the most limiting factor of the study. Because this project was designed as a final component of a Master's Degree program, time was of the essence. University deadlines proved to be a major limitation of the study. As discussed in the "Suggestions for Future Research" section below, it would be interesting to research more long term effects on the classroom environment. In addition, the timing of the project was somewhat problematic. Because of Winter Break, standardized testing, and other factors, even more time was lost.

Other major limitations involved setting and equipment. I could not have predicted the availability of the school's video camera. Because this study took place during the first year that a camera was available at the school, teachers were still experimenting with its many uses. This caused some problems in scheduling videotaping sessions. In relation to this problem, the nature of the study may not have been conducive to the recording necessitated by the project. Because literature circles usually happen simultaneously among the various groups, it was difficult to find a quiet time to record. Early videotapes were useless because of background noise in the classroom. This required finding additional space to record small groups. This caused a more unnatural feel to the recording process as students were removed from the familiarity of the classroom setting and were forced into a fishbowl-like environment for videotaping purposes.

Finally, as each teacher implements literature circles in different ways, generalizations made in this study may not be applicable in all classrooms. The purpose of this study was not to make generalizations about all teachers and/or students in all schools. Rather, it reflects the research of one teacher and a small group of students who wanted to achieve natural discussions that would highlight the use of literature circles to achieve the ultimate goal of student choice and control.

SIGNIFICANCE

As a classroom teacher, this study has great personal significance. The reflection involved with teacher research is time-consuming, demanding, and – often – depressing. However, most importantly, it is rewarding. By encouraging students to voice their opinions, self- and peer-critique, and by evaluating my own instructional practices, I have opened new windows of learning for my students and myself. This project has forced me to take stock of my own continued professional development, to realize the potential of the students with whom I work on a daily basis, and to continue the search for effective instruction.

As I began the project, I hoped to create a piece that would cover some of the elements of literature circles not typically discussed in the literature related to literature circles. The research on literature circles currently in circulation speaks generally to the concepts of student choice and control; however, teachers will encounter any number of problems as they begin to incorporate this technique into their reading instruction. It is imperative that teachers evaluate this instructional strategy and offer solutions to problems they encounter. Through this study, I hoped to empower the children in my classroom to create a format for achieving the goal of natural, effective conversations. One intent of this study was to add to the current selection of readings related to the implementation of literature circles. Ideally, this project will spark additional discussions, foster further reflections, and stimulate new ideas. In essence, it is my hope that this study will assist teachers as they begin to evaluate the implementation of literature circles in their own classrooms.

SUGGESTIONS FOR FUTURE RESEARCH

Because this study was completed in a relatively short time frame, it would be helpful to extend the research over a longer period of time. Within two months, great improvements were made. Who knows what could happen over the course of an entire school year? It would also be interesting to see what would occur if literature circles were removed from the curriculum for a period of time. Without regular participation in the process, would students begin to slip back into old practices, or would the knowledge gained through such a study hold over time?

Finally, I encourage every teacher to take on the professional responsibility of teacher research. Professional development, as it stands today, leaves much to be desired. There is nothing more essential to our schools than empowering teachers to recognize a problem, to study its genesis, its growth over time, its possible solutions, and to share their findings in ways that encourage other professionals to do the same. Teacher research provides the vehicle to continued improvements in curriculum, instruction, and professional development. I encourage all those who bravely call themselves educators to utilize teacher research as a mechanism for change.

EPILOGUE

Fifteen years have passed since the writing of this teacher research study. To ignore the fact that the literature cited is outdated would be careless of me. Since my study took place, a host of scholars has continued to pursue a variety of lines of research related to the implementation of literature circles in classrooms. Please see the "Additional Readings" section for more current writings related to literature circles. The "Additional Readings" section also lists resources for conducting teacher research and a variety of studies that have been conducted by classroom practitioners.

In the fifteen years since this study took place, I have conducted additional teacher research studies, researched teacher research networks, presented at a variety of conferences, published additional pieces (Amtzis, Flessner, & Klehr, 2016; Flessner, 2008; 2009; 2011; 2012; 2013; 2014; Flessner & Horwitz, 2012; Flessner & Stuckey, 2014), and continued to learn about the processes and power of teacher research; yet, this project – my first foray into teacher research – remains close to my heart.

When I arrived at Teachers College, Columbia University to begin my Master's Degree program, I was told I would need to complete a thesis utilizing teacher research methodology. I was mildly irritated, to say the least. I had big dreams. I saw grandiose research projects on my horizon – studies that would change education for the better. I went into the teacher research process with skepticism and bitterness.

Luckily, I was assigned a thesis advisor – Megan Blumenreich – who forever changed my understandings of research, its many manifestations, and its impact on students and schools. Megan assisted me in grounding my research in a true problem of practice. She helped me narrow my focus, design a manageable study, and pushed me to share my findings when my study was finished. I am forever indebted to her as a mentor and as a friend. Luckily, with a little effort, we can all access many of Megan's publications on the topic of teacher research (e.g., Blumenreich, 2011; 2012; 2015; 2016; Blumenreich & Rodriguez, 2016; Falk & Blumenreich, 2005; 2012).

After finishing this project, I read everything I could find about teacher research. I devoured books, articles, conference proceedings, and any other obscure publication I could find. I contacted experts in the field whose names continued to appear in the publications I was scouring. Ken Zeichner, one of those experts, engaged with me in thought provoking conversations, sent me copies of articles he had written and drafts of manuscripts he was preparing, and – ultimately – agreed to serve as my advisor during my doctoral program at the University of Wisconsin-Madison.

Upon arrival in Madison, Ken introduced me to a family of teacher researchers. Cathy Caro-Bruce and Mary Klehr welcomed me with open arms, taught me about the network of teacher researchers they had built, and alerted me to the fact that hundreds of the studies conducted by teachers in this network were freely accessible on the internet (see oldweb.madison.k12.wi.us/sod/car/search.cgi). After many conversations with Ken, Cathy, and Mary, I was entrusted with the responsibility of co-facilitating a group of Madison teachers as they engaged in teacher research topics related to equity in our schools. With my co-facilitator, Sara Parrell, I was blessed with the opportunity to lead a group of educators through the teacher research process. Sara showed me the ropes of facilitating teacher research (see Caro-Bruce, 2000, for further information on this process), mentored me as I navigated the problem of working with practicing teachers from my position as a graduate student no longer engaged in daily classroom practice, and taught me the art of being patient with the research process.

As I look back on this history, I cannot believe the good fortune with which I have been blessed. Beginning with Megan, I have been surrounded by educators (Ken, Cathy, Mary, Sara, and others) who know the power of teacher research, believe that educators can take control of their own professional learning, and work with parents, policy makers, and other stakeholders to empower educators to instigate change in our classrooms, schools, and communities. Alongside Cathy, Mary, and Ken, I co-edited the book *Equity through Action Research* (Caro-Bruce, Flessner, Klehr, & Zeichner, 2007) which highlights the work of several teachers in Madison who used their positions as teacher researchers to make changes in their classroom practices to better attend to issues of equity, diversity, and social justice.

As my journey has continued, I have met others who have impacted my journey: Catherine Compton-Lilly, Julie Horwitz, Pat Maguire, Mary Brydon-Miller, Rebecca Akin, Alan Amtzis, Gerald Campano, Eric "Rico" Gutstein, and my wife and children: Courtney, Abel, and Adelyn. Each of these individuals – as well as others too numerous to name – has taught me much about the value of teaching and teacher research, the importance of teacher and student empowerment, and the need for all of us to support and publicize the work of educators around the globe who are truly making a difference in the lives of the students, families, and communities with whom they engage. I am a better educator and a better person because of my association with each of these individuals.

APPENDIX

Literature Circle Checklist

Book: Circle: Videotape/Audiotape/Live
Group Members:
Evaluator: Date of Evaluation:

Instructions

Place a checkmark next to the goals that are met, "no" next to goals that are not met, and a question mark net to goals that are partially met or met by some members of the group. Remember to give examples to help prove your point.

Getting Ready

_____ When reading, look for important ideas (themes).

_____ Be prepared (be able to prove your point, have page numbers ready, etc.).

_____ Ask questions that have more than one answer (avoid yes/no questions).

_____ Vary the subject of your questions by:

_____ Identifying the plot, setting, characters, and vocabulary.

_____ Making predictions and inferences.

_____ Making connections to other books, your life, and the real world.

_____ Looking for examples of creative writing (alliteration, personification, similes/metaphors, imagery, cliffhangers, etc.).

_____ Take your book, pencil, and discussion topics/questions to literature circles (leave other distractions at your desk).

Group Behaviors

_____ Work together.

_____ Debate, but don't argue.

_____ Focus on the group while doing your personal best.

Discussion Structure

_____ Everyone should speak and participate equally.

_____ Have a discussion rather than a question/answer session.

_____ Avoid interrupting your group members.

When Speaking

_____ Consider the points of others, and add on to their points.

_____ Try to talk about new ideas instead of repeating yourself or others.

_____ When it's your turn, avoid wandering away from the topic.

Other Comments

_____

_____

_____

_____

REFERENCES

Amtzis, A., Flessner, R., & Klehr, M. (2016). Special issue on teaching and learning teacher research. *The Educational Forum, 80*(4).

Atwell, N. (1998). *In the middle: Writing, reading, and learning with adolescents*. Portsmouth, NH: Heinemann.

Babbitt, N. (1969). *The search for delicious*. New York, NY: Scholastic.

Blumenreich, M. (2011). Scholarly research makes education dynamic. *Teacher Education & Practice, 24*(4), 447-450.

Blumenreich, M. (2012). Teacher learners' oral history projects: Exploring how our communities and cultural pasts shape us. In R. Flessner, G. R. Miller, K. M. Patrizio, & J. R. Horwitz (Eds.), *Agency through teacher education: Reflection, community, and learning* (pp. 5-14). Lanham, MD: Rowman & Littlefield Education.

Blumenreich, M. (2015). Commentary: Teacher research as a form of inspiration, influence and mentoring. *Voices of Practitioners, 10*(2), 83-87.

Blumenreich, M. (2016). Assigning reflective memo blogs to support teacher research data analysis. *Voices of Practitioners, 11*(1), 68-75.

Blumenreich, M., & Rodriguez, R. (2016). Research as discovery, teaching as trust: Developing new perspectives through teacher research. *The Educational Forum, 80*(4), 367-379.

Brabham, E., & Villaume, S. (2000). Continuing conversations about literature circles. *The Reading Teacher, 54*, 278-280.

Bruner, J. (1961). *The process of education*. Cambridge, MA: Harvard University Press.

Burns, B. (1998). Changing the classroom climate with literature circles. *Journal of Adolescent and Adult Literacy, 42,* 124-129.

Calkins, L. M. (2001). *The art of teaching reading.* New York, NY: Longman.

Caro-Bruce, C. (2000). *Action research facilitator's handbook.* Oxford, OH: National Staff Development Council.

Caro-Bruce, C., Flessner, R., Klehr, M., & Zeichner, K. M. (Eds.). (2007). *Creating equitable classrooms through action research.* Thousand Oaks, CA: Corwin Press.

Daniels, H. (1994). *Literature circles: Voice and choice in the student-centered classroom.* York, ME: Stenhouse Publishers.

Dewey, J. (1916). *Democracy and education.* New York, NY: Macmillan.

Falk, B. & Blumenreich, M. (2005). *The power of questions: A guide to teacher and student research.* Portsmouth, NH: Heinemann.

Falk, B., & Blumenreich, M. (2012). *Teaching matters: Stories from inside schools.* New York, NY: The New Press.

Flessner, R. (2008). *Living in multiple worlds: Utilizing third space theory to re-envision research in the field of teacher education* (Doctoral dissertation, University of Wisconsin-Madison).

Flessner, R. (2009). Working toward a third space in the teaching of elementary mathematics. *Educational Action Research, 17*(3), 425-446.

Flessner, R. (2011). Pushing the field of practitioner research: Utilizing 'reflective third spaces' to explore educational practice. In I. M. Saleh, & M. S. Khine (Eds.), *Practitioner research in teacher education: Theory and best practices* (pp. 121-140). Frankfurt, Germany: Peter Lang.

Flessner, R. (2012). Addressing the research/practice divide in teacher education. *Action in Teacher Education, 34*(2), 159-171.

Flessner, R. (2013). 'Making the work interesting': Empowerment through ownership in elementary literature circles. In A. Cohan, & A. Honigsfeld (Eds.), *Breaking the mold of classroom management: What educators should know and do to enable student success* (pp.61-67). Lanham, MD: Roman & Littlefield Education.

Flessner, R. (2014). Revisiting reflection: Utilizing third spaces in teacher education. *The Educational Forum 78*(3), 231-247.

Flessner, R., & Horwitz, J. (2012). Easing into the academy: Using technology to foster cross-institutional critical friendships. *The New Educator, 8*(1), 86-103.

Flessner, R., & Stuckey, S. (2014). Politics and action research: An examination of one school's mandated action research program. *Action Research Journal 12*(1), 36-51.

Fountas, I. C., & Pinnell, G. S. (1996). *Guided reading: Good first teaching for all children.* Portsmouth, NH: Heinemann.

Hanssen, E. (1990). Planning for literature circles: Variations in focus and structure. In K. Short & K. Pierce (Eds.), *Talking about books: Creating literate communities* (pp. 198-209). Portsmouth, NH: Heinemann.

Harvey, S., & Goudvis, A. (2000). *Strategies that work: Teaching comprehension to enhance understanding.* York, ME: Stenhouse Publishers.

Noll, E. (1994). Social issues and literature circles with adolescents. *Journal of Reading, 38,* 88-93.

Peralta-Nash, C., & Dutch, A. (2000). Literature circles: Creating an environment for choice. *Primary Voices K-6, 8,* 29-37.

Peterson, R., & Eeds, M. (1990). *Grand conversations: Literature groups in action.* New York, NY: Scholastic.

Piere, K. (1990). Initiating literature discussion groups: Teaching like learners. In K. Short & K. Pierce (Eds.), *Talking about books: Creating literate communities* (pp. 176-197). Portsmouth, NH: Heinemann.

Rieber, R. W., & Carton, A. S. (Eds.). (1987). *The collected works of L. S. Vygotsky: Problems of general psychology.* New York, NY: Plenum Press.

Samway, K., Whang, G., Cade, C., Gamil, M., Lubandina, M., & Phommachanh, K. (1991). Reading the skeleton, the heart, and the brain of a book: Students' perspectives on literature study circles. *The Reading Teacher, 45,* 196-205.

Scott, J. (1994). Literature circles in the middle school classroom: Developing reading, responding, and responsibility. *Middle School Journal, 26,* 37-41.

Short, K., & Pierce, K. (1990). *Talking about books: Creating literate communities.* Portsmouth, NH: Heinemann.

Vygotsky, L. (1978). *Mind in society: The development of higher psychological processes.* Cambridge, MA: Harvard University Press.

Watson, D. (1990). Show me: Whole language evaluation of literature groups. In K. Short & K. Pierce (Eds.), *Talking about books: Creating literate communities* (pp. 156-174). Portsmouth, NH: Heinemann.

ADDITIONAL READINGS

Literature Circles

Batchelor, K. (2012). The 'us' in discuss: Grouping in literature circles. *Voices from the Middle, 20*(2), 27-34.

Casey, H. K. (2008). Engaging the disengaged: Using literature clubs to motivate struggling adolescent readers and writers. *Journal of Adolescent & Adult Literacy, 52*(4), pp. 284-294.

Certo, J., Moxley, K., Reffitt, K., & Miller, J. A. (2010). I learned how to talk about a book: Children's perceptions of literature circles across grade and ability levels. *Literacy Research and Instruction, 49,* 243-263.

Clarke, L. W., & Holwadel, J. (2007). "Help! What is wrong with these literature circles and how can we fix them?" *The Reading Teacher, 61*(1), pp. 20-29.

Daniels, H. (2002). *Literature circles: Voice and choice in book clubs and reading groups* (2nd ed.). York, ME: Stenhouse Publishers.

Pearson, C. (2010). Acting up or acting out?: Unlocking children's talk in literature circles. *Literacy, 44*(1), 3-11.

Stebick, D. M., McCullough, B., & McKowen, J. (2015). Promoting literacy growth through literature circles in second grade. *The Reading Professor, 31*(1), 19-22.

Wiesendanger, K., & Tarpley, P. Developing cultural awareness through implementing literature circles in the classroom. *Race, Gender & Class, 17*(1/2), 110-113.

Teacher Research and Reflective Teaching

Anderson, G. L., Herr, K., & Nihlen, A. G. (2007). *Studying your own school: An educator's guide to practitioner action research* (2nd ed.). Thousand Oaks, CA: SAGE.

Brydon-Miller, M., Maguire, P., & McIntyre, A. (Eds.). (2004). *Traveling companions: Feminism, teaching, and action research.* Santa Barbara, CA: Praeger

Campano, G. (2007). *Immigrant students and literacy: Reading, writing and remembering.* New York: Teachers College Press.

Cochran-Smith, M., & Donnell, K. (2006). Practitioner inquiry: Blurring the boundaries of research and practice. In J. L. Green, G. Camilli, and P. B. Elmore (Eds.), *Handbook of complementary methods in education research* (pp. 503-518). Mahwah, NJ: Lawrence Erlbaum Associates.

Cochran-Smith, M., & Lytle, S. L. (1993). *Inside/outside: Teacher research and knowledge.* New York, NY: Teachers College Press.

Cochran-Smith, M., & Lytle, S. L. (2009). *Inquiry as stance: Practitioner research for the next generation.* New York, NY: Teachers College Press.

Compton-Lilly, C. (2003). *Reading families: The literate lives of urban children.* New York: Teachers College Press.

Compton-Lilly, C. (2007). *Rereading families: Literacy learning in grades four and five.* New York: Teachers College Press.

Gallas, K. (1998). *"Sometimes I can be anything"*: *Power, gender, and identity in a primary classroom.* New York, NY: Teachers College Press.

Gutstein, E. (2006). *Reading and writing the world with mathematics: Toward a pedagogy of social justice.* New York: Routledge.

Horwitz, J. R. (2009). Critical reflection: Uncovering a developmental spiral. In K. Pithouse, C. Mitchell, & R. Moletsane (Eds.), *Making connections: Self-study and social action* (pp. 301-315. New York, NY: Peter Lang.

Horwitz, J. R. (2012). Photovoice as a critical reflection methodology. In R. Flessner, G. R. Miller, K. M. Patrizio, & J. R. Horwitz (Eds.), *Agency through teacher education: Reflection, community, and learning* (pp. 15-24). Lanham, MD: Rowman & Littlefield Education.

Hubbard, R. S., & Power, B. M. (2003). *The art of classroom inquiry: A handbook for teacher researchers* (rev. ed.). Portsmouth, NH: Heinemann.

Klehr, M. (2012). Community engagement as catalyst for reflection and agency within a professional development school clinical setting. In R. Flessner, G. R. Miller, K. M. Patrizio, & J. R. Horwitz (Eds.), *Agency through teacher education: Reflection, community, and learning* (pp. 97-104). Lanham, MD: Rowman & Littlefield Education.

Klehr, M. (2015). Community engagement as catalyst for professional learning, reflection, and agency in preservice-teacher education. *The New Educator, 11*(4), 277-291.

Lyman, K. (2007). Ribbons, racism, and a placenta: The challenges and surprises of culturally relevant teaching. In C. Caro-Bruce, R. Flessner, M. Klehr, & K. Zeichner (Eds.), *Creating equitable classrooms through action research* (pp. 170-201). Thousand Oaks, CA: Corwin Press.

Williams, B. (2007). What teacher behaviors encourage one at-risk African American boy to be a productive member of our classroom community? In C. Caro-Bruce, R. Flessner, M. Klehr, & K. Zeichner (Eds.), *Creating equitable classrooms through action research* (pp. 100-124). Thousand Oaks, CA: Corwin Press.

Zeichner, K. M., & Liston, D. P. (1996). *Reflective teaching: An introduction*. Mahwah, NJ: Lawrence Erlbaum Associates, Inc.

Zeichner, K. M., & Noffke, S. E. (2001). Practitioner research. In V. Richardson (Ed.), *Handbook of research on teaching* (4th ed.) (pp. 404-442). Washington, DC: American Educational Research Association.

ABOUT THE AUTHOR

Ryan Flessner is an Associate Professor of Teacher Education at Butler University in Indianapolis, IN (United States). His teaching and research interests include teacher education, elementary mathematics, practitioner inquiry, and issues of equity, diversity, and social justice.

Prior to his role at the university level, Ryan taught elementary school in Indianapolis, New York City, and Madison, Wisconsin.

In: (Participatory) Action Research   ISBN: 978-1-53613-041-6
Editors: J. Calder and J. Foletta   © 2018 Nova Science Publishers, Inc.

Chapter 3

ACTION RESEARCH: THE RESEARCHER'S ROLE AND ENGAGEMENT IN K-20 STEM EDUCATION

Andrea C. Burrows[1,*], Edd, Meghan Lockwood[2], MSNS, Christina Belardo[3], MSNS and Edward Janak[4], PhD

[1]School of Teacher Education, University of Wyoming, Laramie, WY, US
[2]Wyoming Game and Fish Department, Cheyenne, WY, US
[3]Environmental Education Outreach, New Paltz, NY, US
[4]Educational Foundations and Leadership, University of Toledo, Toledo, OH, US

ABSTRACT

This chapter explores the action research (AR) leaders' roles through two studies. The frame is K-20 science, technology, engineering, and

* Corresponding Author Email: Andrea.Burrows@uwyo.edu.

mathematics (STEM) education and integration and how participant engagement leads to AR project insight. Specifically, we set the stage wih the evolution of science education and then use an informal Girl Scout water quality project and a college level science and art integration project as means of analyzing what worked and what is needed in K-20 science education AR projects. We end the chapter with a focus on AR leaders and offer suggestions to consider. We recognize and value that citizen science, or inclusion of non-professionals in scientific research, as well as unusual stakeholders can increase scientific knowledge and involve communities in solutions to problems. We investigated science education through AR projects that touch on the three dimensions of the Next Generation Science Standards (NGSS) and the progression of new ideas. As a methodology, AR was embraced, and the stakeholders' roles were explored. Results show that the AR leaders' roles should include participating completely in an AR project, embracing conflict as a normal part of the process, accentuating stakeholder voice, promoting process engagement, and actively looking for barriers to the AR process. These are vital factors for contextual understanding. Implications include increased AR impact through action items for K-20 AR leaders and stakeholders, which could impact the success of a science focused AR project.

Keywords: action research, art education, engineering education, informal education, K-12 STEM education, K-20 education, science education, STEM integration, NGSS, researcher engagement

INTRODUCTION

How can an action researcher be involved in the action research (AR) process? Stringer (2014) urges us to "look, think, and act." Hence, completely, is a valued reply to that question. We wanted to know how researchers engaged with the AR process and also what they discovered. More importantly, what might they have missed if they had been an outside observer? In this chapter we explore this immersion through two K-20 (i.e., Kindergarten through college) projects including: 1) a Girl Scout troop performing an informal water quality study, and 2) a college class interacting with a science and art integration project. The AR project leaders were graduate students. Since both projects are science, technology, engineering, and mathematics (STEM) related, later in this chapter we provide a concise look into the evolution of science education as a focus area.

In the two science projects presented, we embraced experiences of AR. For example, past studies show us that there is a wave of interaction with the research process as a researcher engages with a project (Burrows, DiPompeo, Myers, Hickox, Borowczak, French, & Schwortz, 2016; Burrows & Harkness, 2015; Burrows, Thomas, Woods, Suess, & Dole, 2011). We expected the wave of engagement and disengagement as each AR project leader journeyed through the research landscape. Yet, we were curious what pieces of the process mattered the most for the researchers during their travels with AR participants.

As action researchers, we value the three key concepts of democratic participation, community empowerment, and social justice (Brydon-Miller, 1997; DePalma & Teague, 2008; Somekh & Zeichner, 2009; Zeni, 1998). We grasp the importance of participants expressing their voice in *what* is studied and *how* it is studied, including stakeholders in the process, and showing the significance of how wealth and opportunities influence societal behaviors. Throughout the AR process, understanding personal biases is paramount to engage meaningfully and assist in the forward movement of the study (Nyhof-Young, 2000; Nystrom, 2007). Hence, in this chapter, we provide a background history for science education, bring the researcher's AR role and engagement to the reader, describe two scientific projects involving AR studies (i.e., water quality; science and art integration), and offer suggestions when other AR leaders move forward with this type of work. As a note, the use of "we" throughout the chapter refers to the team working on that particular project, not necessarily the four chapter authors.

BRIEF HISTORY OF SCIENCE EDUCATION

To understand the context of the two science-related AR projects described in this chapter, the following information sets the stage for today's scientific study. Throughout its history as a discipline, science education has been a prime site to engage in action research; however, science educators have not thought along these lines until relatively recently. As detailed in the 1937 report published by the Progressive Education Association (PEA) *Science in General Education*, the history of the field was marked by "confusion as to purposes and procedures." As the report authors explain:

> Many differing purposes for instruction in the sciences have been proposed at different periods; that these purposes have been embodied in many differing programs and practices; and that the purposes and practices of any given period have tended to persist, in part at least, into the succeeding periods…The appropriateness of previous goals and procedures to new conceptions and demands has not always been carefully considered, and in some cases incompatible aims and practices are now being carried along side by side. (p. 5)

The teaching of science has been integral in the curriculum of the public schools longer than the United States has been in existence, however, its intent and technique has been highly variable. In its earliest form, the teaching of science had three purposes: descriptive, utilitarian, and religious. As early as the year 1751, for example, Benjamin Franklin called for the teaching of "histories of nature" that would teach merchants to understand the commodities they sold, craftsmen to understand the nature of the raw materials with which they worked, and ministers to understand the nature of the proofs of God (PEA, p. 5-6).

The reforms of the Common School Era did not come at the exclusion of science education; indeed, its purposes shifted away from religious and descriptive to mental training. In the 1892 Committee of Ten report, which codified secondary curriculum, there were two branches of the sciences to be explored: hard sciences (physics, astronomy, chemistry) and life sciences (biology, botany, zoology, physiology). The teaching of these subjects was focused on memorization of facts that students regurgitated during standard recitation periods. In spite of the diversity of content and the emergence of student laboratory work, original research conducted by teachers was still unheard of in educational settings.

With the advent of Progressive Education in the 1930s came new conceptions of curriculum and pedagogy, which much more focus on hands-on learning through problem-solving approaches. Of course, the aims of science education were not exempt from this shift; as the 1937 PEA report explains, the primary aim of science education was "to meet the demands of modern industrial society by emphasizing newer developments in science and seeking to make the sciences play a more active role in the lives of students" (PEA, p. 10). Mental discipline was supplanted (though not entirely replaced) by project method; covering ground or material widely replaced depth of study. As described by then-professor of education Henry Morrison in 1931 (italics in the original):

> The learning process in the science type is essentially *reflection upon experience* in the search for *meaning*. Of course experience is made available in book form and in other schoolroom instrumentalities or activities. The heart of the teaching, whether in the textbook or in the mouth of the teacher, is *explanation*. The outcome, the learning product, is a new understanding, a new attitude of intelligence toward the present environment or toward the historical past, or a new principle to be employed in trained thinking from the study of one of the organized sciences such as physics, chemistry, biology, economics, politics. (p. 180)

However, from the 1930's to the 1950's there was a shift in perception. In the 1950's the U.S. aspired to produce a generation of rocket scientists. The launching of Sputnik I, by the Soviet Union in 1957, was a blow to national pride; the nations' schools were seen to be the salve to this blow. The public of the U.S. turned its attention to the teaching of mathematics and sciences in the public schools. The so-called "new math" and "new science" approaches to the curriculum emerged as a politicians insisted on a back-to-basics approach via the passage of such laws as 1958's National Defense Education Act. This trend gained new vigor with the publication of 1983's *A Nation at Risk*, which stated that the U.S. educational system was at a historical low point and that a back-to-basics approach was once again necessary. Thus, the sciences became highly disciplinary in nature and returned towards the mental discipline approach of the 19th Century.

The 21st Century has seen challenges to the very nature of science education and the rise of high-stakes assessments and highly standardized curricula in U.S. schools. The battle for what happens in science classrooms, and where to focus attention, has not ended. In light of these challenges, Laats and Siegel (2016) remind science educators that their field should have the following student learning aims: 1) students should learn the content of current scientific theories; 2) the path to how those theories/current knowledge were derived; 3) the epistemic status of current theories (How does evidence support or fail to support the theories?, Why should we believe some theories as better supported by evidence than others?); and 4) the nature and role of reason and evidence in the scientific process (p. 75).

In science, the byproduct of the standardization movements is the three-dimensional learning in the Next Generation Science Standards – NGSS (NGSS Lead States, 2013). However, even in light of the rising standardization movements, science educators recognize that science is at its best when it is taught in non-disciplinary frames (integrated as supporting disciplines). Ultimately, as explained by Ault (2015), science educators in the 21st Century have an expanded mission: "Science teaching needs to place the disciplines in service to higher aims." He explains those higher aims as:

- Finding pleasure in knowing the natural world
- Achieving a sense of place
- Gaining confidence in oneself as a clever learner
- Honoring the talents of others
- Valuing attachment to community
- Respecting the diversity of scientific enterprises
- Becoming committed to improving society
- Appreciating objects of scientific interest through aesthetic lenses (p. 191)

While these aims may seem contradictory or controversial to more traditional science educators (e.g., fact memorization), the aims do lend themselves well to those who engage in AR and integrated STEM activities. Integrated STEM education is also frequently referred to as science, technology, engineering, art, and mathematics, or STEAM, and it is a means to accentuate the importance of all disciplines (Belardo, Burrows, & Dambekalns, 2017). However, in this chapter we refer specifically to STEM integration and science education.

THE RESEARCHERS' ROLE AND ENGAGEMENT

While understanding the background history of the science education context, what involvement should an AR researcher have in scientific projects? On the surface, the answer is easy: the researchers create, implement, and analyze the projects' goals, activities, and data while including stakeholders in the process. However, the researchers' processes of filling a role or engaging with participants, while leading a project and those participants, includes variances and challenges that shed light on the studies' progressions as a whole.

Both Belardo and Lockwood, the AR researchers for the two projects, followed similar paths through the AR projects. These two AR project leaders were vested in informal science education as well as discipline integration in more traditional classrooms. Each project lasted an academic year. The leaders felt passionate about helping the K-20 community embrace science as a way to know their natural world, find a sense of place, connect to the community, improve society, and appreciate objects in a holistic way. One AR leader, Lockwood, was already working in an informal setting with a middle school aged Girl Scout troop and wanted desperately to find out what was working to help the girls learn the science content. She was interested in discovering how the informal project lent itself to supporting the more traditional classrooms that the girls attended during the school year. The second AR leader, Belardo, was fervent about the importance of both science and art as a means for learning those disciplines and other subjects. She was invited to participate in an already established science and art integration project for college students. She was curious about the interactions that science students would have with the art content and vice versa how the art students would interact with the science content. Both AR leaders became part of the aforementioned groups, and both involved the project participants in discussions of the data collected, analysis procedures, and meanings of what was found as the projects progressed during the year of implementation.

After the conclusion of the projects, which led to two masters' theses (Belardo, 2015; Lockwood, 2016), both AR leaders reflected on what had helped them to succeed with their projects and participants. They noted the importance of an organizer with an outline of proposed activities, data collection, participant discussions, and data analysis. For example, one leader mentioned that participants "may veer off track or [get] side-lined with other ideas or adding components to the project." As others have found (Schwortz, Burrows, & Guffey, 2015), mentoring during the yearlong science process was instrumental in keeping these AR project leaders focused on the projects' goals as well as engaged and accessible with participants. The juxtaposition of having to concentrate on collecting the data while maintaining a community valuing atmosphere could have derailed these leaders. Yet, both leaders referred to discussions with a mentor as instrumental in maintaining a central goal (remembering that no AR journey is ever straightforward). One leader stated, "you encouraged me to stand up for myself, be confident in myself, and remind myself that I am the expert on the topic [leading others]." This quote not only speaks to mentoring, but also emphasizing the power of voice. Additionally, these two leaders were dedicated to involving the projects' participants in conversations, and they were open to the feedback that they heard. Both leaders asked their groups about their perspectives on moving through the projects, and what they thought about the data collected. The dedication of the AR leaders to the participants first, projects second, and data collection third, allowed them to complete successful projects.

Although successful, both AR leaders also commented on challenges of the projects. The biggest concern raised was that for such inclusive AR projects, there was quite a bit of logistical information to set in place (e.g., IRB approval, data collection methods, discussion meetings). Moreover, once the projects were in full swing, the leaders began to question if they understood themselves and/or AR research methodology. One leader wrote, "I was a bit confused for a large portion of time [on the project] about what AR actually was. ...I have to admit I was always a little skeptical that my project [was adequate for AR]." After discussion, we agreed that these moments of uncertainty were disengagement in the AR process, with root causes of confidence and limited experience. The leaders spoke of bias and what they guarded against, such as "looking to work with people like me." As a team, we talked about the leader challenges, and topics of engagement, voice, and conflict were often heard. In the end, when asked what they would do differently if allowed to re-do the AR projects, both leaders explained that time was a major limiting factor. Although we knew going into the projects that there were time limitations in place, the knowledge of those constraints haunted the leaders instead of pushing them to connect in varied means throughout the AR projects. Even researcher led tasks, such as data analysis, were difficult for the leaders to sometimes complete. One leader lamented, "I was... involved in the [project] that I was performing the research with, so it was difficult for me to try and take a slight step back to look at my data objectively." Thus, although the AR projects were successful, we knew throughout the yearlong processes that the AR leaders could make improvements to increase the effectiveness of their roles in upcoming projects.

THE ACTION RESEARCH GIRL SCOUT WATER PROJECT

The AR Girl Scout project sprang organically from the initial meeting interactions between the Girl Scout leaders, parents, girls, and the AR project leader. The group desired an understanding of the K-12 STEM exposures in informal learning as the girls investigated the restoration of the Laramie River from 2009-2012. After obtaining IRB approval, we settled on these specific research questions:

- Can an informal science project, such as the Girl Scout citizen science project, address the three dimensions of learning from the NGSS?
- What aspects of an informal Girl Scout citizen science water quality project address the NGSS three-dimensions of learning?
- How can the facilitation of citizen science projects be improved in the future to address more explicitly the NGSS' three dimensions of learning?

Scientific inquiry and the use of the entire scientific processes requires a greater focus in science teaching (Burrows, Wickizer, Meyer, & Borowczak, 2013; Houseal, Abd-El-Khalick, & Destefano, 2014). Skills in scientific inquiry range from questioning to sharing conclusions with a larger audience (i.e., dissemination). The importance of these authentic science skills was not lost on us, and we strived to utilize its tenets (Burrows, 2015; Burrows et al., 2016; Spuck, 2014). Thus, the purpose of this study was to explore the Girl Scout water quality project and the scientific offerings (especially relating to the NGSS) that the informal learning situation presented the girls. During the informal setting interactions, we probed for insights into how *informal* science informs *formal* science education, as well as the impact of informal settings on the STEM interest of the girls. This study exemplifies an AR project showing authentic knowledge transforming to action, as it examines research for improving participants' opportunity *for* and access *to* quality informal education.

In this AR project the researchers used Vygotsky's (1978) social constructivist lens. Vygotsky emphasized culture and social context for learning. We investigated questions on the educational science value in this informal education Girl Scout project exploring water quality. The girls were asked questions probing into their cultural beliefs to inform the project. The stakeholders interacted and expressed their thoughts about both the project and the water quality science content, and the researchers interacted with them in order to collect data that was as authentic as possible. With this authentic data, we utilized learning as a social endeavor to view the collected interactions and statements, which allowed the researchers to "step back and critically analyze situations, to recognize and avoid bias, to obtain valid and reliable data, and to think abstractly" (Strauss & Corbin, 1990, p. 18). In this manner, we invite the reader to peer into our use of grounded theory during the AR process, where we as researchers often began with the questions and data collection and then moved to analysis and conclusions, or processed inductively.

In general, researchers and participants conduct AR when they desire change in social situations (Somekh, 1995). During the AR process a plan is devised, action is taken, observations are noted, and reflection is incorporated (Afify, 2008). The two main methods of data collection used in this study were observation and focus group discussion notes. During the Girl Scout activities, we wrote and recorded what we heard and saw. Middle school aged girls (9-15 years) created a research project looking at water quality to determine whether or not river restoration was successful. All of the girls were asked to participate, and of the 14 Girl Scouts, 10 volunteered to participate in the study (71%). Data were collected during 10 interactions from September 2015 through March 2016, as well as during four focus group discussions. During observations, we took notes on the content, topics, participants, and dialogue occurring throughout the meeting. We recorded notes as the meeting progressed, including quotes from participants and facilitators, and invited feedback from participants. Notes included information about the topics being covered, dialogue and quotes from participants and facilitators, engagement of participants, and general actions of participants and facilitators. After these meetings, the researcher typed up the handwritten notes and discussed nuances of bias, engagement, conflict, and voice.

Participants also contributed opinions of the Girl Scout water quality project in focus group discussions. Did the project address the three–dimensional NGSS that includes: Disciplinary Core Ideas (DCI), Crosscutting Concepts (CCC), and Science/Engineering Practices (SEP)? For the participants, the NGSS were described as the set of standards that many states (approximately 18 by the end of 2016) had adopted for teachers to use as benchmarks of student success. The DCI relate to central content, the CCC refer to seven themes found across disciplines (i.e., patterns, cause/effect, scale/proportion/quantity, systems/system models, energy/matter, structure/function, and stability/change), and the SEP highlight skills found in science and engineering. During focus group discussions, we asked the participants questions about the three dimensions, including which ones they thought were addressed during the program, how they were addressed, and if certain situations addressed a dimension.

For analysis, we coded notes taken during observations and focus group discussions. Coding was completed by hand using colored highlighters to code for each component chosen. For DCI, CCC, and SEP, a broad component was coded, and we searched for more specific instances to fit under the umbrella of the broad component. We coded meetings, focus groups discussions, and water quality project activities as addressing the NGSS components if participants and facilitators asked question(s) that led to component discussion, introduced a new topic(s), and addressed the components in theme or action. All participants agreed on the coding of the data collected.

Through AR immersion, the findings show that the three-dimensional NGSS can be used in informal education settings, and that DCIs, CCCs, and SEPs are all present in this informal Girl Scout water quality project. Table 1 (adapted from Lockwood, 2016) shows selected quotes from the Girl Scout participants in relation to each of the three-dimensional NGSS, while Table 2 (adapted from Lockwood, 2016) highlights the facilitator quotes in the same vein.

As AR insiders, we were able to discern what participants were asking and doing with rich detail. If we had been outsiders, this insight would have been lost to self-reported, question-response answers, and most likely uninspired, data. We are encouraged that participants varied in their ability to identify different components of the NGSS three dimensions, as this validates the individual learning efforts needed in science education. For example, some participants focused intently on the CCC "patterns" throughout the program, whereas others were quite interested in the SEP, particularly "planning and carrying out investigations."

Table 1. Girl Scout *participant* quotes relating to the three-dimensions of the NGSS

Learning Dimension	Component	Meeting Observation Girl Scout Quotes	Focus Group Discussion Girl Scout Quotes
DCI	Life Sciences	"I think I know what kind of crane fly larva this is!"	Has life science been addressed? Girl: "Yes, macro-invertebrates are definitely a part of life science. They're alive and we've learned how to identify them."
CCC	Earth/Space Sciences	"Maybe someone put the rocks along the edges of the river here like they did at the park."	How are people involved in the system? Girl: "…in the restoration & making it better."
	Patterns	"I notice that there seems to be more canopy cover here at the restored site than further down at the control site."	"We've seen patterns. Like how in faster water, there are fewer macro-invertebrates than in slower water."
	Cause/Effect	Will fewer rocks have impact? Girl: "… they found lots of macros in the rocks, so maybe they aren't finding as many…"	"The restoration caused the water to be healthier. Or at least that is what we are hoping for, and trying to determine."
SEP	Planning & Implementing Investigations	N/A	"We learned about the science circle, and how to do science." "We …planned an investigation & [are doing] it to complete the science process."
	Asking Questions & Defining Problems	Was the restoration successful? Girl: "We can look at whether or not the water is cleaner and the river healthier or not."	"We developed questions at the beginning of the study, and are answering them as we go. And we're still asking smaller questions all the time"
	Analyzing & Interpreting Data	"When are we going to make more graphs and analyze data that way? That was really fun!"	When we counted macros, [did] we analyze data?" Girl: "Yes, you have to count them before you do any more analysis, so you know what you're working with. It's the first step in analysis."

**Table 2. Girl Scout *facilitator* quotes relating to the
three-dimensions of the NGSS**

Learning Dimension	Component	Meeting Observation Facilitator Quotes	Focus Group Discussion Facilitator Quotes
DCI	Life Sciences	"We could look at plant growth around the river. Why is that important to us?"	N/A
	Earth/Space Sciences	"Why would the restoration team put bigger rocks along the bank of the river?"	"What about Earth Systems Science? What do you think that is?"
CCC	Patterns	"What patterns do you notice as you're observing the site?"	"Patterns are not just cool designs that you see, but places where you notice things occurring."
	Cause/Effect	Will fewer rocks have an impact? (Re-worded)	N/A
SEP	Planning & Implementing Investigations	"Now that we have a question, we need a hypothesis. Who knows what a hypothesis is?"	"Which of the following steps are important parts of planning an investigation? Developing questions and hypotheses, determining data to collect, collecting data, and analyzing data?"
	Asking Questions & Defining Problems	"We need to develop questions. This will guide our study, so what do we want to know?"	"What is the question we are trying to answer? Is this a researchable question?"
	Analyzing & Interpreting Data	"Today we will continue to analyze our data by making figures of the data we collected."	"We used a T-test and statistics to see if we had significant data. Is this a form of analysis?"

In future iterations of similar projects, leaders might also consider minimal content assessment throughout the project to assess what participants grasp about DCI, CCC, and SEP, as well as interacting with the participants to hear what they discuss. This particular informal science project did not address all of the components of the three learning dimensions at all times, but with extensive planning and activity creation – not to mention attention to NGSS - we believe that it is possible for informal science projects to inform formal science instruction. Informal education can also be science education, and through AR this connection was clearly revealed.

Finally, these educational connections are compelling, but so are the discussions of bias, engagement, conflict, and voice, which are important for all stakeholders. One poignant conversation revolved around who had access to join and participate in Girl Scout functions. We discussed access to cars, bias on who "should be" a Girl Scout, and when the activities take place. We were reminded to be as inclusive as possible when creating these informal science community events. We encourage informal and formal science instructors to use this AR project as a springboard for designing authentic science experiences.

THE ACTION RESEARCH SCIENCE AND ART INTEGRATION PROJECT

For this science and art integration project, we utilized an AR approach for one year with approximately 20 college students to gain a deeper understanding of the process, because in other years a mixed methods approach was utilized (Belardo, Burrows, & Dambekalns, 2017). We measured pre-service teachers' perceptions of integrating science and art into future K-12 STEM (or pre-collegiate) classrooms. We worked with college students and specifically, the research questions included:

- How have pre-service secondary teachers' perceptions about this science and art integration project changed over time?
- How has the silk batik activity influenced pre-service teachers' perceptions of science and art incorporation in their future classrooms?

How can science be taught effectively, especially in K-12 schools? One answer is integration with other subjects. The idea of discipline integration of seemingly disparate subjects such as science and art was the focus of this study. We asked if science and art were that different. Although most educators view a disconnection between the two disciplines, and there is often a lack of science visual learning strategies (Baldwin & Crawford, 2010), the stakeholders in this AR project saw potential to truly connect science and art. There is not a large difference between science and art skills, instead there are overlapping similarities and opportunities for the other discipline's enhancement (Lovelace, 2014; Needle, Corbo, Wong, Greenfeder, Raths, & Fulop, 2007; Ursyn, 1997; UW News, 2014). The arts are similar to the STEM fields, and are able to "re-invigorate the educational platform, providing not only an interesting approach, but also opportunities for self-expression and personal connections" (Land, 2013, p. 548) in pre-collegiate schooling. In this mindset, we approached the science and art project (see Table 4 and Table 5 for examples of science and art similarities).

Through an AR approach - including leader field notes, participants' open-response survey answers, participants' informal interview answers, and AR team interactions - we provide pre-service teachers' perceptions and uses of the science and art integration project in this section. To help the reader understand what was occurring during the data collection, an overview of the project here is important. During the six days of the science and art integration project, the science and art pre-service teachers were asked to design and paint images onto silk batik. In addition, they were asked to address the secondary science and K-12 art curricular topics - using both a macroscopic (e.g., satellite image of a delta) and microscopic (e.g., microbe) images. Thus, the pre-service teachers concentrated on choosing, creating, and then explaining beautiful scientific images in both a science and an art environment. Table 3 shows the project objectives. The AR project leader worked in a group that created an ice crystal microscopic image, and written explanations of the science and art integration pieces in the work can be seen in Table 4.

Table 3. Science and Art Integration Project Objectives

1)	Connecting previous knowledge (instruction, teaching approaches, standards, and content) from pre-service teachers' methods courses and relating the knowledge to the integration project.
2)	Creating a small individual and larger group silk batik that represented microscopic and macroscopic scales of scientific phenomena.
3)	Identifying artistic and scientific concepts from their microscopic art product
4)	Explaining the importance of science and art in the classroom based on a hands-on experience and collaboration with others.

Table 4. Project leader's group reflections on the ice crystal microscopic image

Art Discussion	Primary colors, Secondary colors, Visual texture, Actual texture, Composition, Geometirc shapes/lines, Organic shapes/lines, Repitition of color
Science Discussion	Crystalline structure, Atmospheric conditions, Light properties, Scale, Metamorphism, Deposition
Aesthetic Approach to Teaching Science Discussion	<ul><li>Students make discoveries using their aesthetic curiosity.</li><li>Integration activity was not just to provide an educational experience, but to provide opportunities to play and explore.</li><li>Give students materials to not only learn the concept of them (i.e., Marbles down a track for Newton's First law) but for them to explore and play and make their own connections.</li><li>Our experience of art and science – We were given a variety of supplies, materials, information, and we were able to work together, utilize our strengths, and collaborate, and make plan and focus on all the art and science concepts we talked about into creating a beautiful painting.</li><li>Concept is not just about learning science, but it is about experiencing what was happening.</li><li>We can use the science and art concepts to create a science and aesthetic approach for students. Lessons like this that are creative, can help engage students that are academically driven or who are not creative, and can help them understand the world around them.</li></ul>

Although not as rich in detail as conversations, the open-ended questions allowed pre-service teachers to freely voice their opinions, thoughts, and perspectives regarding the science and art integration project. There were several themes identified in the pre-service teachers' open response answers (see Table 5).

Findings show that there was a general increase in overall awareness of benefits in a science and art integrated project. Through AR, and the leader acting as a participant, we learned that pre-service teachers transitioned *from* only seeing interdisciplinary learning as a leading benefit to integration, *to* alternative learning strategies, working together, as well as interdisciplinary learning after the science and art project. Positively, there was a general increase in awareness of similar skills that are shared between scientists and artists. Upon completion of the science and art integrated project, the pre-service teachers' responses included similar methods for problem solving, observational skills, and using visual tools and representations. Importantly, the collective comments echoed a new idea for the pre-service teachers. One participant exclaimed, "I never had an idea that you can take scientific images and use them in art projects. I mean I've seen landscapes, portraits, and more traditional stuff, but...." This sentiment was echoed in different ways through writing and oral interactions by both art and science pre-service teachers.

Over the course of the AR project there was a general decrease of participants' specified challenges. The participants also noted the engagement, or lack thereof, with both parts of the science and art project. One participant noted, "We started out with the science-based snowflake, then during most of the process it was art-based to paint and finish the piece, and it felt as if we did not get to revisit the science-part and go full circle until we were finishing a group commentary about the experience for our presentation." After the science and art integrated project, the participants identified challenges of using interdisciplinary learning, collaborating with other teachers, and lacking a strong scientific background. As stakeholders we discussed our biases about the science and art disciplines, engagement or disengagement with either science or art, voice in what was included and discarded and why, conflicts – often over the process itself - in groups, and barriers to engaging in integration activities with an open mind. Nevertheless, as the process unfolded, we saw two separate groups in the beginning merge into one large group when the project ended (approximately six class periods or eight hours).

Table 5. Common themes of importance and quotes from participants

1)	Importance of creativity	"Using art helps build creativity in science"
2)	Using visual tools and representations	"[A project like this] allows you to visually enhance a science unit."
3)	Engagement with the subject	"[This project] engages students while they learn the same content from different aspects."
4)	Collaboration/teamwork between classroom teachers	"Collaboration is key, each group had something to teach and we complimented each other."
5)	Alternative learning strategies and styles (i.e., new ways to teach)	"This gives students a new way of looking at science if it's not their strongest subject. Allows new form of learning and understanding."
6)	Importance of interdisciplinary learning	"…art and science can tie into each other and they can push what we know from each [subject] even further."
7)	Making real-world connections	"This is real practice and development. It is practice for a real life unit in which I can integrate two subjects."
8)	Observational skills	"There is looking then there is seeing. [This project] helped me to know the difference."
9)	Problem solving by similar methods (different disciplines)	"Science and art work very well together. Both deal with critical, analytical thinking and using them together means that students will make more connections."
10)	Lacking skills in art or science	"What about students like me with low artistic skills?"
11)	Time commitment	"Time. Spending a lot of time on explaining science terms, but using art. Creating a piece with a science subject, but hoping students don't get sidetracked with painting. Handling time is an issue."

As AR insiders, we saw the images and participated in the selection process and silk batik painting of those images. We witnessed firsthand the collaboration between art pre-service teachers and science pre-service teachers, and we watched both groups grow. The growth happened in content knowledge (see Table 4) as well as collaborative skills and new, fresh ideas for the K-12 classroom. If we had been outsiders, we would have missed out on the conversations in the group settings where advantages and disadvantages to a science and art project were discussed without prompting. Most likely, participants would not have been as frank with their responses if the leader had not been one of them. Thus, AR allowed us to view a science and art integration project from inside and experience the successes and challenges ourselves.

DISCUSSION AND SUGGESTIONS

Here we are brought back to our original question: How can an action researcher be involved in the action research (AR) process? Completely is not only the reply that is valued, but it is a necessity. We answer that the more intimately these stakeholders interact with the AR process, the more likely insights into what should be emphasized or deleted come into focus. We hunger to more deeply understand how AR leaders, researchers, and participants engage with projects.

AR often involves tension between stakeholders. During these projects there were times of slight tension between individuals and groups. For example, what should the leader do when the group no longer wants to participate in discussions about the project? Or, what should a participant do when she feels that she is working more diligently than her partners? Our first piece of advice is to follow the loudest lead first without losing sight of the other perspectives. We know that stakeholders need to be heard, so when they speak, we listen. We also know that we must eventually circle around to the other perspectives. So we ask ourselves - and the group - if it is a resource, objective/goal, or identity issue, knowing that identifying that pivotal point clarifies how the situation is handled (Burrows & Harkness, 2015). Depending on the type of conflict, we need to allow feelings to flow (antagonism), resonance to take place (similarities), invention to happen (solutions), action to occur (do something) or a combination of the above (Burrows & Harkness, 2015). For these projects, we experienced resource and objective/goal types of conflict and we embraced the strategies of resonance, invention, and action. These strategies took a few minutes (e.g., getting more supplies) to a few days (e.g., collaborating on how to move forward in a dysfunctional group). However, each intervention allowed the stakeholders to move forward in their AR project, and allowed them to find a voice for project improvement.

We originally asked about the impact of being an AR insider, and in this chapter we explored the AR project leader immersion through two K-20 projects (i.e., water quality; science and art integration). We found, like others (Brydon-Miller & Coghlan, 2014; Reason & Bradbury, 2007; Stringer, 2014), that project immersion is vital to truly understanding what is happening with all stakeholders and the project as a whole. Our second piece of advice is to honor the immersion process, write copious notes on and reflections about what is overheard, and share your interpretations of what is happening with stakeholders. We stick to this advice even when the stakeholders include scientific minds where pushback is expected and evidence is required. Here we refer the reader to the previous paragraph on conflict resolution, along with a gentle reminder that AR is a messy process that scientists often find disturbing. Reminding all of the stakeholders of the identified problem and proposed end goals helps to ease this tension with and among groups.

We experienced the ebb and flow of engagement in the AR process and reminded ourselves and other stakeholders to hold tight to the three main concepts of democratic participation, community empowerment, and social justice. Empowerment is not underestimated in these projects, and our third piece of advice is to seek ways through explicit action and dialogue emphasizing the power of voice. We saw firsthand how impactful it was when participants expressed their perspectives on what was studied (e.g., part of river; chosen image) and how it was studied (e.g., looking for macro-invertebrates; investigating chosen science and art concepts). All stakeholders were involved in the AR projects, and they participated in discussions about the significance of wealth and opportunities for others (e.g., which girls participated; who has access to images). Along with the engagement, voice, and opportunity discussions, we discussed our biases and backgrounds and attempted to address as many as we could identify (e.g., prior participation in informal science; prior exposure to scientists). Our fourth piece of advice is to cling to engagement, promoting voice, and dissecting potential barriers in the K-20 environment to provide as many opportunities as possible. As science educators, we recognize that citizen science, or inclusion of non-professionals in scientific research, as well as unusual stakeholders, such as scientists and artists, can increase scientific knowledge and involve communities in solutions to problems.

In sum, this chapter explained the science education background leading to the two AR projects described here. Then we delved into the role and engagement of the project leaders. Finally, we offered suggestions on moving forward with AR project work in K-20 educational settings. Like Stringer (2014) builds off of "look, think, act," we offer additions to this model. These can be summed up in the phrase, "be kind, thoughtful, and intentional." As AR leaders we should remember to be kind as we look, think, and act, but also thoughtful and intentional when dealing with all aspects of AR projects while learning how to move forward as a community - including the initial euphoria of coming together, inherent biases, eventual conflict, immersion process, ebb and flow of stakeholder engagement, promoting voice, and looking out for others' best interest.

REFERENCES

Afify, M. F. (2008). Action research: Solving real-world problems. *Tourism and hospitality research, 8* (2), 153-159.

Ault, C. R. (2015). *Challenging science standards: A skeptical critique of the quest for unity.* New York: Rowman & Littlefield.

Baldwin, L., & Crawford, I. (2010). Art instruction in the botany lab: A collaborative approach. *Journal of college science teaching, 40* (2), 26-31.

Belardo, C. (2015). *STEM integration with art: A renewed reason for STEAM. Doctoral projects, masters plan B, and related works.* Paper 10. [http://repository.uwyo.edu/plan_b/10/].

Belardo, C., Burrows, A. C., & Dambekalns, L. (2017). Partnering science and art: pre-service teachers' experiences for use in pre-collegiate classrooms. *Problems of education in the 21ˢᵗ century, 75* (3), 215-234.

Brydon-Miller, M. (1997). Participatory action research: Psychology and social change." *Journal of social issues, 53* (4): 657–666.

Brydon-Miller, M., & Coghlan, D. (2014). The big picture: Implications and imperatives for the action research community from the SAGE encyclopedia of action research. *Action research, 12* (2), 224-233.

Burrows, A. C. (2015). Partnerships: A systemic study of two professional developments with university faculty and K-12 teachers of science, technology, engineering, and mathematics. *Problems of education in the 21st century, 65,* 28-38.

Burrows, A. C., DiPompeo, M., Myers, A. D., Hickox, R. C., Borowczak, M., French, D. A., & Schwortz, A. C. (2016). Authentic science experiences: pre-collegiate science educators' successes and challenges during professional development. *Problems of education in the 21ˢᵗ century, 70,* 59-73.

Burrows, A. C., & Harkness, S. (2015). Experiencing action evaluation's cyclic process: Partnering conflict, reflection, and action. *Educational action research, 24* (4), 460-478.

Burrows, A. C., Thomas, J., Woods, A., Suess, R., & Dole, D. (2011). Riding the wave: Student researcher reflection on the action research process. *Educational action research, 20* (2), 291-312.

Burrows, A. C., Wickizer, G., Meyer, H., & Borowczak, M. (2013). Enhancing pedagogy with context and partnerships: Science in hand. *Problems of education in the 21st century. 54,* 7-13.

DePalma, R., & L. Teague. (2008). A democratic community of practice: Unpicking all those words. *Educational action research, 16* (4), 441–456.

Laats, A., & Siegel, H. (2016). *Teaching evolution in a creation nation.* Chicago, IL: University of Chicago Press.

Houseal, A. K., Abd-El-Khalick, F., & Destefano, L. (2014). Impact of a student-teacher-scientist partnership on students' and teachers' content knowledge, attitudes towards science, and pedagogical practices. *Journal of research in science teaching 51* (1), 84-115.

Land, M. H. (2013). Full STEAM ahead: The benefits of integrating the arts into STEM. *Procedia computer science, 20*, 547-552.

Lockwood, M. (2016). *Addressing three-dimensional learning with citizen science projects*. SMTC plan B papers. 46. [http://repository.uwyo.edu/smtc_plan_b/46/].

Lovelace, J. (2014). Art + science. *American craft magazine, 74* (4), 70-77.

Morrison, H. C. (1931). *The practice of teaching in the secondary school (revised edition)*. Chicago: University of Chicago Press.

Needle, A., Corbo, C., Wong, D., Greenfeder, G., Raths, L., & Fulop, Z. (2007). Combining art and science in "arts and sciences" education. *College teaching, 55* (3), 114-119.

NGSS Lead States. (2013). *Next generation science standards: For states, by states*. Washington, D.C.: The National Academies Press.

Nyhof-Young, J. (2000). The political is personal: Reflections on facilitating action research in gender issues in science education. *Educational action research* 8 (3): 471–498.

Nyström, E. (2007). Exclusion in an inclusive action research project: Drawing on student perspectives of school science to identify discourses of exclusion. *Educational action research* 15 (3): 417–440.

Progressive Education Association Committee on the Function of Science in General Education. (1938). *Science in general education: Suggestions for science teachers in secondary schools and in the lower division of colleges*. New York: NY: Appleton-Century Company.

Reason, P., & Bradbury, H. (2007). *Handbook of action research*. Thousand Oaks, CA: SAGE Publications.

Schwortz, A. C., Burrows, A. C., & Guffey, K. (2015). Mentoring partnerships in science education. *Educational action research, 25*(4), 630-649.

Somekh, B. (1995). The contribution of action research to development in social endeavors: A position paper on action research methodology. *British educational research journal 21* (3), 339-355.

Somekh, B., & Zeichner, K. (2009). Action research for educational reform: Remodelling action research theories and practices in local contexts. *Educational action research, 17* (1), 5–21.

Spuck, T. (2014). Putting the "authenticity" in science learning. In T. Spuck, L. Jenkins, & R. Dou (Eds.), *Einstein fellows: Best practices in STEM education* (pp. 118-156). New York, NY: Norton.

Strauss, A., & Corbin, J. (1990). *Basics of qualitative research: Grounded theory procedures and techniques.* Newbury Park, CA: SAGE Publications.

Stringer, E. T. (2014). *Action research* (4th Edition). Los Angeles, CA: SAGE Publications.

Ursyn, A. (1997). Computer art graphics integration of art and science. *Learning and instruction, 7* (1), 65-86.

UW News. (2014, June 11). *Special Saturday U program pairs UW scientists and artists.* Retrieved from http://www.uwyo.edu/uw/news/2014/06/special-saturday-u-program-pairs-uw-scientists-andartists.html.

Vygotsky, L. S. (1978). *Mind in society: The development of higher mental process.* Cambridge, MA: Harvard College Press.

Zeni, J. (1998). A guide to ethical issues and action research." *Educational action research, 6* (1), 9–19.

BIOGRAPHICAL SKETCHES

Andrea C. Burrows

Affiliation: University of Wyoming, College of Education, School of Teacher Education

Education: EdD. 2011, University of Cincinnati, Curriculum and Instruction with Secondary Science Specialization.

Business Address: 1000 E. University Ave., Dept. 3374, Laramie, WY 82071

Research and Professional Experience:

Associate Professor, University of Wyoming – Laramie, WY, 2017-present

Assistant Professor, University of Wyoming – Laramie, WY, 2011-2017

Adjunct Professor, University of Cincinnati – Cincinnati, OH, 2007-2011

Grant Coordinator, University of Cincinnati – Cincinnati, OH, 2007-2011

Adjunct Professor, Northern Kentucky University – Newport, KY, 2006-11

Professional Appointments:

Orange County Learning Resource Specialist - Ocoee, FL, 2003-2005

Ocoee Middle School Science Teacher - Ocoee, FL, 2001-2003

Waynesboro High School Science Teacher - Waynesboro, VA, 1998-2001

Kate Collins Middle School Science Teacher - Waynesboro, VA, 1996-1998

Florida State University High Science Teacher - Tallahassee, FL, 1993-1996

Honors:

2017   Honored College of Education UW Faculty at Fall Convocation

2016   UW Faculty Award: Outstanding Service to Educational Profession

2015   Most Creative ECE Capstone Project: A Block of Code (Sponsor)

2015   UW Faculty Award: Outstanding Research and Scholarship

2015   National Technology Leadership Initiative Finalist Paper (at *ASTE)*

2014   AERA Early Career Award Nominee

2014   UW Dr. James Hurst *Each Student – A Person Award* Nominee

2013   UW Assessment Mini-Grant – AAC&U Conference Award $2,000

2013   Mary Garland Early Career Fellowship Research Award $25,000

2012   UW Science & Math Teaching Center Affiliate Faculty

2010   Lillian Sherman Scholarship: Outstanding Academic Performance
2007-2011   University Graduate Scholarship, University of Cincinnati
2007-2011   NSF GK-12 Grant Coordinator Fellowship, Univ. of Cincinnati
2000-2001   Waynesboro High School Teacher of the Year Nominee (VA)

Publications from the Last 3 Years:

Belardo, C., Burrows, A. C., &. Dambekalns, L. (2017). Partnering science and art: Pre-service teachers' experiences for use in pre-collegiate classrooms. *Problems of Education in the 21st Century, 75*(3), 215-234.

French, D., & Burrows, A. C. (2017). Inquiring astronomy: Incorporating student-centered pedagogical techniques in an introductory college science course. *Journal of College Science Teaching, 46*(4), 24-32.

Burrows, A. C., & Borowczak, M. (2017). *Hardening freshman Engineering Student Soft Skills.* Paper presentation at the American Society of Engineering Education: First Year Engineering Experience (ASEE FYEE), Daytona Beach, FL. August 7, 2017.

Burrows, A. C., & Borowczak, M. (2017). *Teaching teachers to think like engineers using NetLogo.* Paper presentation at the American Society of Engineering Education (ASEE), Columbus, OH. June 25, 2017.

Borowczak, M., & Burrows, A. C. (2017). *Interactive web notebooks using the cloud to enable CS in K-16+ classrooms and PDs.* Paper presentation at the American Society of Engineering Education (ASEE), Columbus, OH. June 28, 2017.

Leonard, J., Buss, A., Burrows, A. C., & Unertl, A. (2017). *Pathways to equity in engineering and computer science: Fostering STEM in rural learning environments.* Paper presentation at the Annual Meeting of the American Educational Research Association (AERA), San Antonio, Texas. May 1, 2017.

Walwema, G.B., French, D. A., Verley, J. D., & Burrows, A. C. (2016). Is classical mechanics a prerequisite for learning modern physics? *Physics Education*, 51. [H index: 11; Q3] [http://dx.doi.org/10.1088/0031-9120/51/6/065022].

Schwortz, A., Burrows, A. C., & Guffey, K. (2016). Mentoring partnerships in science education. *Educational Action Research, 25*(4), 630-649.   doi:10.1080/09650792.2016.1221838   [http://www.tandf online.com/doi/full/10.1080/09650792.2016.1221838]   [H   index:16; Q2]

Burrows, A. C., DiPompeo, M., Myers, A., Hickox, R., Borowczak, M., *French, D., & *Schwortz, A. (2016). Authentic science experiences: Pre-collegiate science teachers' successes and challenges during professional development. *Problems of Education in the 21ˢᵗ Century, 70*(70), 59-73.

Borowczak, M., & Burrows, A. C. (2016). Enabling collaboration & video assessment: Exposing trends in science pre-service teachers' assessments. *Contemporary Issues in Technology and Teacher Education (CITE), 16*(2), 127-150. [Eric Index: EJ1103980].

Borowczak, M., & Burrows, A. C. (2016). Developing and sustaining computing based outreach experiences. *VLSI Circuits and Systems Letter* (VCAL), 2(2), 21-25. https://www.computer.org/cms/tcvlsi/ newsletters/2016/VLSI_Circuits_and_Systems_vol2_issue2_Oct2016. pdf.

Borowczak, M., & Burrows, A. C. (2016). Are we still teaching VLSI the same way that we were in the mid-90s? *VLSI Circuits and Systems Letter* (VCAL), 2(1), 25-27. https://www.computer.org/cms/tcvlsi/ newsletters/2016/VLSI_Circuits_and_Systems_vol2_issue1_Apr2016. pdf.

Burrows, A. C., & Borowczak, M. (2016). *Arduinos & sensors: K-12 teachers explore computer science.* Paper presentation at the American Society of Engineering Education (ASEE), New Orleans, LA. June 27, 2016.

Borowczak, M., & Burrows, A. C. (2016). *Developing a creative K-12 manipulative: An ECECS capstone.* Paper presentation at the American Society of Engineering Education (ASEE), New Orleans, LA. June 29, 2016.

Borowczak, M., & Burrows, A. C. (2016). *GIS technology + socio-scientific issues = teacher and student learning: The lake.* Paper presentation at the Society for Information Technology and Teacher Education Conference (SITE), Savannah, GA. March 21-26, 2016.

Burrows, A. C., & Slater, T. (2015). A proposed integrated STEM framework for contemporary teacher preparation. *Teacher Education and Practice, 28*(2-3), 318-330.

Burrows, A. C., & Harkness, S. (2015). Experiencing action evaluation's cyclic process: Partnering conflict, reflection, and action. *Educational Action Research, 24*(4), 460-478. doi.org/10.1080/09650792.2015.1108211 [H index:16; Q2].

Burrows, A. C. (2015). Partnerships: A systemic study of two professional developments with university faculty and K-12 teachers of science, technology, engineering, and mathematics. *Problems of Education in the 21st Century, 65*(65), 28-38.

Borowczak, M., & Burrows, A. C. (2015). Methods to approach outreach: Help for the classroom and beyond. *VLSI Circuits and Systems Letter* (VCAL), 1(2), 29-31. https://www.computer.org/cms/tcvlsi/newsletters/2015/VLSI_Circuits_and_Systems_vol1_issue2_Sep2015.pdf.

Borowczak, M., & Burrows, A. C. (2015). K-20 education. *VLSI Circuits and Systems Letter* (VCAL), 1(1), 28-29. https://www.computer.org/cms/tcvlsi/newsletters/2015/VLSI_Circuits_and_Systems_vol1_issue1_Apr2015.pdf.

Meghan E. Lockwood

Affiliation: Wyoming Game and Fish Department, Habitat Protection Program - Cheyenne, Wyoming

Education:
BS Environmental Studies, Linfield College, McMinnville, Oregon
Graduate Program of Teton Science Schools, Kelly, Wyoming
MS Natural Science with a concentration in Natural Science Education, as well as Environment and Natural Resources, University of Wyoming in Laramie, Wyoming, 2016

Business Address:

Wyoming Game and Fish Department, 5400 Bishop Blvd., Cheyenne, WY 82006

Research and Professional Experience:

While a graduate student in the University of Wyoming's Science and Math Teaching Center, Lockwood worked with Dr. Andrea C. Burrows to complete a Master's thesis titled "Addressing Three-Dimensional Learning with Citizen Science Projects," an evaluation of the ability of a particular citizen science program at the University of Wyoming to address the three dimensions of learning from the Next Generation Science Standards. This thesis work influenced this NOVA book chapter. She also worked as a graduate assistant to the Biodiversity Institute at the University of Wyoming from 2015-2016. Since receiving her Master's Degree, Lockwood has gone on to work at the Teton Science Schools in Kelly, Wyoming, and the Wyoming Game and Fish Department in Cheyenne, Wyoming.

Professional Appointments:

Program Assistant, Kelly Campus of the Teton Science Schools, 2016
Conservation Educator, Wyoming Game and Fish Department, 2017
Administrative Assistant, Habitat Protection Program at the Wyoming Game and Fish Department, 2017

Publications from the Last 3 Years:

Paper presented at the *American Educational Research Association Meeting, 2017* - "Citizen Science, Informal Education, and Action Research: Next Generation Science Standards, Girl Scouts and Water"

Poster presented at the *National Alliance of Broader Impacts*, 2016 - "Girl Scouts in Science: Discovering Wyoming Water"

Poster presented at the *Ecological Society of America Meeting*, 2014 - "Twenty years of change in the urban tree community in Forest park, Portland, Oregon"

Christina M. Belardo

Affiliation: Education Outreach Coordinator, Mohonk Preserve

Education: BS Environmental Science, University of Delaware; Graduate Student of the Tetons Science Schools Graduate Program; MS Natural Science Education, University of Wyoming, 2015

Business Address: P.O. Box 715, New Paltz, NY 12561

Research and Professional Experience:

- Education Outreach Coordinator, Mohonk Preserve, 2017-present
- Citizen Science Education Coordinator, Mohonk Preserve, 2015-17
- Wildlife Safaris Guide, Jackson Hole Wildlife Safaris, 2015
- WITS - NOYCE Graduate Assistant, University of Delaware, Science and Math Teaching Center, 2014-2015
- Field Instructor, Teton Science Schools, 2013-2014
- Volunteer Coordinator, Delaware Nature Society, 2010-1013
- Teacher Naturalist, Delaware Nature Society, 2009-2013

Honors:

- Outstanding Graduate Student, University of Wyoming, Science & Math Teaching Center, 2015

Publications from the Last 3 Years:

Belardo, C. A. (2015). *STEM Integration with Art: A Renewed Reason for STEAM.* Doctoral Projects, Masters Plan B, and Related Works, Paper 10. http://repository.uwyo.edu/plan_b/10.

Burrows, A. C., Belardo, C. & Dambekalns, L. (2017). Partnering Science and Art: Pre-Service Teachers' Experiences for Use in Pre-Collegiate Classrooms. *Problems of Education in the 21st Century*. 75. 215-234.

Edward Janak

Affiliation: University of Toledo, Judith Herb College of Education, Department of Educational Foundations and Leadership

Education: PhD 2003, University of South Carolina

Business Address: Gillham Hall 5000-C, Mail Stop 921, 2801 W. Bancroft St., Toledo OH 43606-3390

Research and Professional Experience: 2015- present, Associate professor/department chair at the University of Toledo; 2012-2015, Associate Professor, Department of Educational Studies, University of Wyoming; 2006-2012, Assistant Professor, University of Wyoming

Professional Appointments: 2003-04 Adjunct, Laramie County Community College, Laramie WY; 1995-2002 English Teacher, Swansea High School, Swansea SC; 1993-95 English Teacher, Marlboro County High School, Bennettsville SC

Honors: Popular Culture Association/American Culture Association Felicia F. Campbell Area Chair Award, 2014; University of Wyoming Mortarboard Society "Top Prof," 2006, 2011 & 2012; University of Wyoming College of Education Faculty Award for Outstanding Advising, 2011; University of Wyoming Promoting Intellectual Engagement Award, 2009 & 2011; University of Wyoming College of Education Faculty Award for Outstanding Teaching

Publications from the Last 3 Years:

Monograph:

Janak, E. (2014). *Politics, Disability and Education Reform in the South: The Work of John Eldred Swearingen*. New York: Palgrave-MacMillan Press.

Edited Collection:

Janak, E. & Sourdot, L. Eds. (2017). *Educating through Popular Culture: You're Not Cool Just Because You Teach with Comics*. Lanham, MD: Lexington Press.

Chapters:

Sourdot, L. & Janak, E. (2017). Introduction. In Janak, E. & Sourdot, L. Eds. *Educating through Popular Culture: You're Not Cool Just Because You Teach with Comics* (pp. ix-xxii). Lanham, MD: Lexington Press.

Janak, E. (2014). "Your dreams were your ticket out": How mass media's teachers constructed one educator's identity. In Ryan, K. M., Macey, D., and Springer, N.J. (Eds). *How television shapes our worldview: Media representations of social trends and change* (pp. 69-86). Lanham, MD: Lexington Press.

Articles in Print:

Janak, E. & Helmsing, M. (2017). Problematizing philanthropy: How a historical study of the General Education Board in the U.S. West puts the 'social' in race and region as social constructs. *Race Ethnicity and Education, 20*(2), 277-288. (Published online November 30, 2015).

Janak, E. (2016). "Democracy is Beautiful": Using a Historical Framework to Examine Preserve Teachers' Attitudes about Teaching for Democracy. *Learning for Democracy, 6*(2), 5-22.

Articles in Press:

Janak, E. & Pescara-Kovach, L. (2017). Four decades, three songs, too much violence: Using popular culture media analysis to prepare preservice teachers for dealing with school violence. *Dialogue: The Interdisciplinary Journal of Popular Culture and Pedagogy, 4*(1), 5-18.

Janak, E. (accepted July 2017). Bracketing and bridling: Using narrative reflexivity to confront researcher bias and the impact of social identity in a historical study. Accepted by *Philanthropy and Education*.

Essays/Editorials:

Janak, E. (2015). Being a proud academic dinosaur: My career in the foundations of education. *The Journal of Educational Foundations, 29*, 87-102.

Non-Refereed:

Janak, E. (October 11, 2016). "A century of preparing educators: Judith Herb College of Education celebrates 100 years." *UT News*: http://utnews.utoledo.edu/index.php/10_11_2016/a-century-of-preparing-educators-judith-herb-college-of-education-celebrates-100-years.

Book Reviews:

Janak, E. (2017). [Review of the book *The history of American higher education: Learning and culture from the founding to World War II* by Roger Geiger]. *The Journal of American Culture 40*(2), 199-200.

Janak, E. (2016). [Review of the book *The first U.S. history textbooks: Constructing and disseminating the American tale in the nineteenth century* by Barry Joyce]. *The Journal of American Culture, 39* (4), 476-77.

Janak, E. (2015). [Review of the book *Uncivil youth: Race, activism and affirmative governmentality* by Sooh Ah Kwon]. *The Journal of American Culture, 38* (2), 199-200.

In: (Participatory) Action Research
Editors: J. Calder and J. Foletta

ISBN: 978-1-53613-041-6
© 2018 Nova Science Publishers, Inc.

Chapter 4

TEACHING PARTICIPATORY ACTION RESEARCH: THE SEARCH FOR PEDAGOGICAL INSIGHTS

*Lawrence Susskind**, Dayna Cunningham*
and Isadora Araujo Cruxên
Department of Urban Studies and Planning,
Massachusetts Institute of Technology, Cambridge, MA, US

ABSTRACT

Most graduate social science departments and professional degree programs require their students to study both qualitative and quantitative research methods. This binary focus typically glosses over questions such as who defines the subject matter and scope of the research and who owns or controls research findings. In this chapter, we discuss how teaching Participatory Action Research (PAR) in MIT's Department of Urban Studies and Planning has pushed us to focus on (1) the

---

* Corresponding Author Email: susskind@mit.edu.

responsibilities of action researchers and their obligations to the communities and places in which they work; and (2) the importance of building the capacity of community members so that they can take control of the research being done about, with, and for them. While various manuals have suggested the best ways of doing this kind of work in practice, very little attention has been given to how to teach PAR methods to graduate students and research partners. We offer six considerations that we consider central to PAR pedagogy and, in the remainder of the chapter, describe how each of these considerations has informed the intellectual framework and pedagogical strategies at the heart of our teaching. One of the big surprises for us has been the extent to which a half-semester PAR module can radically alter the way professional degree candidates think about the rest of their course work and future careers. We conclude with an invitation to our academic colleagues who teach quantitative and qualitative research methods, but do not include any discussion of PAR-oriented issues and approaches in their courses.

Keywords: pedagogy, teaching, participatory action research

INTRODUCTION

Most graduate social science departments and professional degree programs require their students to study both qualitative and quantitative research methods. However, this binary focus typically glosses over other methodological, epistemological, and ethical considerations including questions such as who defines the subject matter and scope of the research and who owns or controls research findings. In this chapter, we discuss how teaching participatory action research (PAR) in MIT's Department of Urban Studies and Planning has pushed us to focus on (1) the responsibilities of applied social researchers and their obligations to the communities, groups, and places in which they work; and (2) the importance of building the capacity of community or group members so they can take control of the research being done about, with, and for them.

We begin this chapter with a brief overview of the intellectual history of action research (AR) and PAR. While various manuals have suggested the best ways of doing this kind of work in practice,[1] very little attention has been given to how to teach PAR methods to graduate students and research partners. We offer six considerations that we consider central to PAR pedagogy and, in the remainder of the chapter, describe how each of these considerations has informed the intellectual framework and pedagogical strategies at the heart of our teaching. One of the big surprises for us has been the extent to which a six-month PAR module can help professional degree candidates sharpen their own theories of practice and radically alter how they think about what they are learning and how they want to define their future work. We conclude the chapter with an invitation to our academic colleagues who teach quantitative and qualitative research methods, but do not take into account PAR-oriented considerations in their teaching.

PARTICIPATORY ACTION RESEARCH: HISTORICAL ROOTS AND PEDAGOGICAL VALUE

The development of action research as an approach to enhanced scientific understanding cannot be traced to a singular point in time or to a particular discipline. Its origins tie together insights from various intellectual influences such as philosopher John Dewey's "pragmatism",[2] urban planner and philosopher Donald Schön's "reflective practice", general systems thinking, and critical theory (Schön, 1984; Greenwood & Levin, 2006; Reason & Bradbury, 2008). AR and PAR practitioners have also drawn inspiration from grassroots organizing and processes of social mobilization such as the civil rights movement in the United States and the

---

[1] See, for example, Fals-Borda & Rahman, 1991; Greenwood & Levin, 2006; Reason & Bradbury, 2008; Kemmis, McTaggart, & Nixon, 2013; Chevalier & Buckles, 2013.

[2] See also, the work of sociologist and social activist W.E.B. Du Bois, such as in Du Bois and Eaton's *The Philadelphia Negro: a social study* (1899).

liberationist movement derived from the work of Brazilian pedagogue Paulo Freire (Fals-Borda, 1991; Reason & Bradbury, 2008).[3] The common thread linking these sources is a critique of scientific positivism and analytic rationality, and a call for reorienting social science more towards context-specific, experientially-based, and collectively-produced knowledge aimed at promoting social change.

John Dewey's conception of science as a form of inquiry that is fundamentally connected to practice is perhaps the most foundational contribution to the development of action research. Dewey construed inquiry as incessant "cycles of action and reflection" dedicated not simply to the production of new knowledge, but to the resolution of concrete, practical problems in society (Dewey & Rogers, 2012). In this sense, Dewey suggested that inquiry was intrinsically related to the exercise of democracy—that is, to enable an active citizenry (or public) to engage in problem-solving and to deal with conflicts through public debate. From Dewey and the work of those who followed, action research derives its orientation towards production of knowledge that communities can use to solve the problems they face—what Greenwood and Levin (2006) call "actionable knowledge."

The effort to tie inquiry more closely to action also entails an epistemological shift away from the search for generalizable knowledge or objective truth that is typically associated with the traditional application of scientific methods. As an alternative, action researchers believe that social science should place a premium on context-specific knowledge along with local ways of knowing acquired through lived experience (Greenwood & Levin, 2006). This is sometimes elaborated through the Aristotelian idea of *phronesis* or practical wisdom (Reason & Bradbury, 2008). As Flyvbjerg explains, *phronesis* "goes beyond both analytical, scientific knowledge (*episteme*) and technical knowledge or know-how (*techne*) and involves judgements and actions" derived from contextual experience (Flyvbjerg,

---

[3] See also, Horton and Freire's *We make the road by walking: Conversations on education and social change* (1990) and Hale's *The Freedom Schools: Student Activists in the Mississippi Civil Rights Movement* (2016).

2001, p. 2). This kind of knowledge—based on values rather than technical rationality—is considered essential for capturing the intuitive and situational dimensions of human action and helping to improve "social and political praxis" (Flyvbjerg, 2001).

What Is Special About PAR?

A variety of approaches to the theory and practice of action research[4] have developed over the years. In particular, the emergence of PAR can be traced to participatory research initiatives in Latin America and to the activities of leftist social movements in the 1960s and 1970s that were concerned with relationships between knowledge, individual empowerment, and societal transformation (Fals-Borda & Rahman, 1991). A key influence in this regard was the work of Paulo Freire regarding the role of popular education in social and political liberation.

In *Pedagogy of the Oppressed* (Freire, 2000 [1970]), Freire criticized traditional educational models that viewed students as mere recipients of knowledge—victims of what he called "the banking model" of education. He argued that "knowledge emerges only through invention and re-invention, through the restless, impatient, continuing, hopeful inquiry human beings pursue in the world, with the world, and with each other" (Freire, 2000 [1970], p. 72). For Freire, collective inquiry through dialogue is the means through which people develop a critical awareness (*conscientização*) of their position in the world. As he explained, such awareness enables "people to discuss courageously the problems of their context and to intervene in that context" (Freire, 1973, p. 36).

Building on these kinds of insights, participatory action research is a form of action-oriented inquiry that seeks to involve community-partners in all stages of the research process—from defining the questions, to analyzing and communicating findings. It aims to both place greater

---

[4] Reason and Bradbury's (2008) edited volume on action research reunites a collection of texts covering various approaches.

control over the research process in the hands of those directly affected by the problem under investigation and to build democratic capacity for collective problem-solving within these communities. As Rahman observes, "an immediate objective of PAR is to return to the people the legitimacy of the knowledge they are capable of producing through their own verification systems, as fully scientific, and the right to use this knowledge (…) as a guide in their own action" (Rahman, 1991, p. 15). In this sense, PAR challenges conventional notions of "expertise" and aims to disrupt expert (power) hierarchies in the production and circulation of knowledge.

In this chapter, we argue that the pedagogical value of PAR as an approach to applied social science and practical problem-solving resides precisely in pushing faculty and students to think more deeply about the process of knowledge production and their responsibilities towards the communities they work in or with—particularly if there is a commitment to promoting long-term social change. Within our own discipline, urban studies and planning, professional degree candidates are typically taught the importance of public participation and community engagement for constructing democratic planning processes. Yet, we often shy away from discussing with students the ways in which they can work directly and collaboratively with communities, not simply to consult them about a pre-defined problem or plan, but rather to involve them in the very definition of problems or elaborations of plans. Even when action research has been used explicitly as a planning tool to facilitate community dialogue and explore new forms of knowledge generation—such as in Sandercock and Attili's (2014) five-year action research and film-making project with indigenous peoples in British Columbia—outside researchers have retained control over the research, engaging the community only in select ways and failing to use action research to build local problem-solving capacity for the long-term.

Incorporating PAR or a PAR-like orientation into graduate planning education—and in applied social science departments more broadly—can prompt students to think critically about at least four key dimensions of public engagement in the realm of policy: formulation, evaluation, intervention, and long-term implementation. Who should define which problems deserve attention? Who will control the evaluation of the effectiveness of policy or strategy? What outcomes of policy intervention should be given priority, especially in the long-term? How will affected communities ensure ongoing commitment to original policy goals and outcomes? What are the obligations of researchers and practitioners towards the communities with which they work, or that will be affected by their interventions? The teaching of PAR to graduate students can serve as a setting for the exploration of these questions and of the ways in which collaborative research with partner-organizations and communities can facilitate social transformation.[5] Thus, the central question confronting college and university professors is: what key principles should inform the structure and operation of such an educational space?

Elements of a PAR Pedagogy

While proponents and practitioners of AR and PAR have produced many grounded accounts of their research, a discussion of the pedagogical strategies that should be used to teach PAR to graduate students has generally been overlooked (Greenwood, 2007; McNicoll, 1999; Sankaran, Hase, Dick, & Davies, 2007). Much of the published work linking action research to educational practice stems from educational research and focuses on how educators can use AR to find answers or solutions to problems faced in the classroom or in educational settings (McKernan, 1991; Mertler, 2016; Reed, 2007; Zuber-Skerritt, 1992). For example, Reed (2007) describes three examples of situations in which teachers used action research to a) collect and analyze data, and b) devise an action plan for addressing curriculum issues, school dropout, and student behavior in the classroom.

---

[5] This is not to suggest that that there is a particular PAR model to be followed or to assume that PAR will necessarily be more beneficial to communities (Winkler, 2013). Rather, we propose that the teaching of PAR can alter the ways students approach their own practice and think about the outcomes of their interventions beyond the short-term.

Taking note of the gap in pedagogical documentation,[6] some scholars have written reflective accounts of their experiences teaching AR or PAR courses (Etmanski & Pant, 2007; Fine & Torre, 2008; Greenwood, 2007; Kur, DePorres, & Westrup, 2008; McKernan, 1994; McNicoll, 1999; Sankaran et al., 2007; Winkler, 2013). These are extremely valuable because they illuminate particular pedagogical "challenges and pleasures", as McNicoll (1999) calls them. Having reflected on our own experience, we offer six considerations that we consider central to the design of PAR instruction. We think these can lead to the creation of educational spaces in which students can challenge conventional ways of approaching knowledge production and community engagement.

The first consideration is ethics. A pedagogy of participatory action research needs to confront moral questions such as who controls knowledge production and for what purposes, what counts as knowledge, and what are the obligations of outside researchers to the communities and groups with whom they work. It also requires us to consider, particularly when the research is controversial, how risks are distributed within the research team (Fine & Torre, 2008). Building on Cahill, Sultana, and Pain (2007), we argue an ethics of PAR should be characterized by a commitment to collaboration and joint-learning, by an openness to diverse forms of knowing and a recognition that people have valuable knowledge about their experiences, and by a responsibility for critical reflection, action, and capacity building. Further, an ethics of participatory action research needs to involve, in our view, continuous negotiation with the co-researchers of the conditions of collaboration and discussion of their concerns (Cahill, Sultana, & Pain, 2007; Public Science Project, 2013). As with any discussion of ethics, there are no correct answers. However, we do not think faculty and students should enter into a discussion of AR and PAR without making explicit their ethical and epistemological assumptions.

---

[6] In a survey of different academic databases, for example, Sankaran et al. (2007) found only five articles explicitly focused on the teaching of AR.

A second consideration in the design of a pedagogical approach to PAR instruction should focus on the discussion of multiple ways of interacting with communities or groups to decide what research questions ought to be asked and how they can be answered. How do we begin a PAR process with a community or group? As co-researchers, what are some of the strategies we can use to engage people in problem definition and research design? What forms should translation or exchange take when different forms of knowledge are in conversation? What kinds of skills—for example, facilitative or organizational—are necessary to enable joint-learning? These are some of the central questions that need to be addressed in the design of a course about PAR.

Relatedly, the third consideration refers to ways of involving communities and groups in data gathering, which often requires training in various research methods (Public Science Project, 2013). Although PAR is often thought of primarily in terms of qualitative research, there is no reason that it should favor qualitative research strategies over quantitative methods of data analysis. As an approach to applied social science research, PAR can embrace a multitude of methods. The choice of a particular methodological strategy ought to depend on the choice of the research questions made by the co-researchers. In addressing methodological choices, it is often important to discuss with students the possibility that research methods used in a single project can evolve during the course of the project. As Kur, DePorres, and Westrup (2008) have observed in their experience teaching AR, students often struggle with the necessary lack of linearity in action-based research processes. They may need help seeing how different methods can be useful at different stages of a research effort.

The fourth consideration refers to guidelines regarding the best way to prepare case studies, particularly the importance of drawing on story-telling and narrative techniques. Since PAR places a premium on context-based knowledge, case studies can be an especially valuable tool for investigating certain issues in depth and for highlighting place-specific or context-specific factors that might define a problem and potential ways of resolving it (McKernan, 1994; Flyvbjerg, 2001). Taking context seriously does not mean that case studies have no theoretical or policy relevance beyond the context to which they refer. Rather, taking context seriously allows one to draw insights from multiple contexts through careful comparative analysis. This often requires noting differences but also emphasizing meaningful similarities across distinct contexts. Within the realm of urban planning, Sandercock (2003) has also called attention to the power of stories and story-telling as ways of engaging communities, resolving conflicts, and informing problem-solving.

These techniques may also constitute part of a strategy for collaborative data analysis and joint-presentation of findings—what we think of as the fifth consideration in a PAR pedagogy. How might co-researchers work together to define the key audiences for the research, and interpret and represent research findings? When reporting results, how might findings be displayed in compelling and actionable ways for particular audiences? How should decisions about the use of findings be made?

Finally, a pedagogy of PAR needs to address the question of how to balance the sometimes-competing professional needs and interests of outsiders (usually the academics) and those of the community-based partners. As Cahill, Sultana, and Pain (2007) observe, academic researchers face specific institutional demands that pose challenges (often in the form of university requirements) regarding the design of collaborative research projects. These include requirements imposed by Institutional Review Boards (IRBs) that are usually aimed at upholding conventional standards of scientific work in the natural sciences. If a scholar wants approval from an IRB for a particular community-based research design, she or he will need to ensure that the IRB's mandates are met while accommodating the preferences of the community partners. So, how can scholars be accountable to their community partners as well as to their university?

To summarize, we propose that a pedagogy of PAR needs to address concerns about research ethics and knowledge ownership as well as ways of interacting and collaborating with partner-communities in making decisions about question definition, data collection and analysis, and reporting of findings. University-based PAR instruction needs to introduce students to a range of analytical techniques that are consistent with PAR's commitment to producing context-dependent knowledge, often drawing on very different ways of knowing. And, finally, PAR pedagogy needs to confront the tensions and challenges that arise when outside researchers seek to reconcile their obligations to their university responsibilities with their obligations to their community partners. Applied social scientists, in particular, have great difficulty reconciling what their university colleagues might think is "high quality" research with what the community needs. We have written elsewhere about the tensions faced by doctoral students and faculty, otherwise known as "pracademics", who want to engage primarily in community-based research (Susskind, 2013). In the next section, we describe the structure of two half-semester courses about PAR we have taught at MIT over the past four years.[7]

TEACHING PAR THEORY AND PRACTICE AT MIT

Our teaching of PAR at MIT is organized into two modules. The first, typically taught in the Fall semester, introduces students to theories of AR and PAR and exposes them to competing ideas about social inquiry and the role of applied social science in promoting social change. The focus is on the epistemological foundations of PAR, the role of the academic researcher, and the arguments for and against PAR as a scientific method. The second module, taught in the Spring semester, examines the application of PAR principles in practice, especially through the analysis of cases of knowledge co-creation with community research partners. It focuses on appropriate methods for doing PAR in practice and on the ethical dilemmas at the heart of partnerships between applied social scientists and community members.

---

[7] Lawrence Susskind and Dayna Cunningham originally formulated the course in 2013. Isadora Cruxên served as teaching assistant for the course for the academic year of 2015–2016.

Despite the difference in focus, the foundation for both modules is the introduction of a theoretical framework for thinking about PAR in relation to the practice of social science and the exercise of democracy. Through an exploration of the work of Dewey and Freire as well as contributions from Appadurai (2006)[8] and Santos, Nunes, and Meneses (2007),[9] we encourage students to interrogate the concepts of science, knowledge, and democracy as well as the relationships among them. This not only immerses students in the intellectual history of PAR, but it helps to situate the practice of PAR within a broader set of epistemological concerns. Most importantly, it serves as the starting point for the examination of the ethical questions we raised earlier. We discuss how social science research can be used to create knowledge, the role of expertise and local knowledge in knowledge production, the relationship between knowledge—or multiple forms of knowledge—and democracy, and the role of power in configuring such relationships. While we offer no clear-cut answers, the debates that emerge allow us to plumb the value of contextual knowledge and lived experience, and the chances of building democratic capacity through collective inquiry.

After laying this foundation, we draw from manuals such as Greenwood and Levin (2006) and Reason and Bradbury (2008) to introduce general principles of AR and PAR, and explore variants such as Critical PAR and Feminist PAR. In both modules, we use cases from practice—both domestic and international—to illustrate how practitioners have carried out participatory action research on the ground. We also invite PAR practitioners to speak directly with students about their experiences.

---

[8] Appadurai (2006) argues that research, understood as a form of disciplined inquiry, can empower individuals by improving their capacity to understand—and, by extension, to effectively change—their environment through active citizenship. In this sense, we might think of the democratization of inquiry at the individual level as being necessary for the exercise of democracy at a broader scale.

[9] In "Opening up the Canon of Knowledge and Recognition of Difference," Santos, Nunes, and Menezes (2007) argue that the struggle for social justice globally cannot happen independently from a struggle for "global cognitive justice," that is, a recognition of the epistemological diversity that exists in the world. They suggest there is a need to replace a Western-centric "monoculture of scientific knowledge" with an "ecology of knowledges." They observe that, "The very action of knowing, as pragmatist philosophers have repeatedly reminded us, is an intervention in the world, which places us within it as active contributors to its making" (Santos, Nunes, & Menezes, 2007, p. xxxi).

For example, Cory Greene, a formerly incarcerated PhD student at the Graduate Center of City University of New York (CUNY) and a member of the Public Science Project,[10] spoke to our students about his engagement in Critical PAR projects that "sit at the intersection of race, class, education and the criminal punishment system" (Mehta, 2015). This includes the Morris Justice Project in the Bronx, New York. Greene discussed his relationship with the groups and communities he works with along with the variety of strategies his blended community and academic research team uses for knowledge co-production. Similarly, we invited Alison Coffey and Jenna Harvey from the Community Innovators Lab (CoLab) at MIT to share their experiences working on a PAR project with young people at PalmasLab, an innovation space located in a neighborhood on the periphery of Fortaleza, Brazil—we discuss this project further below. This conversation focused on the co-definition of a research question, the choice of methodological strategies for data collection, and translation of research findings into meaningful action.

The discussion of cases of PAR in practice is a useful means of drawing students into the discussion of the five considerations we raised at the outset of this chapter. The cases also bring to life the ethical dilemmas that we think are so challenging. The conversations with Greene and the team from CoLab prompted students to reflect on the question of whether outside researchers should adopt a neutral stance toward particular problems or whether PAR's implied commitment to social change—and often social justice issues—requires a different approach to positionality in social research.[11] We also encouraged students to address these issues in their final papers or presentations (due at the end of the course).

Particularly in the second module, we seek to expose students to examples from practice that employ a multiplicity of approaches to data

---

[10] The Public Science Project engages in what they call "Critical Participatory Action Research (CPAR), a theoretical, epistemological, and ethical commitment of accountability to those most closely related to, and affected by, the issue(s) under study" (Mehta, 2015). See more at http://publicscienceproject.org/.

[11] The issues of neutrality and positionality surfaced in reflection memos written by students, which were posted online to the course forum, and during in-class debates. We discuss the reflection memos further in the chapter.

collection and analysis. This helps to impress upon students that the choice of research methods—whether qualitative or quantitative—ought to be contingent on the chosen research questions. Almost every year, regardless of what we say about the value of mixed methods, there is, for some students, an epistemological dissonance in using quantitative methods in a PAR project. As one student observed when reflecting about the use of a survey in the Morris Justice Project, "Since PAR is inevitably done with groups and not whole communities, it seems that one group applying a large-scale survey to a larger community without channels for engagement and contestation in the process could in some cases reproduce the same information extraction dynamic that PAR seeks to contest."[12] We try to address such issues during in-class discussion and raise broader questions regarding scientific rigor in PAR as compared to other forms of social research. For instance, are the concepts of validity and generalizability applicable to PAR or should PAR-related research only be assessed in terms of what Greenwood and Levin call "workability", that is, "its capacity to resolve problems in real life"? (Greenwood & Levin, 2006, p. 75) Who decides which standards to use in evaluating PAR project findings?

We dedicate several sessions to discussing the importance of case study research for social science and for PAR, and ask students to prepare a narrative analysis of a theme of their choice. In our view, narrative analysis is a critical skill for all PAR practitioners. It enables a systematic harvesting of knowledge from storytelling—one of the most basic forms of human communication—and can serve as a means of building empathy between the outside researchers and the community. We focus on representativeness in narrative analysis and review different narrative forms including thematic, structural, dialogic, and performance analysis (Riessman, 2008). Students in our course have prepared narrative analyses of documentaries, book chapters, and even Twitter hashtags. These exercises are especially helpful for addressing issues of representation and meaning-making. As Flyvberg (2001) suggests, social scientists are

---

[12] Reflection memo written by a student and posted to the course forum on October 20th, 2015.

generally tasked (or embrace the task) of codifying and generalizing meaning that other people have created. However, that creates a fundamental dilemma: should social scientists decide what something means? Narratives and case studies provide space for the discussion of how research findings should be presented and how to engage partner-communities and groups in telling their own stories about problems they seek to resolve.

Throughout our courses, we ask students to write reflection memos that comment on the readings and raise questions for in-class discussion. These are posted online to a collective forum and shared ahead of class. One key objective of these memos is to stimulate students to continuously reflect about what they are learning. Like other teachers of AR and PAR (Beisser & Connor, 2004; Etmanski & Pant, 2007; Kur et al., 2008), we see reflection and reflective practice as a crucial dimension of PAR. In addition to the reflection memos, we draw on Schön's *The Reflective Practitioner* (1984) and Scharmer's *Theory U: Leading from the Future as it Emerges* (2009) to discuss how cycles of reflection-action-reflection can be incorporated into PAR practice. PAR practitioners must be able to turn the beam of observation back on themselves to better understand their responsibilities in bringing about social change and confronting any tensions that may arise. Reflection memos, coupled with examples from practice and in-class discussion, have also helped students think about the transformative potential—and the limits—of PAR research in a range of different contexts.

At the conclusions of each module, we ask students to reflect with us on ways in which the course can be improved. Several students have mentioned how the course has provided one of the few opportunities during their graduate education to discuss in depth their roles in knowledge production and their responsibilities toward the communities with which they engage. Many have thanked us for the opportunity to explore their own personal theories of practice as planners. Some suggested that we expand the scope of the course to discuss PAR as an approach to professional planning education and practice more broadly. This has prompted us to think about how a PAR-orientation might be incorporated more generally into methods courses in the master in city planning program at MIT. In the next section, we draw on the experiences of some of our former students to illustrate how the courses have helped shape their personal theories of practice and professional development.

Helping Students Develop Their Theories of Practice

Teachers of AR and PAR have written about the challenge of structuring courses that allow sufficient time for students to discuss theory, learn different methods, and engage in meaningful practice (McKernan, 1994; McNicoll, 1999). McKernan (1994), for example, noted that, in his experience, a single semester was simply not enough to cover these three areas. It has been surprising to us, however, how completing even one of the half-semester PAR modules we offer at MIT can shape the ways students approach the rest of their graduate education and professional practice.

Our students have noted, for example, that the PAR courses have served as spaces where they could talk through tensions and ethical dilemmas they encountered in their exposure to planning practice in previous work or in other courses but which they had had little opportunity to explore in depth. Importantly, our students have emphasized that such discussions were fundamental for helping them develop their own theories of practice, that is, the sets of principles and values they thought should guide their actions and professional endeavors.

According to Andrew Binet, a former master's (and current PhD) student who took both modules and also served as a teaching assistant for the course, the idea of a theory of practice was "spoken a lot about as an important thing in [other classes in the department] but in terms of actually articulating it for myself and actually having a personal and real system of value orientations, the PAR class is what enabled me to do that, especially as someone who had zero planning experience."[13] Binet noted, in particular, how important it was for him that the course was co-taught by two professors with very different views about PAR, which allowed him to "triangulate", as he called it, and develop his own thinking about PAR and its connection to planning practice. For Binet, "planning that doesn't have a PAR-like orientation risks exacerbating systems of oppression. If planning is about intentional social action, the only way it can do this is through PAR-like processes" that help define scopes of inquiry and engage issues of power and inequality.[14]

Eventually, this "triangulation" became central to Binet's own professional work. Since 2015, he has been involved in a multi-methods research process supported by the Healthy Neighborhood Equity Fund (HNEF) and implemented through a collaboration with DUSP faculty-member, Mariana Arcaya, the Conservation Law Foundation, and MIT's CoLab. The goal is to examine the ways in which urban development impacts community health in different neighborhoods across the Boston metropolitan area. Binet has been responsible for coordinating the PAR component of the project, which involves collaborative research design, data collection, and analysis alongside an "inter-generational, multi-community group of resident researchers" (Community Innovators Lab, 2017). Reflecting on how the course has influenced his work in the project, Binet observed:

> By virtue of taking that class I became able to talk about power in a way that I would not otherwise have. Ultimately what was necessary within the [HNEF] PAR process was the ability to actually and meaningfully talk about power both [with residents] and within our own team—like, I'm a white person from a different country coming into your community—and to be able to have a frank conversation about what that means for research ethics. I have no doubt that I didn't do it perfectly but the only reason I was able to do it in the first place was because of this

---

[13] Interview with Andrew Binet, September 26th, 2017, Cambridge, MA, United States.
[14] Interview with Andrew Binet, op. cit.

class. And related to that, the other piece was learning to map out the different types of knowledge and value simultaneously and create an understanding about what types of knowledge were in play.[15]

Another way in which the course supported students in developing their personal theories of practice was by providing an avenue by which they could reflect about PAR in relation to different strands of theory or practical experiences they were invested in. For example, Jenna Harvey, a former master's student who took the PAR theory module, observed that the course helped her place her previous experience with participatory research within a broader contextual and theoretical framework for how to approach this kind of work.[16]

Prior to taking the PAR module, Harvey had been involved in the aforementioned collaboration between MIT's CoLab and PalmasLab in Fortaleza, Brazil. Along with Alison Coffey (a former master in city planning student who had taken the PAR practice module), Harvey worked with youth leaders at PalmasLab to design and implement a collaborative research project "focused on understanding how residents of Conjunto Palmeiras experience and engage with multiple "wealths" and "poverties" shaping the landscape of local development" (Community Innovators Lab, 2017). According to Harvey, taking the PAR course pushed her to consider more carefully her positionality as an outside researcher, the issue of accountability to her research partners, and what it meant to build democratic capacity at PalmasLab and in Conjunto Palmeiras.[17] Ultimately, such reflections and the conceptual tools she learned through the course formed the foundation for her view, articulated in her master's thesis (Harvey, 2016a), that collective inquiry through PAR can foster the development of what she calls "projective agency" as an important democratic capacity, particularly for marginalized communities. For Harvey:

---

[15] Interview with Andrew Binet, op. cit.
[16] Interview with Jenna Harvey, September 23th, 2017, Somerville, MA, United States.
[17] Interview with Jenna Harvey, op.cit.

> PAR as a process [has] the potential for building up and strengthening capacity – the capacity to see present circumstances as susceptible to change, to think beyond them, and to imagine something new. Through the research process, the PalmasLab team exercised this capacity, and through discussion, survey implementation, collaborative analysis and reflection, they led others in their community in doing the same. (…) [PAR] as a political stance about who has the right to produce credible knowledge, and as an approach that joins together inquiry, reflection and action, has the potential to form the foundation for [a] new model of practice [based on knowledge co-creation]. Understanding PAR as just an alternative approach to social science research and knowledge production is limiting. PAR values and key principles should be at the center of planning practice, not the margins. (Harvey, 2016b)

The experiences of Binet and Harvey, while singular, help illustrate the pedagogical value of PAR for helping students situate themselves within their field and develop their own understanding of what it means to construct a transformative and democratic professional practice. While not all of our students have gone on to do PAR as part of their professional careers, many have related to us that the course was fundamental to helping them define what kinds of practitioners they wanted to become.

CONCLUSION

We have sought to highlight the importance of focusing attention on what a pedagogy of PAR ought to entail and why it is an important part of applied social science education. We have proposed various questions we believe are essential for students to think about: who owns and controls research and any knowledge produced, why context matters, what are the responsibilities of outside researchers towards partner-communities and groups, how to structure interactions with these partners, and how to conduct research in a collaborative way that builds democratic capacity in the long-term. By teaching the theories and practice of PAR to graduate students at MIT, we have found, as have others (Greenwood, 2007; Kur et al., 2008), that learning about PAR can profoundly change—or reinforce—students' personal theories of practice, and shape the way they approach their graduate education and professional careers.

We invite our academic colleagues who teach quantitative and qualitative research methods in applied social science departments to consider incorporating PAR-oriented material into their courses. We understand, of course, that there are important institutional challenges to teaching PAR or PAR-like approaches in academic settings, many of which do not value the principles we have discussed here (Greenwood 2007). For example, many social science departments remain attached to a positivistic approach to research, and might think of PAR as lacking the kind of "objectivity" or generalizability they associate with top-notch scientific work. Further, as Greenwood (2007) observes, the "banking model of education" continues to be the prevalent pedagogy in educational institutions. Nonetheless, we hope to provoke a conversation not just about PAR as an approach to research, but also as a way to rethink the roles and responsibilities of applied social scientists who want to engage with communities.

Unless graduate students learn how to interact with partners from the outset of a research effort, they might not learn to communicate *with* as opposed to unidirectionally convey messages *to* the groups, organizations, and communities with which they are working. Unless graduate students learn to take context into account and to build relationships and trust with those who are affected by problems or have the capacity to act on the knowledge that is shared, their contribution to social change will be extremely limited. Finally, unless students learn to think about their responsibilities toward their community partners and the possibility of building community capacity as a by-product of research, the solutions or interventions they generate are likely to have little long-term impact. These points were compellingly articulated by our former student, Jenna Harvey, in an essay about how PAR might inform a theory of planning practice. We conclude with her words:

In my experience as a student of planning, too often skills such as reflective practice and facilitation are marginalized and discounted in favor of "hard skills" that are marketable and more easily quantifiable. This kind of pedagogy often produces practitioners that think they know the solutions before actually understanding the issues, perpetuating a cycle that is often oppressive and unproductive in affecting lasting change. To break out of this cycle we must first develop the critical ability to recognize the way it confines us in the first place. Only then can we embark on a planning approach that centers on the knowledge of those closest to the problems. (Harvey, 2016b)

REFERENCES

Appadurai, A. (2006). The right to research. *Globalisation, Societies and Education*, 4(2), 167–177.

Beisser, S. R., & Connor, K. (2004). Impact of teaching an action research course. *Academic Exchange Quarterly*, 8(3), 80–86.

Cahill, C., Sultana, F., & Pain, R. (2007). Participatory ethics: politics, practices, institutions. *ACME: An International Journal for Critical Geographies*, 6(3), 304–318.

Chevalier, J. M., & Buckles, D. (2013). *Participatory action research: Theory and methods for engaged inquiry*. Routledge.

Community Innovators Lab. (2017). *Participatory Action Research*. Retrieved September 29, 2017, from http://colab.mit.edu/our-work/participatory-action-research.

Dewey, J., & Rogers, M. L. (2012). *The public and its problems: An essay in political inquiry*. Penn State Press.

Du Bois, W. E. B., & Eaton, I. (1899). *The Philadelphia Negro: a social study* (No. 14). Published for the University.

Etmanski, C., & Pant, M. (2007). Teaching participatory research through reflexivity and relationship. *Action Research*, 5(3), 275–292. http://doi.org/10.1177/1476750307081018.

Fals-Borda, O. (1991). Some basic ingredients. In *Action-research, Action and knowledge: breaking the monopoly with participatory*. New York: Apex Press.

Fals-Borda, O., & Rahman, M. A. (1991). *Action and knowledge: breaking the monopoly with participatory action-research*. New York: Apex Press.

Fine, M., & Torre, M. E. (2008). Theorizing Audience, Products and Provocation. In P. Reason & H. Bradbury (Eds.), *The SAGE Handbook of Action Research* (2nd ed., pp. 407–419). London: SAGE Publications Ltd. http://doi.org/10.4135/9781848607934.n35.

Flyvbjerg, B. (2001). *Making social science matter: Why social inquiry fails and how it can succeed again*. Cambridge university press.

Freire, P. (1973). *Education for critical consciousness* (Vol. 1). Bloomsbury Publishing.

Freire, P. (2000 [1970]). *Pedagogy of the oppressed*. Bloomsbury Publishing.

Greenwood, D. J. (2007). Teaching/learning action research requires fundamental reforms in public higher education. *Action Research, 5*(3), 249–264.

Greenwood, D. J., & Levin, M. (2006). *Introduction to action research: Social research for social change*. SAGE publications.

Hale, J. N. (2016). *The Freedom Schools: Student Activists in the Mississippi Civil Rights Movement*. Columbia University Press.

Harvey, J. A. D. (2016a). *Deepening Democratic Capacity through Collective Inquiry: Community-led Research at PalmasLab*. Massachusetts Institute of Technology.

Harvey, J. A. D. (2016b). *Participatory Action Research as a Theory of Practice for Planners*. Retrieved September 29, 2017, from http://colabradio.mit.edu/participatory-action-research-as-a-theory-of-practice-for-planners/.

Horton, M., & Freire, P. (1990). *We make the road by walking: Conversations on education and social change*. Temple University Press.

Kemmis, S., McTaggart, R., & Nixon, R. (2013). *The action research planner: Doing critical participatory action research.* Springer Science & Business Media.

Kur, E., DePorres, D., & Westrup, N. (2008). Teaching and learning action research: Transforming students, faculty and university in Mexico. *Action Research, 6*(3), 327–349.

McKernan, J. (1991). *Curriculum Action Research: a Handbook of Methods and Resources for the Reflective Practitioner* (1st ed.). Routledge.

McKernan, J. (1994). Teaching educational action research: a tale of three cities. *Educational Action Research, 2*(1), 95–112.

McNicoll, P. (1999). Issues in teaching participatory action research. *Journal of Social Work Education, 35*(1), 51–62.

Mehta, A. (2015). *Exploring Participatory Action Research: Speaker Series.* Retrieved September 28, 2017, from http://colabradio. mit.edu/exploring-participatory-action-research-speaker-series/.

Mertler, C. A. (2016). *Action research: Improving schools and empowering educators.* Sage Publications.

Public Science Project. (2013). PAR Map. Retrieved September 28, 2017, from http://www.publicscienceproject.org/files/2013/04/PAR-Map.pdf.

Rahman, M. A. (1991). The theoretical standpoint of PAR. In *Action and knowledge: breaking the monopoly with participatory action-research.* New York: Apex Press.

Reason, P., & Bradbury, H. (2008). *Handbook of action research: Participative inquiry and practice* (2nd ed.). London: SAGE Publications Ltd.

Reed, C. (2007). Action research: A strategy for instructional improvement. *Teaching and Learning, 4*(2).

Riessman, C. K. (2008). *Narrative methods for the human sciences.* Sage.

Sandercock, L. (2003). Out of the closet: The importance of stories and storytelling in planning practice. *Planning Theory & Practice, 4*(1), 11–28.

Sandercock, L., & Attili, G. (2014). Changing the lens: Film as action research and therapeutic planning practice. *Journal of Planning Education and Research*, *34*(1), 19–29.

Sankaran, S., Hase, S., Dick, B., & Davies, A. (2007). Singing different tunes from the same song sheet: Four perspectives of teaching the doing of action research. *Action Research*, *5*(3), 293–305.

Santos, B. de S., Nunes, J. A., & Meneses, M. P. (2007). Opening up the Canon of Knowledge and Recognition of Difference. *Another Knowledge Is Possible. London: Verso, XIX-LXII*.

Scharmer, C. O. (2009). *Theory U: Leading from the Future as It Emerges*. San Francisco: Berrett-Koehler Publishers, Inc.

Schon, D. A. (1984). *The reflective practitioner: How professionals think in action* (Vol. 5126). Basic Books.

Susskind, L. (2013). Confessions of a pracademic: Searching for a virtuous cycle of theory building, teaching, and action research. *Negotiation Journal*, *29*(2), 225–237.

Winkler, T. (2013). At the coalface: Community--university engagements and planning education. *Journal of Planning Education and Research*, *33*(2), 215–227.

Zuber-Skerritt, O. (1992). *Action Research in Higher Education: Examples and Reflections*. ERIC.

ABOUT THE AUTHORS

Lawrence Susskind, Ford Professor of Urban and Environmental Planning, Department of Urban Studies and Planning, Massachusetts Institute of Technology. Professor Susskind's research interests focus on the theory and practice of negotiation and dispute resolution, the practice of public engagement in local decision-making, entrepreneurial negotiation, the resolution of science-intensive policy disputes, and socially-responsible real estate development. Professor Susskind is the author or co-author of twenty books including *Good for You, Great for Me* (Public Affairs Press), *Breaking Robert's Rules* (Oxford), *The Consensus*

Building Handbook (Sage), and *Dealing with An Angry Public* (Free Press). Professor Susskind is currently Director of the MIT Science Impact Collaborative, Director of the MIT-UTM Malaysia Sustainable Cities Program (MSCP) and Co-director of the Water Diplomacy Workshop. He is Founder of the Consensus Building Institute, a Cambridge-based, not-for-profit that provides mediation services in complicated resource management disputes around the world. He also was one of the founders of the inter-university Program on Negotiation at Harvard Law School.

Business Address: Department of Urban Studies and Planning, Massachusetts Institute of Technology, 77 Massachusetts Avenue, Cambridge, MA, 02139. Building/Room 9-432.

Dayna Cunningham, Executive Director of the Community Innovators Lab (CoLab) and Lecturer, Department of Urban Studies and Planning, Massachusetts Institute of Technology. Dayna Cunningham is the Executive Director of the Community Innovators Lab (CoLab). CoLab is a center for planning and development within the MIT Department of Urban Studies and Planning (DUSP), that supports the development and use of knowledge from excluded communities to deepen civic engagement, improve community, inform policy, and mobilize community assets. Prior to CoLab, as Program Director of the ELIAS Project, an MIT-based collaboration between business, NGOs and government, she worked with leaders using profound innovation processes to create multi-sector initiatives for economic, social, and environmental sustainability. Before that, Dayna worked as an Associate Director at the Rockefeller Foundation supporting efforts to explore changing racial dynamics and new conceptions of race in the U.S., as well as civil rights legal innovation. Prior to the Rockefeller Foundation, as a voting rights lawyer with the NAACP Legal Defense and Educational Fund, she litigated cases in Arkansas, Tennessee, Louisiana, Mississippi, and elsewhere in the South. Dayna is a 2004 graduate of the Sloan Fellows MBA program of the MIT Sloan School of Management. She has an undergraduate degree from Harvard and Radcliffe Colleges and a juris doctor degree from New York

University School of Law. She currently serves as a board member for the Emerald Cities Collaborative, Beloved Community Center, Restaurant Opportunities Council (ROC) United, and Presenting Institute.

Business Address: Department of Urban Studies and Planning, Massachusetts Institute of Technology, 77 Massachusetts Avenue, Cambridge, MA, 02139. Building/Room 9-238.

Isadora Araujo Cruxên, Doctoral Student in International Development, Department of Urban Studies and Planning, Massachusetts Institute of Technology. Isadora Cruxên is a PhD student in International Development at MIT's Department of Urban Studies and Planning. Her current research interests focus on interactions between state and financial actors and the ways in which they influence urban development and access to services in cities in Latin America. Her master's thesis, "Fluid dynamics: Politics and Social Struggle in São Paulo's Water Crisis", explored social mobilization around a two-year long water supply crisis in the metropolitan area of São Paulo, Brazil's most populous region and main economic center. Isadora holds a Bachelor's degree in Political Science from the University of Brasília, Brazil, and a Master in City Planning from MIT. Prior to coming to MIT, she worked as a research fellow at the Institute for Applied Economic Research in Brazil on projects about public participation in policy development. She was also involved in organizing and facilitating participatory processes, such as the elaboration of Brazil's Second Plan of Action for the Open Government Partnership.

Business Address: Department of Urban Studies and Planning, Massachusetts Institute of Technology, 77 Massachusetts Avenue, Cambridge, MA, 02139. Building/Room 9-320.

In: (Participatory) Action Research
Editors: J. Calder and J. Foletta

ISBN: 978-1-53613-041-6
© 2018 Nova Science Publishers, Inc.

Chapter 5

USING ACTION RESEARCH AND AN IMPORTED CONCEPTUAL FRAMEWORK TO STUDY THE INDIVIDUAL DIMENSION OF CURRICULUM RELEVANCE

Francisco Sousa[*]

Faculty of Social and Human Sciences,
University of the Azores, Angra do Heroísmo, Portugal
Research Center on Child Studies,
University of Minho, Braga, Portugal

ABSTRACT

Curriculum relevance has not been presented as a priority topic in Curriculum Studies. Nevertheless, some researchers within this field have addressed that same topic in ways that suggest that there is much work to be done in its conceptualization. Interestingly, potential contributions to

[*] Corresponding Author Email: francisco.jr.sousa@uac.pt.

such conceptualization can be found in other fields, within the wider field of Education. For example, some research on both Mathematics Education and Science Education has addressed issues of content relevance in these specific contexts. The conceptual frameworks that directed the studies can be considered in the context of Curriculum Studies in general, although the above-mentioned researchers do not usually call for such generalization. Accordingly, the chapter starts out by examining how Curriculum Studies have addressed relevance and by proposing a framework for the study of curriculum relevance in general, which was adapted from literature on Science Education. The proposal considers three dimensions of relevance: societal, vocational, and individual. Then the text narrows the focus to the individual dimension and presents some notes related to its meaning. The chapter proceeds with a discussion on the importance of action research in the study of the individual dimension of curriculum relevance. Finally, an action research project, which was focused on students' acknowledgement of curriculum relevance, is presented. The project took place in the Azores Islands, Portugal, and was carried out by a team that included researchers from the only university located in the region, as well as teachers of elementary schools from that same region. The problem that prompted the emergence of the project was some teachers' complaints about some students' alleged lack of interest for the school and the curriculum. Action research allowed the team to deepen the participants' understanding of the problem, which, in turn, facilitated the design of instructional strategies that took the students' views of curriculum relevance into consideration. Data reveal a tendency towards both future relevance and extrinsic aspects of relevance. Nevertheless, the outcomes of the project include evidence of improvements in the students' acknowledgment of both present relevance and intrinsic aspects of relevance.

Keywords: curriculum relevance, action research

1. INTRODUCTION

Curriculum relevance "is inherent to the very concept of curriculum" (Roldão, 2011, p. 10). In fact, if curriculum is defined as "all the learning which is recognized as being socially necessary at a certain moment in time and within a certain context," then it is "socially justified by its necessity and usefulness" (Roldão, 2011, p. 10). However, as time goes by and contexts change, parts of the curriculum might become obsolete. The evolution of society, culture and technology requires changes in the curriculum. But such changes tend to be relatively slow. Because tradition and routines tend to dispel the need to justify the curriculum all the time, educational communities are not necessarily aware of the reasons why the curriculum has certain characteristics. In other words, they might lose sight of curriculum justification and regard the curriculum as a given.

Therefore, although relevance is inherent to the concept of curriculum, paradoxically, curriculum relevance is not always ensured or recognized. If this assumption is correct, curriculum relevance should be a major topic in the field of Curriculum Studies. However, not many scholars in the field have systematically addressed this topic in explicit ways. Although issues of curriculum relevance are implicit in a large portion of the literature, including the work of the most outstanding curricularist, few publications address curriculum relevance directly and tackle it as a central issue.

The present chapter revisits some of the few explicit conceptualizations of curriculum relevance that have already been proposed, as well as some of the indirect contributions to such conceptualization that can be derived from the work of outstanding curricularist across the history of Curriculum Studies. Considering that interesting conceptualizations can be found outside Curriculum Studies, the chapter explores some discussions of curriculum relevance in other fields, within the wider field of Education: Geographical Education, Mathematics Education, and Science Education. The possibility of adapting some of the theoretical constructs that emerge from those discussions to the analysis of curriculum at large – not only to specific parts of the curriculum, such as Geography, Mathematics, or Science – will be discussed.

Special attention will be paid to the individual dimension of relevance. Data from an action research project will be commented in light of a conceptual framework that emerged in the field of Science Education but might guide analyses of the whole curriculum. Such account of the project will be preceded by a brief discussion on the importance of action research for studying curriculum relevance.

2. CURRICULUM RELEVANCE: A RELEVANT TOPIC WITHIN CURRICULUM STUDIES?

Historical overviews of Curriculum Studies reveal that a number of researchers in different historical periods were interested in curriculum relevance, although such interest has been predominantly stated in implicit rather than explicit ways and the topic has not been frequently stated as a priority.

The question that represents the pre-history of Curriculum Studies is, after all, a question of curriculum relevance. By asking "What knowledge is of most worth?," Spencer (1866) calls for the identification of knowledge that deserves to be included in the curriculum. In light of Spencer's interests, the question could have been phrased as "What knowledge should a relevant curriculum include?"

For Spencer, in order to find answers to the question he raised, the first step should be to identify and to rank the main kinds of activity that constitute human life. Spencer himself proposed the following ranking: (1) activities that directly contribute to self-preservation; (2) activities that indirectly contribute to self-preservation; (3) caring for offspring; (4) maintaining one's political and social relations; (5) leisure activities. Spencer claimed that, in order to fulfil human needs through activities of these kinds, the most relevant knowledge is scientific knowledge, especially knowledge produced by the Natural Sciences.

This embryonic proposal on how to make a curriculum already includes the main traits of activity analysis, which "is one of the most powerful and enduring ideas in the field of curriculum" (Null, 2010, p. 9). Indeed, such idea was incorporated into curriculum theory when Curriculum Studies emerged as an autonomous field and is still very influential nowadays.

"The basic idea of activity analysis it that the best place to begin when creating curriculum is by looking at the daily activities of adults" (Null, 2010, p. 9). This assumption is at the core of Bobbitt's thought:

Human life, however varied, consists in the performance of specific activities. Education that prepares for life is one that prepares definitely and adequately for these specific activities. However numerous and diverse they may be for any social class, they can be discovered. This requires only that one go out into the world of affairs and discover the particulars of which these affairs consist. This will show the abilities, attitudes, habits, appreciations and forms of knowledge that men need. The curriculum will then be that series of experiences which children and youth must have by the way of attaining those objectives. (Bobbitt, 1918, p. 42)

By stating this commitment to activity analysis, Bobbitt, implicitly, values societal and vocational dimensions of curriculum relevance. His approach to curriculum development is fundamentally aimed at fulfilling the needs of society, although he also considers educational experiences that "expand and unfold the nature of the individual" (Bobbitt, 1918, p. 3). Indeed, he discusses a tension between proponents of curricula that value subjective results and proponents of more utilitarian curricula. After characterizing these sides of the tension, Bobbitt (1918) states that "both are right," but he also locates the former at "the play-level" and the latter at "the work-level." In addition, he states that "one precedes the other" (p. 6). From this perspective, curricula based on subjectively rich educational experiences are only considered valuable inasmuch as they contribute to making utilitarian curricula even more effective in their utilitarianism.

Another tension, which has both similarities and dissimilarities with the one addressed by Bobbitt, is discussed by Dewey – a tension between different "educational sects." One of them "fixes its attention upon the importance of the subject-matter of the curriculum as compared with the contents of the child's own experience" (Dewey, 1990, p. 185). For the other one, "the child is the starting-point, the center, and the end" (Dewey, 1990, p. 187). In order to resolve this tension, Dewey develops a notion of instruction as a continuous reconstruction of the child's present experience, based on the expansion of the embryonic elements of subject-matter that it already contains:

From the side of the child, it is a question of seeing how his experience already contains within itself elements – facts and truths – of just the same sort as those entering into the formulated study; and, what is of more importance, of how it contains within itself the attitudes, the motives, and the interest which have operated in developing and organizing the subject-matter to the plane which it now occupies. From the side of the studies, it is a question of interpreting them as outgrowths of forces operating in the child's life, and of discovering the steps that intervene between the child's present experience and their richer maturity. (Dewey, 1990, p. 189)

This notion of instruction as continuous reconstruction of the child's present experience entails, to a large extent, an appreciation of the individual dimension of curriculum relevance, inasmuch as such reconstruction is only possible if subject-matter is presented in ways that allow students to relate it to their present experiences.

Ralph Tyler is another author whose contribution to curriculum theory is outstanding. His well-known *rationale* for curriculum development is structured upon three sources from which educational objectives can be derived: studies of the learners themselves, studies of contemporary life outside the school, and suggestions about objectives from subject specialists (Tyler, 1949). Objectives derived from studies of contemporary life outside the school are likely to contribute to the enhancement of societal and vocational relevance. Objectives derived from studies of the learners might contribute to the enhancement of individual relevance, for they include the investigation of students' needs and interests.

Tyler was involved with the Eight Year Study, which was conducted in the USA between 1930 and 1942. Some characteristics of this study suggest consideration for the students' acknowledgment of curriculum relevance. Integrated core curricula, organized around broad problems, were designed in some of the participating schools; flexible curricular materials were developed; and teacher-pupil planning was practiced. In the context of such innovations, learning was conceived as "a series of experiences, balancing student interests with societal and educational needs" (Kridel, 2010, p. 324).

Among many other issues, the social movements that emerged in the USA during the 1960s addressed issues of curriculum relevance, which raised the interest of scholars. In that period, "college and high-school students began demanding curriculum relevance," for "the discipline-centered curriculum at the secondary level was now regarded as irrelevant to the social situation" (Tanner & Tanner, 1995, p. 324).

In the context of his call for the reconceptualization of Curriculum Studies, Schwab (1973) implicitly values different dimensions of curriculum relevance, by asserting that "defensible educational thought must take account of four commonplaces of *equal* rank: the learner, the teacher, the milieu, and the subject matter" (pp. 508-509).

More recently, Erickson and his co-authors (2008) reviewed studies on students' experience of school curriculum. One of the main topics addressed was student disaffiliation with learning. After citing researchers who claim that affiliation with learning depends, to some extent, on race and social class, the authors suggest that more attention should be paid to within-school and within-classroom variables: "It seems that we need to look much more closely and thoroughly at the conditions within school life itself, in which students affiliate and disaffiliate with the project of school learning" (p. 207).

In order to understand within-classroom conditions that might enhance or inhibit student engagement with the curriculum, researchers need detailed information on what happens in the classroom. Teachers, as insiders, access such information all the time, as they do their job. Therefore, research approaches that entail the involvement of teachers in projects as members of research teams (not just their superficial participation as providers of data) is potentially important both in terms of knowledge production and in terms of problem solving. Action research is expected to combine these two purposes.

This is one of the main reasons why action research has been used by some curricularist who intend to narrow the gap between theory and practice. Lawrence Stenhouse is a case in point. His conceptualization of curriculum as a hypothesis that must be tested in practice, his commitment to using action research to address curricular problems, and his vision of "an educational science in which each classroom is a laboratory, each teacher a member of the scientific community" (Stenhouse, 1975, p. 142) have inspired many other researchers.

By addressing curricular problems from the perspective of practitioners who want to solve them and by, at the same time, aiming at knowledge production through research, action research follows, to some extent, the deliberative tradition within Curriculum Studies (McCutcheon, 1995, 1999; Reid, 1999; Walker, 2003). In this tradition, curricular problems faced by teachers in schools and classrooms tend to be studied under the assumption that "neither the problems nor the decisions are known well in advance" (Parker, 2004, p. 433). "The fundamental *purpose* of deliberative inquiry is to reach justified decisions about curricular action in particular contexts" (Harris, 1991, p. 293), rather than obtaining generalizable results. Assumptions of this kind underlay the action research project presented in the fifth section of this chapter.

3. A FRAMEWORK FOR THE STUDY OF CURRICULUM RELEVANCE

Although, as previously suggested, curriculum relevance is an important topic in Curriculum Studies, it has been addressed in implicit rather than explicit ways by curricularist. Indeed, Curriculum Studies' *raison d'être* is to tackle the question "What to teach?," that is, the problem of deciding which knowledge is relevant enough to be included in the curriculum. However, it is difficult to find comprehensive conceptualizations of curriculum relevance in the field. Such conceptualization is needed, in order to enhance awareness of implicit assumptions about the meaning of relevance, considering that the literature is loaded with implicit, and sometimes conflicting, assumptions on what curriculum relevance means. Such assumptions tend to be committed to different kinds of interests and, therefore, are usually held by different kinds of stakeholders. For example, employers might be tempted to assume that a relevant curriculum is one that directly prepares students for the world of work.

In order to make sense of different meanings, to facilitate deconstruction of the interests that fuel them, and to discuss them in an explicit way – one that takes the notion of curriculum relevance itself as the focus of the analysis, rather than suggesting what relevance means in implicit ways –, an organizing scheme would be useful.

Roldão (2013) addresses curriculum relevance as a question of cognition, considering that learning occurs "when one acquires new knowledge, and only when such knowledge is significantly incorporated into the cognitive devices that the individuals employ in order to act, to understand reality, and to expand their knowledge" (p. 20). She adds that learners' acknowledgment of curriculum relevance depends on five variables: relation between the curriculum and the learner's cultural references; meaning of new information in light of the individual's cognitive journey; relation between the curriculum and the student's interests; students' perception on the social usefulness of the curriculum; and logical sequence and connections between different topics.

An empirical study of curriculum relevance in higher education was carried out by Malagón-Plata (2009). He studied three academic programs implemented at a Colombian university in light of a number of categories that allegedly represent characteristics of a relevant curriculum in higher education – for example, emphasis on practice, research, and extension.

Some authors address curriculum relevance in more indirect ways. For example, Fernandes, Leite, Mouraz, & Figueiredo (2013) focus on curriculum contextualization, which is conceptualized as a means for promoting curriculum relevance. They carried out a literature review which disclosed five kinds of contextualization: based on place, based on the student, based on pedagogical practice, based on attention to cultural diversity, and based on disciplinary content.

Interestingly, curriculum relevance is occasionally studied in the specific context of certain curricular areas. For example, a study on the relevance of the Mathematics curriculum for students between the ages of 14 and 16 (Sealey & Noyes, 2010) concluded that the meaning of the word "relevance" varies according to social groups to which students belong. Based on this study, the authors identified three categories of relevance. One of them is practical relevance, which is focused on the usefulness of knowledge for the present. Another category is process relevance, that is, the quality of curricula that facilitate transfer of knowledge and skills to new contexts, rather than immediate applicability. In the specific case of Mathematics, the authors highlight the importance of the subject for the development of logical reasoning, which facilitates problem solving in a wide range of contexts. The third category consists of professional relevance. This category is based on the assumption that the acquisition of certain kinds of knowledge and the development of certain competences is likely to facilitate access to the world of work in the future. Sealey & Noyes (2010) did not find, in the sample selected for their study, data that might be included in a fourth category: political relevance. Based on the assumption that students should develop critical awareness on how Mathematics is used by society, they call for the incorporation of this fourth dimension into the curriculum.

Roselimo (2017) studied the relevance of Geography curriculum in Lesotho secondary schools, through an analysis of curriculum documents. This study was carried out under the assumption that "geography is not only relevant to the goals of further education, but it also prepares learners for a meaningful life in the fast changing world with complex environmental, economic and social changes" (p. 131).

A thorough framework for the study of curriculum relevance has been proposed by Science Education researchers (Stuckey, Hoftein, Mamlok-Naaman, & Eilks, 2013). Although the authors' focus is, indeed, Science Education, and they never claim that their approach should be generalized to curriculum in general, apparently there is no reason why such generalization should not be considered.

The above-mentioned framework includes three dimensions of relevance: individual, societal, and vocational. The individual dimension consists of satisfying the learner's curiosity and interests. The societal dimension is based on the assumption that students are expected to use knowledge that they acquire in school for contributing to society's development. The vocational dimension is the potential of curriculum for maximizing students' chances of finding rewarding jobs and careers.

When discussing curriculum in light of these dimensions, one may consider its relevance both for the present and for the future. For example, a curriculum with a strong vocational dimension is expected to have these two qualities: (1) it maximizes students' chances of finding a rewarding job in the future; (2) it provides the students, in the present, with clear clues on its importance in the pursuit of potential careers.

In the framework proposed by Stuckey, Hoftein, Mamlok-Naaman, & Eilks (2013), the above-mentioned three dimensions, besides being crossed by a present versus future axis, are crossed by an intrinsic versus extrinsic axis. From an intrinsic perspective, a relevant curriculum fulfils students' interests; from an extrinsic perspective, a curriculum is considered relevant inasmuch as it helps students meet goals originally set by others, such as achieving good grades.

The possibility of using this framework for analyzing the curriculum in general (not the Science Education curriculum only) should be considered, for various reasons, although the authors do not claim that it can be used beyond their field.

The framework is very encompassing, for it covers three dimensions of curriculum relevance in a balanced way. By considering many possibilities (e.g., curricula that emphasize vocational relevance versus curricula that emphasize individual relevance; relevance in the present versus relevance for the future), the framework facilitates comparisons of different curricula in terms of the aspects of relevance that they value.

Furthermore, the proposal is based on a literature review that, despite being, to a large extent, focused on specific issues of Science Education, contextualizes them in debates related to the curriculum in general, including debates that played a central role in the history of Curriculum Studies.

For all these reasons, the adoption of the conceptualization developed by Stuckey, Hoftein, Mamlok-Naaman, & Eilks (2013) is being proposed in the present chapter. Other contributions might strengthen this approach. For example, Roldão's (2013) conceptualization is likely to deepen one's understanding of the individual dimension of curriculum relevance. Likewise, a deeper understanding of the other dimensions might benefit from studies that have been specifically focused on those same dimensions. For example, Hiim (2017) has provided important contributions to the conceptualization of the vocational dimension. For her, a "relevant curriculum can be defined as a curriculum that provides students with the opportunity to develop vocational knowledge in their chosen occupations" (p. 13). Additionally, she advocates that a vocationally relevant curriculum should provide counselling on choices related to occupations early in vocational programs, besides being based on analyses of "work demands, core competences, and the need for qualifications in the actual vocations" (p. 4).

4. THE INDIVIDUAL DIMENSION OF CURRICULUM RELEVANCE: TENSIONS AND MISUNDERSTANDINGS

As Stuckey, Hoftein, Mamlok-Naaman, & Eilks (2013) note, the term "relevance" has frequently been used as a synonym for student interest, meaningfulness, satisfaction of the student's needs, and motivation. Accordingly, the curriculum tends to be considered relevant inasmuch as it is considered meaningful by students, because it fulfils their interests, because they understand their real-life applications, and because it is representative of their culture.

Accordingly, Roldão (2013) identifies meaningfulness as one of the variables that influence curriculum relevance. In order for new information to become meaningful, the learner must be able to relate it to previously acquired and consolidated concepts and conceptual structures – advanced organizers, according to Ausubel (cited by Rodão, 2013); *schemata*, according to Piaget (cited by Roldão, 2013). Such ability to develop meaningful networks of knowledge depends, to a large extent, on a logical organization of content.

Another source of relevance considered by Roldão is the students' interest, under the assumption that "the affective dimension is an integral part of learning" (Roldão, 2011, p. 12).

Students' interests might be related to their perception of the social usefulness of the curriculum. It is certainly impossible that students perceive the usefulness of every piece of curricular content for their lives outside school all the time. Accordingly, this variable – the extent to which students consider the curriculum useful – needs to be understood in a broad sense, not in the restricted sense of immediate usefulness and practical applicability. In that broad view, knowledge provided by a relevant curriculum is likely to be "used and/or questioned in new situations, capable of encouraging the acquisition of new knowledge" (Roldão, 2011, p. 14).

Culture acts as filter through which students from different cultural backgrounds separate curricula that they consider relevant from curricula that they consider irrelevant. Assuming that the curriculum "reflects to a great extent the dominant culture(s)" (Roldão, 2011, p. 15), ensuring curriculum relevance for students from cultural minorities is especially challenging. Many of these notions of relevance have strong connections with the concept of intrinsic motivation, which is based on students' inner willingness to learn, regardless of external rewards. Extrinsic motivation – which is based on external goals and rewards – is also considered in the literature. Furthermore, some researchers in the field of Psychology have moved beyond the intrinsic-extrinsic dualism and developed multifaceted theories of motivation (Reiss, 2012). Sometimes appreciation of instruction wherein meaningfulness, student interest, and cultural diversity are taken into consideration is criticized, or even scorned, by some authors, especially outside the field of Education (e.g., Crato, 2006; Mónica, 1997), for allegedly devaluing knowledge and encouraging facileness. Although it is obvious to most scholars in the field of Education that meaningful learning and attention to cultural diversity are compatible with academic rigor, such compatibility is not always made explicit in the literature.

Further research on curriculum relevance might contribute to making that idea more explicit. In addition, a conceptual framework that represents the multiple ways in which a curriculum can be relevant (from the students' point of view, from a societal perspective, etc.) is likely to reinforce the idea that student interest and society's needs are not necessarily incompatible.

The framework proposed by Stuckey, Hoftein, Mamlok-Naaman, & Eilks (2013) incorporates those tensions in a very balanced way. If researchers of curriculum use it to analyze data or, at least, keep it in mind, probably the distinction between relevance, motivation, meaningfulness and related concepts will become clearer. This is another reason why the adoption of the framework in the study of curriculum relevance in general (not only curriculum relevance within Science Education) should be considered.

A rough test of this possibility will be presented in the fifth section of this chapter. Some data from a research project will be commented in light of the framework. It will not be a presentation of the project's findings, considering that most aspects of the project have already been presented in other publications (Sousa, Alonso, & Roldão, 2013; Sousa, 2016). What is presented in this chapter is a simple test of the applicability, *a posteriori*, of the framework proposed by Stuckey, Hoftein, Mamlok-Naaman, & Eilks (2013) in the context of Science Education to some data from the above-mentioned project. This framework was not applied to the original analysis because it was not known when the project was carried out.

Since action research was the approach used in the project, the above-mentioned comments on some of its data will be preceded by some considerations on the importance of action research for studying the individual dimension of curriculum relevance.

5. UNDERSTANDING CURRICULUM RELEVANCE IN THE CLASSROOM: THE POTENTIAL OF ACTION RESEARCH

Classrooms are probably the best sources of data related to the individual dimension of curriculum relevance. Students' talk and behavior in the classroom provide information on the extent to which they are engaged with the curriculum. Concentration on tasks might suggest engagement and acknowledgment of curriculum relevance; lack of concentration or open resistance might suggest disengagement. Interviews with students may perhaps follow classroom observation, in order to obtain data on reasons for the observed behaviors, from their own perspective.

External researchers may eventually employ the best techniques of data collection, but, in order to obtain detailed information on what happens in the classroom, they need teachers' collaboration. Teachers, as insiders, can access such detailed information more easily than external researchers. Based on their professional knowledge, they can also interpret it in revealing ways. Accordingly, teachers might help researchers understand important aspects of students' engagement or disengagement in the classroom, which, in turn, might contribute to the emergence of richer data on students' (lack of) acknowledgment of curriculum relevance. It might also contribute to the development of instructional strategies that enhance curriculum relevance.

Similar assumptions underlie action research projects focused on vocational relevance that have been conducted in Norway. The results of these studies show that "according to the students, the lack of practical experience makes it difficult for them to make informed vocational choices" (Hiim, 2017, p. 4). Many of the vocational education teachers involved in the projects used action research as a means for trying "to develop a more practice-based, integrated curriculum, in cooperation with vocational firms" (Hiim, 2017, p. 5). Action research allows external researchers to work with teachers and therefore to take advantage of their professional knowledge in order to obtain rich data on the individual dimension of curriculum relevance. If teachers are integrated into action research teams (instead of just providing data requested by external researchers) they might contribute to knowledge production with regard to curriculum relevance, and with regard to many other issues.

There is a high potential of collaboration between teachers and university researchers in this approach. However, there are also tensions, obstacles and challenges. Teachers tend to focus "on situation-specific issues with short-term benefits," whereas "academics seek to produce more generalizable knowledge over a longer timetable" (Bevins & Price, 2014, p. 273). In the specific case of action research projects focused on curriculum relevance, this implies that, if a project team includes teachers and academics, probably the academics' effort will be predominantly directed towards the production of research findings that allow them to enrich an academic knowledge base related to this issue, whereas the teachers' effort will be predominantly directed towards solving problems related to student disengagement. The existence of these different agendas is one of the reasons why some authors (e.g., Elliot, 1991; McNiff & Whitehead, 2010; Stenhouse, 1975) have portrayed action research as an enterprise led by practitioners. From this perspective, the participation of academics is discouraged. In some cases, it is explicitly rejected; in other cases, it is tolerated, as long as academics play the role of outside facilitators only. However, action research is sometimes initiated by academics. For example, Espido Bello (2006) reports a collaborative action research project that she initiated as a university researcher. The starting point was her wish to put a collaborative action research project into operation at a school, "in order to know its impact on the professional development of the teachers involved" (p. 4). Hawkins (2015) also initiated an action research project as an academic. In this case, the project addressed education for social justice through children's literature at pre-school. Interestingly, as the project progressed, the other participants – educators and pre-schoolers – revealed that their ownership of the project increased. The action research project that will be briefly presented in the next section of this chapter was also initiated by academics, with the justification that there are contexts in which "if the initiative is not taken by university researchers, it can hardly come from elsewhere" (Sousa, 2016).

6. AN EXAMPLE: THE RRC PROJECT

The action research project "Research for a Relevant Curriculum" (RRC) was conducted between 2007 and 2012 by a team that included assistant professors from the University of the Azores, Portugal, and elementary school teachers. The number of participants changed overtime. The period when the team had more members was the school year 2009-2010 – four university researchers and 10 elementary school teachers. The problem that prompted the emergence of the project was some teachers' complaints about some students' alleged lack of interest for the school and the curriculum. Those teachers' willingness to solve or decrease the problem converged with university researchers' interest in understanding how students from Azorean schools viewed curriculum relevance.

Accordingly, the main objectives pursued by the project were to identify causes of the alleged student disengagement with regard to the curriculum, to understand the extent to which the students considered the curriculum relevant, and to develop instructional strategies that contribute to the enhancement of curriculum relevance from the students' perspective.

In the five action research cycles of RRC (each cycle corresponded to one school year) the team selected students whose behavior suggested lack of concentration on the tasks and lack of interest for the curriculum. Although this kind of behavior was very frequent, the team members did not have time to collect and analyze data related to many students. Therefore, few students were selected – usually three from each class. Subsequently, those students were interviewed. Data obtained from the interviews were then used to support decisions on new instructional strategies.

The team assumed that content is frequently not presented "as a means of understanding the world around us, but as a series of separate pieces of information (...) that they are subsequently incapable of using" (Esteve, 2000, p. 12). In the context of this approach, it is difficult for many students to regard curriculum relevance as something that exists beyond school and its routines. As Dewey suggests, absence of learning is not necessarily the cause of this problem. Possibly school subjects

were learned at least sufficiently to enable a pupil to pass examinations in them. One trouble is that the subject-matter in question was learned in isolation; it was put, as it were, in a water-tight compartment. When the question is asked, then, what has become of it, where it has gone to, the right answer is that it is still there in the special compartment in which it was originally stowed away. If exactly the same conditions recurred as those under which it was acquired, it would also recur and be available. But it was segregated when it was acquired and hence is so disconnected from the rest of experience that it is not available under the actual conditions of life. (Dewey, 1997, pp. 47-48)

In light of these assumptions, one of the most important questions included in the interviews consisted of asking students about the usefulness of what they learned in school for their lives outside school in the present.

Many interviewees did not identify any instance of usefulness. Among those who acknowledged usefulness, some tended to relate it to the future, as the following transcript illustrates.

Q: Think about what you learn here, at school... Math, Portuguese Language... Is it useful for anything?

A: No.

Q: It's not useful for anything?!

A: It allows us to learn things...

Q: Yes... And what are those things useful for? Why is it important to learn such things?

A: Because it's important that we know those things when we grow up.

Q: When you grow up? What about now? You are still a child. Are those things that you learn at school useful for something that you do outside school? [Pause] When you do something outside school, are some of the things you learned at school useful? [Pause] For example, you told me that sometimes you help your mother... When you're helping your mother is any of the things you learned at school useful?

A: No.

Q: So you think that what you learn at school will only be useful later on... Are you sure it is not useful now?

A: Yes, I am.

(6-year-old girl, 1st grade)

Not all the answers were as vague as these ones. The next transcript explicitly identifies access to a driver's license as a source of extrinsic motivation in the future.

> Q: These things that you learn at school... What are they useful for? Are they important? [Pause] Are these things that you learn at school useful for anything in your life outside school? [Pause] To read, to write...
> A: If one doesn't know how to read and write, one can't get a driver's license.
> Q: Hmmmm... So, what you learn at school will be useful when you grow up, for getting a driver's license. Right?
> A: Yes.
> Q: Is it useful for anything else?
> A: No.
>
> (8-year-old boy, 2nd grade)

As these transcripts illustrate, the students' answers suggest that curriculum relevance is not frequently evident for them. When some relevance is acknowledged, answers tend to emphasize future relevance and extrinsic aspects of relevance.

Some students also tended to restrict relevance to school-related contexts – for example, by stating that what they learned at school was useful because it enabled them to help their younger siblings with homework –, even when interviewers reminded them that the question was related to relevance outside school.

Data obtained from the interviews was combined with data obtained from other sources – for example, official files that provided information about the students and their families – to support decisions on new instructional strategies. Those strategies always entailed some kind of connection between the formal curriculum and selected aspects of students' lives outside school.

For example, one of the team members – a primary school teacher – used data on the students' families when he designed a new strategy for teaching proportionality. More specifically, the fact that some students' fathers were masons was taken into consideration. The teacher handed those students a table and asked them to fill it in at home with their fathers' help. By filling in the table, the students were expected to show a proportional quantification of materials that are needed to produce given amounts of concrete.

By the end of each action research cycle, that is, by the end of each school year, the selected students went through a second round of interviews. In this context, some of the questions that had been asked in the first round were repeated. The answers given in the second round suggest improvements in the students' acknowledgment of both present relevance and intrinsic aspects of relevance.

CONCLUSION

Although relevance is inherent to the very concept of curriculum, conceptualizations and discussions of curriculum relevance have been implicit rather than explicit within the field of Curriculum Studies. However, a clear and encompassing conceptualization of curriculum relevance has been presented in the context of Science Education by Stuckey, Hoftein, Mamlok-Naaman, & Eilks (2013). Although the authors have not claimed that their approach should be generalized, there is apparently no reason why it cannot be used in the analysis of the whole curriculum.

This possibility was roughly tested by applying the framework to some data from RRC project, *a posteriori*. Accordingly, transcripts from interviews with students who had participated in the project were analyzed in light of the categories included in the framework. The examples provided in the present chapter are related to the individual dimension of relevance because that was the focus of RRC. As the examples suggest, the framework was helpful in making sense of the data. Without this framework interpretation of data exemplified in this chapter would have been poorer. If the framework was known before 2013 and had been applied to data analysis in the context of RRC itself, the analysis would have been richer.

The interplay between the three dimensions of relevance (individual, societal, and vocational) and the two axes (relevance in the present versus relevance in the future; intrinsic versus extrinsic aspects of relevance) makes the framework at the same time easy to handle and able to capture multiple aspects of relevance in their complexity.

Possibly the framework will be applied to new studies, which will provide opportunities for empirical testing, for refinement, and for consolidation.

REFERENCES

Bevins, S., & Price, G. (2014). Collaboration between academics and teachers: a complex relationship. *Educational Action Research*, 22 (2), 270-284.

Bobbitt, F. (1918). *The curriculum*. Boston: Houghton Mifflin.

Crato, N. (2006). *The educationalists' jargon: a critique of romantic and constructivist pedagogy*. Lisbon: Gradiva.

Dewey, J. (1990). *The school and society* and *the child and the curriculum*. Chicago: The University of Chicago Press.

Dewey, J. (1997). *Experience and education*. New York: Touchstone.

Elliott, J. (1991). *Action research for educational change*. Buckingham: Open University Press.

Erickson, F., Bagrodia, R., Cook-Sather, A., Espinosa, M., Jurow, S., Shultz, J., & Spencer, J. (2008). Students' experience of school curriculum: The everyday circumstances of granting or withholding assent to learn. In F. M. Connellly (Ed.), *The SAGE handbook of curriculum and instruction* (pp. 198-218). Thousand Oaks, CA: SAGE.

Espido Bello, X. E. (2006). Initiating a Collaborative Action Research Project: From Choosing a School to Planning the Work on an Issue. *Educational Action Research*, 14 (1), 3-21.

Esteve, J. M. (2000). Culture in the school: assessment and the content of education. *European Journal of Teacher Education*, 23 (1), 5-18.

Fernandes, P., Leite, C., Mouraz, A., & Figueiredo, C. (2013). Curricular contextualization: tracking the meanings of a concept. *Asia-Pacific Education Researcher*, 22 (4), 417-425.

Harris, I. (1991). Deliberative inquiry: the arts of planning. In E. Short (Ed.), *Forms of curriculum inquiry* (pp. 285-307). Albany: SUNY Press.

Hawkins, K. (2015). The complexities of participatory action research and the problems of power, identity and influence. *Educational Action Research*, 23 (4), 464-478.

Hiim, H. (2017). Ensuring curriculum relevance in vocational education and training: epistemological perspectives in a curriculum research project. *International Journal for Research in Vocational Education and Training*, 4 (1), 1-19.

Kridel, C. (2010). The eight year study. In C. Kridel (Ed.), *Encyclopedia of Curriculum Studies, Volume I* (pp. 323-325). Thousand Oaks, CA: SAGE.

Malagón-Plata, L. A. (2009). La pertinencia curricular: un studio en tres programas universitarios. *Educación y Educadores*, 12 (1), 11-27. [Curriculum relevance: a study of three university programs. *Education and Educators*, 12 (1), 11-27].

McCutcheon, G. (1995). *Developing the curriculum: Solo and group deliberation*. White Plains, NY: Longman.

McCutcheon, G. (1999). Deliberation to develop school curricula. In J. G. Henderson & K. R. Kesson (Eds.), *Understanding democratic curriculum leadership* (pp. 33-46). New York: Teachers College Press.

McNiff, J., & Whitehead, J. (2010). *You and your action research project* (3rd ed.). Abingdon: Routledge.

Mónica, M. F. (1997). *Os filhos de Rousseau: ensaios sobre os exames* [Rosseau's children: Essays on exams]. Lisbon: Relógio d'Água.

Null, J. W. (2010). Activity analysis. In C. Kridel (Ed.), *Encyclopedia of Curriculum Studies, Volume I* (pp. 9-10). Thousand Oaks, CA: SAGE.

Parker, W. (2004). Diversity, globalization, and democratic education: Curriculum possibilities. In J. Banks (Ed.), *Diversity and citizenship education: Global perspectives* (pp. 433-458). San Francisco: Jossey-Bass.

Raselimo, M. (2017). Situating the Lesotho secondary school geography in curriculum relevance debate. *International Research in Geographical and Environmental Education*, 26 (2), 121-134.

Reid, W. (1999). *Curriculum as institution and practice: Essays in the deliberative tradition.* Mahwah, NJ: Lawrence Earlbaum Associates.

Reiss, S. (2012). Intrinsic and extrinsic motivation. *Teaching of Psychology*, 39 (2), 152-156.

Roldão, M. C. (2011). What is a relevant curriculum? In D. Potolea, I. Neacsu, L. Ciolan, & I. Rusenescu (Eds.), *Enhancing curriculum relevance* (pp. 7-18). Bucharest: Editura Universitara.

Roldão, M. C. (2013). O que é um currículo relevante? In F. Sousa, L. Alonso & M. C. Roldão (Orgs.), *Investigação para um currículo relevante* [What is a relevant curriculum? In F. Sousa, L. Alonso & M. C. Roldão (Eds.), *Research for a relevant curriculum*] (pp. 15-28). Coimbra: Almedina.

Schwab, J. (1973). The practical 3: translation into curriculum. *School Review*, 81 (4), 501-522.

Sealey, P., & Noyes, A. (2010). On the *relevance* of the mathematics curriculum to young people. *The Curriculum Journal*, 21 (3), 239-253.

Sousa, F. (2016). Is action research necessarily collaborative? Changing mutuality within a project. *Educational Research and Evaluation*, 22 (3-4), 234-250.

Sousa, F., Alonso, L., & Roldão, M. C. (2013) (Eds.). *Investigação para um currículo relevante* [*Research for a relevant curriculum*]. Coimbra: Almedina.

Spencer, H. (1866). *Education: intellectual, moral and physical.* New York: D. Appleton and Company.

Stenhouse, L. (1975). *An introduction to curriculum research and development.* London: Heinemann.

Stuckey, M., Hoftein, A., Mamlok-Naaman, R., & Eilks, I. (2013). The meaning of 'relevance' in science education and its implications for the science curriculum. *Studies in Science Education*, 49 (1), 1-34.

Tanner, D., & Tanner, L. (1995). *Curriculum development: Theory into practice* (3ʳᵈ ed.). Upper Saddle River, NJ: Merrill/Prentice Hall.

Tyler, R. (1949). *Basic principles of curriculum and instruction.* Chicago: The University of Chicago Press.

Walker, D. (2003). *Fundamentals of curriculum: Passion and professionalism* (2ⁿᵈ ed.). Mahwah, NJ: Lawrence Earlbaum Associates.

BIOGRAPHICAL SKETCH

Francisco Sousa

Affiliation: Faculty of Social and Human Sciences, University of the Azores, Portugal; Research Center on Child Studies, University of Minho, Portugal

Education:
Doctor of Education

Business Address:
Campus Universitário de Angra do Heroísmo
Rua Capitão João d'Ávila, Pico da Urze
9700-042 Angra do Heroísmo
Açores, Portugal

Research and Professional Experience:
Teaches Curriculum Theory and Development, Educational Technology, and Organization of Educational Systems in graduate and undergraduate programs;

Co-convenor of Network 3 (Curriculum Innovation), European Educational Research Association (EERA).

Publications from the Last 3 Years:

Sousa, F. (2016). Is action research necessarily collaborative? Changing mutuality within a project. *Educational Research and Evaluation*, 22 (3-4), 234-250.

Sousa, F. (2016). Reasserting curriculum design through virtual learning environments: The case of MAPE. *European Journal of Curriculum Studies*, 3 (1), 407-417.

In: (Participatory) Action Research   ISBN: 978-1-53613-041-6
Editors: J. Calder and J. Foletta   © 2018 Nova Science Publishers, Inc.

Chapter 6

TRANSFORMING UNIVERSITY TEACHING: PARTICIPATORY ACTION RESEARCH TO PROMOTE DISRUPTIVE PRACTICES

Elia Fernández-Díaz[*], *Carlos Rodríguez-Hoyos*
and Adelina Calvo
Department of Education, University of Cantabria,
Santander, Spain

ABSTRACT

The work presented in this chapter forms part of an innovation project in Higher Education focused on Lesson Study (LS). Through a process of action-research we have succeeded in generating actions to transform our teaching practice and reflect on the knowledge that has emerged during the course of the actions we devised. In addition to describing the process of action-research we have designed, this chapter fully addresses the analysis of one of the cases developed in our work, in

---

[*] Corresponding Author Email: fernandez.elia@gmail.com.

which students have to reconstruct their memories about the experiences they had during compulsory education in order to compare them with the experiences they have during the practicum. Likewise, we have been able to share our concerns about the process of accompaniment, the process of student participation in the design and assessment of the subjects and the search for situated and transformative learning in a university context, among other issues. Finally, based on the review of critical incidents that have concerned us we have proposed improvements we consider appropriate in order to continue the next cycle of action-research.

Keywords: participatory action research, higher education, innovation, lesson Study

1. INTRODUCTION

The practical experience which is analysed in this chapter forms part of the project "Innovating in Higher Education: a proposal based on the Lesson Study model," funded by the University of Cantabria. It is an educational innovation project developed over two academic years by a group of teachers from the Faculties of Education and Teacher Training at the Universities of Cantabria and Oviedo, in the north of Spain. The main objective of this project is to improve assessment activities in different subjects and areas of study in the field of education as well as contributing to rethinking scenarios for the exchange of experiences in university teaching and promoting collaboration in our professional development (Calvo & Rodríguez-Hoyos, 2016).

As some studies on action research in Higher Education have shown, more research on improving university teaching itself is needed (Gibbs et al., 2017). In an educational system which is increasingly defined by its homogenizing and institutionalizing tendencies, we need to assert the political, social and ethical dimensions of the University through models of reflection capable of combatting the reproduction of decontextualized learning situations which are hardly emancipatory or disruptive (Giroux, 2016).

The relevance of the LS model has not only been demonstrated in on-going training involving in-service teachers but also in the field of initial training (Dudley, 2015) in which the need to incorporate a greater number of studies on university practices and continue in-depth research in this area has been acknowledged (Wood & Cajkler, 2016). In this regard, the experience presented here aims to contribute to the discussion on the strengths and limitations in the university field based on the analysis of the case under study. Involving students, systematizing their participation in mixed teams, increases the number of situations in which students can experience the role of researcher, in such a way that an integrative theoretical and practical approach could be encouraged (Vaughan & Burnaford, 2016). It also benefits our pedagogical relationship with students (Moore & Gayle 2010; Villacañas 2014) as well as the development of the teaching process ensuring that student voices are heard (Bovill, Cook-Sather, & Felten, 2011) and guaranteeing their participation and involvement (Kur, De Porres & Westrup, 2008; Niemi, 2002).

Furthermore, the accompaniment of other university teachers, who take on the role of critical friends, constitutes an essential strategy for fostering improvement in teaching practice and lifelong student learning (Curry 2008; Key 2006; Wennergren, 2016). On the one hand, it increases professional development in a contextualized way, training which is characterized because it arises from the questioning of the participants themselves and distances itself from external training models, giving leading roles to the participants based on the review of their own practice (Lewis, 2002). On the other hand, it encourages situations in which students see the relevance of lifelong learning in professional teacher development, observing their own teachers, as learners and researchers (Elliot, 2015).

As we will now demonstrate, shared reflection has allowed us to identify the main findings and gaps in the process with the objective of introducing modifications in the next cycle of action. In the following sections, we will describe the general framework of our work and analyse one of the cases, outlining the dilemmas that were observed and the improvement proposals for future action.

2. CONTEXTUALIZATION: DESCRIPTION OF THE ACTION-RESEARCH PROCESS

In the research process we design a set of actions for reflecting collaboratively on the meaning and functionality of the group activity we carry out in our subjects for student learning. Although each subject is considered as a case study, we aim to agree on a common scheme of work with the objective of systematizing a dynamic of on-going training.

Our first task consists of constituting a mixed team in order to create a collaborative working environment in which the teacher from each subject takes part, other university teachers and students representing the different groups in which they are organized for the development of the activity. We began the design process by explaining the concerns and the starting budgets that we shared, asking ourselves what motivates us to change in order to be able to select specific areas of intervention with the objective of improving student learning. Once we had established the context of our work, together we designed an itinerary for improvement, including the specification of information collection and production techniques, ensuring the integration of the students' voices and the accompaniment of other university teachers. In this process of reflection on action, the deconstruction of actions carried out for improving pedagogical relationships with our students plays a crucial role. Through teachers' accounts we aim to address the issues raised and analyse how our concerns have evolved. Finally, following reflection on our practice, we have come up with an improvement proposal which includes changes to be implemented and a new course of action based on the questions that have arisen from the process carried out. In the design process, inquiry is regarded as an essential element, constituting a guiding thread which helps us to systematize the training process and collaboratively reflect on this. By way of example, in the following table we have included a summary of the main shared questions which we used as a starting point for decision making in the different phases of the process:

Table 1. Initial questions shared by the mixed team

Actions	Questions
Definition of the problem	• What concerns us about our teaching practice? • What aspects do we need to improve? • What do the students think?
Collaborative design of the lesson and data gathering	• How have I planned this lesson? Which aspects do I need to clarify? How am I going to carry out assessment? • What role do the students play in the whole process? • What methods do we use for data gathering? Who will do this? How and when will we do it?
Shared monitoring; feedback	• How will we share the data generated and reflect together during the process?
Data analysis	• How have these teacher concerns evolved or developed?
Improvement proposal	• What changes will we introduce in the next cycle of action? What new questions have arisen?

3. DECONSTRUCTING THE LEARNING PROCESS IN A CLASSROOM: REFLECTIONS ON ONE OF THE CASES DESIGNED

3.1. A Brief Description of Classroom Practice and the Identification of Initial Concerns

The case that we will analyse forms part of the subject "Curriculum, Society and Teaching Teams" which is taught in the second year of the Degree in Primary Education at the University of Cantabria.

During the time the subject is taught the students carry out their first period of teaching practice, something which offers us a unique opportunity to establish links between theory and educational practice. In addition, given these circumstances, we consider it a priority to design classroom activity based on the experiences gained within the context of the school. We reflect on our memories during a process which is full of concerns, trying to untangle teaching models and comparing them with the actual experiences during practical teaching. In this regard, we aim for our students to experience the role of teacher-researcher, generating situations in the classroom to encourage reflection on action.

The process is developed over three stages. During the first stage, we begin our learning history by identifying links between our initial questions on the subject, our concerns regarding the practicum, the memories of our experiences as students during compulsory education and the model of the teacher role that we would like to achieve to enable the promotion of curriculum development in a changing society. In the second stage, we continue navigating, trying to evoke our own experiences while progressively establishing relationships in our process of documentation between theory and educational practice, based on the analysis of two curricular proposals. These proposals which are antagonistic are deliberately chosen by the university teachers to facilitate the identification of the underlying curricular focus and its theoretical foundations. At the end of the training period, in the final stage, we return to the discussion on curricular proposals that the students have been able to experience in the schools and we try to select those which we consider to be the most suitable, from a critical curricular perspective.

The activity is carried out in work groups consisting of 4 to 5 students and is developed throughout the semester, using face-to-face sessions to guide the bibliographic analysis and the confrontation between theoretical and practical experiences. In addition, in these sessions we aim to accompany the students in the process of virtual documentation, to encourage raising awareness about the complete learning path followed. We select evidence from some learning situations and visually narrate the process, in the space available to each group on the subject webpage.

With the objective of encouraging the students to work autonomously we designed a script for guidance purposes only. It is a practical tool which promotes reflection on the contents covered in the subject and the learning situations experienced by each of the groups. We proposed the elaboration of a report for the evaluation of the activity which recounts the reconstruction of knowledge experienced by each work group based on the questions which were initially raised, the issues which have emerged from the bibliographical analysis and the confrontations with teaching practice. Lastly, it should be noted that we proposed a staggered delivery of the report over three stages which correspond to the end of those previously mentioned. Thus, we aimed to promote a training assessment in order to incorporate the improvements identified by the review and assess the process followed by the group.

Having broadly outlined the context of action, the teachers' concerns which formed the basis of the process of shared reflection during the 2016/2017 academic year need to be clarified within the framework of the innovation project referred to earlier:

- How can questioning be promoted and how can the feeling of the activity in the classroom be shared?
- How can the theoretical basis, the analysis of the stories and the topics which emerge be accompanied without hindering the creative and autonomous development of the group?
- How can collaboration in the mixed group be improved and how can the design of the action-research process be given greater flexibility?

3.2. How Our Questions Are Developed

Once the mixed teams of critical friends were established, various seminars were held in order to publicize the case study and share initial concerns with the objective of discussing possible alternatives and rethinking the improvement of the activity collaboratively. Following this, a roadmap was established for the collection and analysis of information based on what is specified in Table 1. Narrative techniques and interviews conducted in follow-up seminars were used to complement our main tools (diaries and discussion groups) for data compilation. In the following sections we will explain the initial results, highlighting the main findings and limitations of the process.

3.2.1. The Questioning of the Status Quo and the Actions Carried Out to Share the Meaning of the Activity

Without a doubt, one of our main concerns relates to the need to build a working environment in order to find a concordance in our objectives and start the process of generating a pedagogical relationship which shows both sides as learners and questions our own roles in the university context. The narrative of the actions carried out in the classroom has enabled us to retrace our steps in the initial stages, in which we basically try to generate some links for beginning the learning path:

> "During this long process I begin by sharing my journey, forged from my experiences as a teacher and researcher at the University (…). It's in this first moment when I try to share the purpose of the teaching innovation project on LS and raise the importance of collaboration in the transformation and improvement of teaching practice." (University teacher's story)

In this process of approaching one another, students try to rethink who they are and why they are studying a Teaching degree. To this end, they obtain objects and photos from their past which are analysed by the group and narrated through the group Web. The use of a visual story allows us to immerse ourselves in the memories of our school experiences and share common questions about the subject. We began the construction of our collective stories comparing the different experiences we had at school. Later on, we contrast our intuitive ideas as the process of documentation progresses, through the critical analysis of the experiences from the practicum and the confrontation of the teaching approaches that underlie them. Thus, the reflection by the students in the discussion groups allowed us to become aware of the understanding achieved in the identification of the meaning and functionality of the activity in initial teacher training in so far as the students have experienced the role of researcher and questioned the status quo:

> "It's helped me reflect on the type of teacher I want to become (...) we come from a traditional conception of education and we've seen that there are other better ways of carrying it out, but the activity has confirmed that the general situation continues to be the same (..) The most important thing is that we see that there are other ways of working, different to those that we normally observe; that it's possible to do it, in other words, that we don't think the text book is essential, quite the opposite (...) we can see that there are other ways; there isn't a single way to carry out educational processes." (Student c_discussion group)

> "It's very interesting because it doesn't require following a specific, clearly defined path. There are some theoretical guidelines that serve as a basis, but it's an activity that, throughout all its phases, invites reflection and the analysis of the experiences of the members of the group. It's so important, both in terms of the theoretical content and analysis, what each individual does in his or her academic life, and that's reflected really well when carrying out the activity." (Student d_discussion group)

In the follow-up seminars, in which we carried out a shared reflection on the information extracted from the classroom stories and the discussion group, we contrasted the students and teachers assessments. The following quotation shows how the university teacher (UT) interprets the feedback provided by the students:

> "It's allowed me to have a global vision of what the activity has meant to them [students] and what they have been able to experience when carrying out their practice, as well as its implications in the construction of their teaching identity; it's helped me to understand how the students interpret the repercussions of all this in their initial training. I definitely think their contributions were very relevant." (UT_follow-up seminar_1)

3.2.2. The Process of Accompaniment and the Development of Student Autonomy

Another of the main concerns that we share as university teachers is closely related to the design of a pre-established script and its use as a tool to accompany the student process of reflection. The need to facilitate a working environment to promote student autonomy as well as the development of information skills and creative production makes us question its usefulness. During the review of the script design we discussed the degree of structuring, reflecting on improvements to be implemented in the next cycle of action to guarantee greater flexibility and ensure student participation in the design of the subject:

"I tried to get them to separate themselves from the script questions so that they could find their own way. Although I think it needs to be used, because of the number of teachers who teach the subject and because it helps facilitate coordination, I think it's quite structured. Now, I think, as you point out, we are in a faculty where, in certain subjects, students have become used to having too many guidelines (…). Basically, we have to ask ourselves how we want them [the students] to participate in the design of the subject, how we are going to integrate what emerges in what we have planned. If they are provided with everything in a very structured way, they won't intervene in the design of the subject which more or less means that we are going to be encouraging them to always have a handbook book to refer to, and that doesn't happen in educational practice. Unless, later on, you want to choose a technical model of teaching and then you'll always want to see it like this. It is impossible then to make the leap. It's necessary for them to experiment with our accompaniment, with our support, with our guidelines for improvement, always accompanied, they can find their own learning path (…) but during the accompaniment they have to have that freedom to choose from those alternatives. We need to understand that they already need to be building that role; they need space to work autonomously and with uncertainty and the activity model should promote this." (UT_follow-up seminar_2)

The opinions expressed by the students in the discussion group confirm the relevance of giving a high degree of flexibility to the guidelines provided for the activity as this significantly contributes to the development of the skills required for their professional future as teachers:

> "We see it as something open, to let the imagination fly; I think it wasn't an objective of the script, but it's made us see that as students, at first, you come across difficulties when you have an open script, but later on, it's much more useful for your learning, especially when we are faced with being teachers: we can't give everything to children in a structured way. Perhaps it's going to be quite difficult to start off with and generate a lot of work, because they'll question you, because they'll get confused...like us, they'll learn about the practice, because one day it's going to stop being closed, both for them and for us. One day, there won't be a person who tells us A, B, or C, either to the children or us. So we have to learn to take charge, to have to ask questions and try to do our best and if we do it wrong, then we did it wrong, but we are the ones who made the mistakes." (Student a_discussion group)

In short, the follow-up work through face-to-face time has enabled a training assessment process focused on the improvement of the theoretical foundations, the analysis of the stories and the topics that emerge.

> "She's been very on top of our group [the university teacher] in that subject, because she observed that there were shortcomings in my group during the first stage; the teacher needs to be aware of these shortcomings, and the truth is that we needed it, and she was there in those moments when we needed it." (Student d_discussion group)

Nevertheless, we continue to identify certain contradictions in the design of the activity. On the one hand, we are concerned about that part of the course in which the students have to analyse the proposals which have been previously selected in order to contrast curricular approaches. To a certain extent, it continues to be something external to personal experiences and the group's own biography, which is why we need to rethink this stage to prevent it ending up as a juxtaposed link, blurring the trajectory of that situated learning we want to achieve.

"We give them that experience already generated, from other teachers, so that they can analyse it, but ... how can something which is externally sought relate to their own memories, with their current experiences? Trying to link it to your own learning history in the classroom is quite complicated." (UT_follow-up seminar_2)

On the other hand, the joint review of the development of the activity provides us with the opportunity to improve our intervention as university teachers, to move away from a managerial model and to give a leading role to the students, integrating strategies that enhance peer learning:

"I think that I intervene too much in the analysis of the issues that emerge from the accounts of their experiences, directing them towards certain issues, aspects ... obviously this forms part of the intended assessment process ... but we should offer scenarios which allow them to analyse their stories together and even if we help them in the process of identifying these categories, they also have to lead more so that they can continue spinning their own learning history themselves." (UT_follow-up seminar_2)

Lastly, the students' contributions will be used as a reference to explain the internal discrepancies in the group of teachers regarding the subject assessment process. We question how to overcome a technical vision of assessment, in which a crucial role is still given to the final exam (designed to promote memorized content), and move towards a global training model:

"Basically because it goes against what they want to convey in the subject, the subject talks about open education, education which is different to what is regarded as traditional, and in the end you have to memorize content and regurgitate it in an exam." (UT_follow-up seminar_3)

3.2.3. Critical Incidents Related to the Action-Research Process Itself

Throughout the process of investigation into the case studied, we have identified a series of dilemmas linked to the design of the research process.

Firstly, we have become aware of the need to move towards a more disruptive vision of design, in the face of hermetic planning which prescribes the sequence of phases and actions to be implemented at each moment. Similarly, we believe it is necessary to give a greater degree of democratization to the composition of the teams, ensuring negotiation on the topics to be debated, the incorporation of emerging issues and the improvement of collaboration through the systematization of the meetings during the development of the process.

"When following a structured design format it's difficult for the process, based on the action itself, to provide you with feedback (...) the sessions should be more flexible and with more encounters. Because flexibility doesn't mean that you are going to lose your way, as it encourages a lot more meetings it also allows for many other issues to emerge that you hadn't previously thought about." (UT_follow-up seminar_3)

"We need to rethink the specific interventions by the students in the mixed team of critical friends; for us it's crucial to listen to their voices...something much more systematic would allow us to carry out that process of reflection on action with more continuity and get much more out of it." (UT_follow-up seminar_3)

Secondly, from the critical incidents with students, we have become aware of the urgent need to rethink their participation in the research process as well as finding ways to promote their role as researchers. Some of the critical incidents referred to are related to the selection of the discussion groups' representatives and the repercussions in the collaborative working environment.

"The discussion group was designed for a small group of students, which meant that not all the representatives of the work groups could participate, so I previously thought that perhaps this could be a difficulty because we are creating a discourse in which our intention is to promote a curriculum model for everyone, inclusive education and, a tremendous paradox, it turns out that later on some representatives of other groups questioned me about their exclusion within the discussion group. Honestly, you're left with the feeling that there's been a contradiction between what you're trying to achieve in the subject and what you've done ... At least, those contradictions are the ones which help you rethink how to improve it." (UT_follow-up seminar_3)

Table 2. Contributions of the case under study: new questions shared by the mixed team

Actions	Questions
Definition of the problem	• What makes us change?
	• What concerns and starting budgets do we share?
	• How can we involve students in the innovation project?
Collaborative design of the lesson; data gathering	• How can I integrate what is emerging? How can time and space be temporarily improved to promote intergroup discussion?
	• How can we encourage refection and follow-up by the group itself?
	• How can student voices be integrated in order to introduce changes in the design?
Shared monitoring; feedback	• How do the students become aware of the learning path, the findings in the process and the mistakes?
Data analysis	• What traces allow us to reconstruct the process? What dilemmas emerge?
Improvement proposal	• How can shared reflection on the improvement of practice beyond the temporary limitations of the innovation project be systematized?
	• What do our students think about the research process?
	• Which factors have created obstacles when thinking about the next cycle?

In short, our reflection on the development of teaching has allowed us to consider the need to introduce changes in the activity for the next academic year. Moreover, new concerns have surfaced in relation to the research process, therefore we need to continue investigating collaboratively in transforming teaching practice and implementing improvements on our new route.

CONCLUSION

This work is part of a research process for the improvement of university teaching. The experience presented here illustrates how concerns about teaching practice in a specific subject evolve as teaching develops by virtue of the joint reflection fostered within a collaborative working environment on LS.

Through action research, we generate actions to transform our teaching practice and reflect on the knowledge that has emerged during the course of the actions we devised (Fernández-Díaz, Calvo, & Rodríguez-Hoyos, 2014). To this end, we have designed a research process, organized in mixed teams, aimed at systematizing a dynamic of ongoing training and the improvement of educational work in which we learn while trying to transform ourselves. In this working environment, joint reflection based on teaching-learning situations in our subjects has allowed us to identify concerns, plan and document the development of the process and analyse the continuities and changes in the next cycle of action, something which has positive repercussions on the improvement of teaching practice (Elliot, 2012; Pérez, Soto, & Serván, 2010; Tan 2012; Thorsten, 2017).

The initial results show the improvements that have been achieved so far. Throughout the process we manage to promote the creation of spaces outside the classroom in which we give students a voice, providing them with the opportunity to take the lead and offering them situations so that they can take on the role of researcher (Cochran-Smith, 2001). Thus we enable students to experience a situated practice (Ng, Nicholas, & Williams. 2010; Olin, Karlberg-Granlund, & Furu, 2016) during their initial training, something which is critically important for their future professional development. On the other hand, we have started to incorporate other tools for the deconstruction of the actions carried out in the classroom, such as the use of the stories (Clandinin & Connelly, 2004; Sparkes & Smith, 2008) which has allowed us to enrich the analysis of how our teaching concerns have evolved (Sancho & Hernández, 2013).

Consequently, we are not only able to integrate improvements in the activities we do with our university students, but also in the process of action-research itself, as we reflect on the design and become more aware of the need to rethink the underlying focus in order to embark on a process which promotes negotiated decision making, takes into account uncertainty and favours the democratization of knowledge as well as disruptive actions in the university context.

As we said in the previous section, we have observed some dilemmas linked to the development of the process of action research itself. Together with the promotion of greater flexibility in the design of the research process, we think that improving the horizontality of relationships in the mixed team is necessary in order to increase collaboration in our budding learning community (Lieberman, 2009) and promote student participation in subject design and assessment, among other issues. Therefore, we will continue investigating the composition of the mixed teams and the role of the critical friend with the objective of rethinking the improvements for the next cycle of action (Wennergren, 2016). We will also attempt to address both the study of the emotional aspects and the appropriateness of taking risks which, while disturbing our comfort zones, constitute the driving force behind the transformation and improvement of practice (Furu 2008; Swaffield 2007), to the extent that we are capable of perceiving inherent dilemmas and obstacles as learning opportunities (Harrison, 2013).

REFERENCES

Bovill, C., Cook-Sather, A., & Felten, P. (2011). Students as co- creators of teaching approaches, course design, and curricula: implications for academic developers, *International Journal for Academic Development, 16* (2), 133-145.

Calvo, A., & Rodríguez-Hoyos, C. (2016). *Innovating in higher education: a proposal based on the LS model.* Retrieved from: http://innouniversidad.unican.es/#proyectos.

Clandinin, D. J., & Connelly, F. M. (2004). *Narrative inquiry: Experience and story in qualitative research.* San Francisco: Jossey-Bass.

Cochran-Smith, M. (2001). The outcomes question in teacher education. *Teaching and Teacher Education, 17* (5), 527-546.

Curry, M.W. (2008). Critical Friends Groups: The Possibilities and Limitations Embedded in Teacher Professional Communities Aimed at Instructional Improvement and School Reform. *Teachers College Record, 110* (4), 733-774.

Dudley, P. (2015). *Lesson Study. Professional Learning for Our Time.* Routledge, London and New York: Routledge.

Elliot, J. (2012). Developing a science of teaching through lesson study. *International Journal for Lesson and Learning Studies, 1* (2), 108-125.

Elliott, J. (2015). Lesson and Learning Study and the idea of the teacher as a researcher. In K. Wood, & S. Sithamparam (Eds.), *Realising Learning* (pp. 148-167). New York and London: Routledge.

Fernández-Díaz, E., Calvo, A., & Rodríguez-Hoyos, C. (2014). Towards a collaborative action research in Spain to improve teaching practice. *Educational Action Research, 24* (3), 397-411.

Furu, E. M. (2008). Teachers Regaining Their Power: Professional Development through Action Learning. In K. Rönnerman, E. M. Furu, & P. Salo (Eds.). *Nurturing Praxis Action Research in Partnerships between School and University in a Nordic Light.* Rotterdam, The Netherlands: Sense Publishers.

Gibbs, P., Cartney, P., Wilkinson, K., Parkinson, J., Cunningham, S., James-Reynolds, C., Zoubir, T., Brown, V., Barter, P., Sumner, P., Macdonald, A., Dayananda, A., & Pitt, A. (2016). Literature review on the use of action research in higher education. *Educational Action Research, 25,* (1), 3-22.

Giroux, E. (2016). Higher Education and the Politics of Disruption. *Frameworks: Education and Society*, *3*, 15-26.

Harrison, C. (2013). Collaborative the KREST project Collaborative action research as a tool for generating formative feedback on teachers' classroom assessment practice: The KREST project. *Teachers and Teaching: Theory and Practice*, *19* (2), 202-213.

Key, E. (2006). *Do they make a difference? A review of research on the impact of critical friends groups.* Paper presented at the National School Reform Faculty Research Forum. Retrieved from http://www.schoolreforminitiative.org/wp-content/uploads/2011/12/.

Kur, E., De Porres, D., & Westrup, N. (2008). Teaching and Learning Action Research: Transforming Students, Faculty and University in Mexico. *Educational Action Research*, *6* (3), 327–349.

Lewis, C. (2002). *Lesson Study: A Handbook of Teacher-Led Instructional Change.* Philadelphia: Research for Better Shools.

Lieberman, J. (2009). Reinventing teacher professional norms and identities: the role of Lesson Study and Learning Communities. *Professional Development in Education*, *35* (1) 83-99.

Ng, W., Nicholas, H., & Williams, A. (2010). School experience influences on pre-service teachers' evolving beliefs about effective teaching. *Teaching and Teacher Education*, *26* (2), 278-289.

Moore, T., & Gayle, B. (2010). Student Learning Through Co-curricular Dedication: Viterbo University Boosts faculty/student research and community services. *Transformative Dialogues: Teaching & Learning Journal*, *4*, 1-7.

Niemi, H. (2002). Active learning–a cultural change needed in teacher education and schools. *Teaching and Teacher Education*, *18* (7), 763-768.

Olin, A., Karlberg-Granlund, G., & Furu, E. M. (2016). Facilitating democratic professional development: exploring the double role of being an academic action researcher. *Educational Action Research*, *24* (3), 424-441.

Pérez, A., Soto, E. & Serván, J. (2010). Participatory Action Research and the Reconstruction of Teachers' Practical Thinking: Lesson Studies and Core Reflection. An Experience in Spain. *Educational Action Research, 18* (1), 73-87.

Sancho, J. M., & Hernández, F. (2013). Developing autobiographical accounts as a starting point in research. *European Educational Research Journal, 12* (3), 342-353.

Sparkes, A. C., & Smith, B. (2008). Narrative constructionist inquiry. In J. Holstein, & J. Gubrium (Eds.), *Handbook of constructionist research* (pp. 295-314). London: Guilford Publications.

Swaffield, S. (2007). Light touch critical friendship. *Improving Schools, 10* (3), 205-219.

Tan, Y. S. M. (2014). Enriching a collaborative teacher inquiry discourse: exploring teachers' experience of a theory-framed discourse in a Singapore case of lesson study. *Educational Action Research, 22* (3), 411-428.

Thorsten, A. (2017). Generating knowledge in a Learning Study from the perspective of a teacher researcher. *Educational Action Research, 25* (1), 140-155.

Vaughan, M., & Burnaford, G. (2016) Action research in graduate teacher education: a review of the literature 2000–2015. *Educational Action Research, 24,* (2), 280-299.

Viñacañas, L. (2014). Meta-action research with pre-service teachers: a case study. *Educational Action Research, 25,* (1), 3-22.

Wennergren, A. (2016). Teachers as learners – with a little help from a critical friend. *Educational Action Research, 24* (2), 241-260.

Wood, P., & Cajkler, W. (2016). A participatory approach to Lesson Study in higher education. *International Journal for Lesson and Learning Studies, 5* (1), 4-18.

In: (Participatory) Action Research   ISBN: 978-1-53613-041-6
Editors: J. Calder and J. Foletta   © 2018 Nova Science Publishers, Inc.

Chapter 7

ACTION RESEARCH TO IMPROVE HIGHER EDUCATION

Alecsandra Ventura, PhD*

Postgraduate Management Department,
University Hospital of the Federal University of Alagoas,
Maceió, Brazil

ABSTRACT

Action research in higher education can improve students' critical thinking and promotes innovation. However, many teachers do not know the method or do not know how to use it to make teaching and learning more effective. This paper proposes the use of action research in higher education, especially in programs that use practical approaches such as residency programs in health care. With a clear and results-oriented approach, the text presents the educational advantages of action research and the challenges to overcome. It also proposes an innovative model of learning assessment based on integrating theory and practice. For this, the paper uses the two juxtaposed and interdependent cycles of action

---

Corresponding Author Email: alecsandra.ventura@gmail.com.

research, the first cycle focused on problem-solving and the second describing the research process. Within this context, the text discusses similar themes such as andragogy, meaningful learning, active learning, and systemic thinking.

Keywords: action research, higher education

1. INTRODUCTION

Has higher education effectively developed in students the skills they need to fit in as good professionals in the 21st century job market? Are teachers prepared to help develop students' competences such as initiative, critical and creative thinking, teamwork, leadership, and a problem-solving orientation?

Teaching entails not transferring knowledge, but creating possibilities for knowledge production or construction (Freire, 1996). In this context, higher education teachers should also be researchers and understand that the more students develop research that solves real-world problems, the more they will develop the skills they will need as professionals.

In this constructivist and aggregator educational process, the use of action research (AR) provides more effective and lasting results in students' professional formation and in this way can improve the quality of higher education. AR enhances both teachers' and students' competences because it focuses on the search for solutions to problems, while at the same time developing scientific studies related to them in a coordinated association between theory and practice. AR is possible because of the researcher's greater involvement, which does not occur in other traditional research methods.

2. THE ACTION RESEARCH METHOD

The goal of AR is to study and influence society at the same time, promoting the interaction between science and practice (Kyro, 2006). AR uses a constructivist approach in which knowledge is built from experience and interaction with the environment. It is constructed, not just "delivered" as a ready and unalterable commodity. McNiff and Whitehead (2009) explain the main differences between traditional investigations and investigations using AR:

1. One feature of the traditional methods is that the researcher adopts a viewer position, observing, describing, and explaining what happens. In contrast, in AR, researchers insert themselves in the research context and can analyze their own practices and learning. This posture becomes clear even in the style of narrative given that traditional methods use the third person whereas AR uses the first person "I" and "we."

2. The intentions of studies that use traditional research methods are to predict and control practices and to show causal relationships between variables; the idea is to apply theory to practice and ensure that practice fits into theory. In contrast, AR intends to develop the practices and expand the knowledge of the researchers themselves and to explain their activities.

Ventura (2014) presents an application of the AR method, demonstrating how researchers can develop their knowledge using action research methodology and how AR investigative practices allow not only for testing theory but also for generating theory. AR is currently used in many areas such as education, political science, social communication, social service (where it is more traditional), management, and information technology.

As a practical improvement process, AR is sometimes considered to be theoretical, but although it is true that traditional disciplinary theory is not a major priority, it is nevertheless important to draw on it for understanding situations, planning effective improvements, and explaining results (Tripp, 2005).

The usual representation of the AR process is a single cycle of planning, action, evaluation, and reflection. Some researchers believe they are doing AR when they plan, act, evaluate, and reflect about a problem, but this usually involves no method, and AR consists of more than just this. According to Mckay and Marshall (2001), AR has two juxtaposed and interdependent cycles, action and research, theory and practice, with activities that occur simultaneously. The authors argue that the dual-cycle view dispels the criticism that AR is the same as consulting because unlike with AR, consulting has no interest in scientific research. This paper presents a proposal to use AR in education, specifically higher education.

3. Using Action Research in the Education Process

3.1. Advantages and Challenges

AR promotes reflection and new knowledge and can bridge the gap between theory and practice. It is a form of development that encourages and develops educators' skills to become more reflective practitioners, more methodical problem solvers, and more thoughtful decision makers (Sparks & Simmons, 1989).

The use of AR has advantages for both teachers and students. Greenbank (2004) says that educational AR has the potential to help improve teaching and learning in higher education and to contribute to redefining teachers' professional roles. According to Vaughan and Burnaford (2015), AR provides teachers with opportunities to build and sharpen the dispositions that create reflective and collaborative leaders.

The solutions-based focus, emphasis on fostering practitioner empowerment, and pragmatic appeal of AR collectively render this research methodology a worthwhile professional development activity for teachers (Hine, 2013), and Hensen (1996) explains that action research can expand teachers' pedagogical repertoires. As a result, teachers who undertake AR become more motivated (Schratz, 1993a).

Similarly, AR also promotes students' professional development in that practicing AR improves competences such as initiative, teamwork, systemic thinking, and goal orientation. The meaningful learning that results from AR comes from the importance attached to participants' prior knowledge and the motivation resulting from the searches for solutions to problems and answers to research questions. In addition, reflecting on actions seems to help student-teachers develop their practical and theoretical understanding in a way that gives their experiences transfer value (Ulvika & Riese, 2016).

Despite so many benefits, the use of AR still has many challenges to overcome. First, educational institutions need to recognize these benefits and promote teacher training for their effective use in the classroom, highlighting the importance of AR not only as a research method but also as a valuable teaching tool that can develop important skills in students and prepare them for the job market.

AR demands somewhat more from researchers in terms of their personal skills. According to Zuber-Sherrit and Fletcher (2007), researchers who use AR need to have leadership skills and be engaging. The University of Notre Dame Australia in Fremantle recognizes the importance of this method and the need to prepare teachers to use it. For this reason, the school offers a core unit in AR methodology as part of its eight-unit masters of education degree (Hine, 2013).

3.2. A Proposed Use of Action Research in Higher Education

A Chinese proverb says: "I hear and I forget, I see and I remember, I do and I understand." This means that active learning and teaching are more effective because they directly involve students and engage them actively in learning. There are many active teaching methodologies, and a common feature among them is that the focus is on the learner and learning, just as it occurs in AR, in which the researcher's learning is one of the main objectives (Ventura, 2012). Teachers can use AR as an active teaching methodology, and the advantage is that teaching and researching are possible with a single methodology; in this way, the teacher should give all necessary support and guidance to students to develop the activities in both cycles of the AR method.

However, it is necessary to enable teachers to use AR so that they understand their objectives, their characteristics, and how to develop each activity in the research and problem-solving cycles. Hine (2013) argues that providing teachers with the necessary skills, knowledge, and focus to engage in meaningful inquiry about their professional practice will enhance this practice and effect positive changes concerning the educative goals of the learning community

Elliot (1994) argues that educational AR has a pedagogical aim that embodies an educational ideal that all those participating are committed to realizing; it focuses on changing practice to make it more consistent with the pedagogical aim. As such, the way of using AR proposed in this article is especially interesting in courses with practical approaches such as medical residency programs and other residency programs in health care. In these courses, residents detect problems in health care systems and study these problems through AR. AR is gaining increasing credibility in health care settings (East & Robinson, 1994). According to Street (2003), AR specifically addresses practical health issues with the intention to provide practical, context-specific knowledge and strategies to improve health care and the environments in which care is conducted.

3.3. Following the Steps of the Two Cycles of Action Research

AR, as a form of action inquiry, is an ongoing, repetitive process in which what is achieved in each cycle provides the starting point for subsequent improvement (Tripp, 2005). In AR, the researcher develops research while attempting to resolve problems. The activities, problem-solving and research, are cyclical (Mckay & Marshall, 2001), and both cycles have eight steps and a common structure, as shown in Figure 1.

According to Mckay and Marshall (2000) the steps of the problem-solving cycle are identify the problem (1), gather information (2), plan interventions (3), take action (4), implement the action (5), monitor the problem-solving efficacy (6),evaluate (7), and either exit if the problem is solved (8a) or amend the plan if it is not (8b).

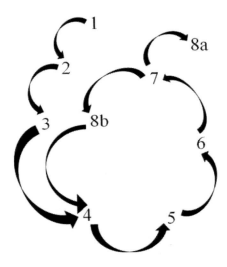

Figure 1. Action research cycle structure (adapted from Mckay & Marshall, 2001).

Then, the research cycle steps are to select the research topics (1), conduct the literature review (2), plan the research (3), take action (4), implement the plan (5), monitor the research interests (6), evaluate (7), and again, exit if the research goals have been achieved (8a) or amend the research plan if not (8b).

The problem-solving and research cycle activities should be developed concomitantly. For each activity in a cycle, there is a corresponding action in the other cycle, for example, identifying a problem (the first activity in the problem-solving cycle) and selecting research themes related to the problem (the first activity in the research cycle).

From an action research perspective, teaching is a form of research and vice versa (Elliot, 1994); teachers who wish to use AR in the teaching process should give students all the support they need to follow each step of the problem-solving and research cycles of the action research method. The next few topics present some suggestions of how higher education teachers can use AR in the teaching and learning process. Each topic addresses an activity in the problem-solving cycle and its corresponding activity in the research cycle.

3.3.1 Identify the Problem and Select the Research Topic

The first step is to identify a problem, and teachers should challenge students to identify a problem to overcome and make a checklist of research topics related to the problem identified. Students should think about their daily practice and if there is something to change or improve. Unlike with the traditional methods, AR starts not from a hypothesis but from a research question directly related to the problem to be investigated. According to Prasad et al. (2001), a research question is essentially a hypothesis asked in the form of a question. The authors contend that these kinds of questions use words such as "what" or "how," have a single focus, and are open-ended without reference to the literature or theory.

In order for the quality of scientific research to be clear to all the actors involved, research objectives must be well defined from the beginning of the process. However, in defining these objectives, students should propose significant and feasible research methods and designs according to the constraints of time and resources. The research problem should be concise and clearly stated, and the benefits of the study need to be clear to all involved. The desire to find this solution will motivate students and develop their creativity.

3.3.2. Gathering Information and Literature Review

To better understand the identified problem, it is necessary to revise the theory and structure the problem. To construct a literature review, it is necessary to locate sources and read articles, books, and other sources directly related to the investigation. Teachers should emphasize the importance of seeking the state of the art of each subject addressed. Action researchers aim to link theory to practice and connect what happens in their educational settings with the broader knowledge about teaching and learning (Efron & Ravid, 2013).

Is there some guidance in the literature about how to solve the identified research problem? If it exists, the next step will be the attempt to put into practice the theorists' recommendations obtained. Segal (2009) says that AR is a very useful and effective way to investigate problems or test new ideas. As such, if there is no guidance on a solution to the problem, it is recommended that the group conduct a brainstorming session and define what strategy it will test in practice throughout fieldwork. The teacher should encourage the students' creativity by proposing solutions to problems based on similar experiences described in the literature or based on the practice of experienced professionals

Structuring problems facilitates understanding their causes and consequences, so that the problems become more comprehensible to everyone. For this, it is necessary that the investigator seek maximum information on the problem by talking with the actors involved, preferably using problem-structuring methods, a broad group of problem-handling approaches whose purpose is to assist in structuring problems rather than directly solving them (Rosenhead, 2013). Teachers should therefore enable students to use one or more of these methods, such as SODA, which uses cognitive maps, or soft systems methodology, which uses rich figures. Franco and Meadows (2007) emphasize that problem-structuring methods should be selected according to their characteristics and the type of task to be developed.

3.3.3. Planning the Intervention and Developing the Research Project

It is now necessary to define actions and prepare a schedule of the activities to be developed. It is important to prepare a checklist of the necessary resources (time, money, personnel, materials, equipment), also measuring the budget necessary for developing the work. In the research cycle, this planning should focus on how to use theoretical sources, such as preparing forms for data collection, making observations, preparing seminars, and other research activities. It is also recommended at this stage to prepare the research evaluation form. In order for students to be able to develop this phase well in the action-research method, teachers should develop timelines, flowcharts, budgets, and other tools commonly used in planning actions, as well as techniques for designing research projects.

In the planning phase, the research objectives should be clearly defined, as well as the results expected to be achieved with the proposed solution to the problem detected. Defining these objectives is extremely important so that in the evaluation phase, it will be possible to evaluate the effectiveness of the implemented solution and the results obtained in relation to the research interests.

It is therefore recommended in this phase to prepare a form to be used in the monitoring phase. This form should list variables to be observed regarding implementing the proposed solution and about the research during the implementation process. Teachers should guide students in preparing this form, which will be essential for understanding the whole process developed throughout the AR. Efron and Ravid (2013) say that a meaningful and efficient research plan usually necessitates reflecting on the following elements:

- Considering your role as a researcher, taking into account ethical values, relationships with actors involved in the problem, etc.
- Establishing the research scope (the purpose of the study)
- Identifying the research site and participants
- Choosing data collection procedures
- Ensuring the study's validity and trustworthiness
- Developing ethical guidelines including how to obtain permissions and ensure confidentiality
- Creating a to-do list (including a timetable)

3.3.4. Action in Both Cycles

In the action phase, the researcher begins to interact with the actors involved in the problem situation, including enabling them to use the tools and theories that will be implemented in the next phase (implementation). One of the main activities of this phase is promoting the AR seminar. According to Ortsman (1978), the role of the researcher in these seminars is to:

- make available to the participants the theoretical and practical knowledge necessary to facilitate the discussion of the problems;
- record information collected during the application of this technique;
- design and implement actions related to developing the project; and
- generate reflections on the problem investigated.

In addition to the seminar technique, it is also important to use other data collection tools such as observation, artifacts, and forms with written questions defined for interviews (individual and collective) with the actors involved; such data collection tools are known as questionnaires or surveys. According to Fraenkel et al. (2016), data collected from observations can lead to additional follow-up data collected with interviews or surveys, but in order to develop this phase, students will need to know how to develop these seminars, how to conduct interviews, and how to document this process.

3.3.5. Implementation in Both Cycles

The implementation phase consists of testing the proposed solution and documenting the results obtained. Each activity should be documented and analyzed in comparison with the theoretical approaches related to the theme. Unlike other social research methods that only seek to describe the context of the study, AR promotes organizational change by involving the participants in a cycle of learning and reflection on the problem investigated (Cassel & Johnson, 2006).

This promotion of changes in the organizational context is what makes AR often criticized and compared with consulting. Therefore, Barskerville and Wood-Harper (1996) find it important to note that in this method, unlike in consulting, the documentary record of interventions is more rigorous and requires theoretical justifications, a cyclical process that entails both intervention and research actions, as presented in section 2.3.

3.3.6. Monitoring in Both Cycles

The monitoring phase consists of collecting information about the intervention and about the research throughout the implementation; the factors to be observed can be planned; in addition to the monitoring factors defined in the planning phase, the researcher may also include other observed variables that could affect the implementation results of the proposed solution or the research being developed.

3.3.7. Evaluation in Both Cycles

Evaluation is necessary for all research (Fraenkel et al. 2016), but how can we evaluate the quality of AR? According to Meyer (2000), any evaluation of AR needs to use appropriate methods and criteria such as authenticity, relevance, involvement, methodological rigor, practical improvement, and transformation of consciousness, that is, understanding, learning, development, and personal growth.

Dick (1993) and Collis and Hussey (2005) clarify that the objectives of AR are to provide changes in some environment and to increase understanding about the research object, that is, to promote the researcher's learning. Therefore, it is imperative to verify that the results were effectively achieved and, if not, which variables interfered negatively in the process. This evaluation should be based on the goals that were defined in the planning phases of the research and problem-solving cycles.

3.3.8. Amending the Plan or Leaving the Cycle

If the results observed in the evaluation phase are not satisfactory in terms of implementing the proposed solution or in terms of research interest, it is possible to amend the plan and continue the cycle in the action phase; if the results are satisfactory, the AR intervention can be finished. It is important to know what has not occurred as planned or what, if it has occurred as planned, did not bring the expected results. At the conclusion of the research and problem-solving cycles, it will be necessary to write the AR report, and teachers should guide their students on how to properly draft this report. A major difference in writing an AR report in relation to other types of research is the verbal voice used by researchers.

In traditional research, researchers use the third person to present studies in which he acted as observers. In AR, the researchers are also actors in implementing proposed actions and should therefore report findings in the first person that is, "me," "I," "us," etc.

According to McNiff and Whitehead (2009), an AR report should focus on the researchers' learning throughout the research and problem-solving cycles. Because AR aims to develop the researchers' practices and increase their knowledge, reports on this research must explain its activities and even generate theory through these investigative practices. Researchers should explain the implications of their findings for practice and suggest changes based on their study results (Efron & Ravid, 2013). Thus, writing research reports requires extreme organization of data and attention to the chronology of events and processes based on the need to "tell the story" in a trustworthy and organized way (Ventura, 2012).

3.4. An Innovative Model of Learning Assessment Using Action Research

AR promotes organizational change by engaging participants in a cycle of learning and reflection on problems (Cassel & Johnson, 2006). According to Ventura (2012), a striking feature of AR is the learning process it triggers, which is configured as one of its primary purposes. Therefore, in educational AR, it is important to establish a process of evaluating the participants' learning throughout the AR process. This evaluation should focus on the learning about the problem detected and also about the research method and the tools used in each phase of the research and problem-solving cycles. It should focus not only on evaluating the AR (authenticity, relevancy, involvement, methodological rigor, practical improvement) but also on the learning developed at every step of the intervention. Teachers can evaluate students' learning through processes such as

- The quality of the literature review

- The use of problem-structuring methods
- The intervention plan
- The quality of the research project
- The use of seminars and other data collection tools
- The implementation of the problem-solving proposed
- The action research report, especially considering what the students have learned from the AR, what skills they believe they have developed, and how they presented this in the report.

A whole process of teaching and assessment can be developed throughout each step of both cycles of AR. Teachers can develop evaluation forms that indicate which criteria will be evaluated so that the evaluation will be objective and clear to all involved.

CONCLUSION

AR provides rich learning for teachers and students as well as developing skills, motivating research, and real-world problem-solving. This motivation is attributable to the significant learning that results from applying AR, in which students clearly perceive the applicability of their interventions in solving day-to-day problems. However, it is necessary for higher education teachers to be properly trained to use AR as a teaching and learning tool in order to develop in students the skills necessary for their professional training, such as creativity, teamwork, and goal orientation.

This teacher training should begin during undergraduate and postgraduate courses, but it may also be promoted by educational institutions that want their teachers to use AR as a valuable teaching and learning tool. AR provides many ways to assess student learning throughout each stage of the research and problem-solving processes, and evaluating AR should focus mainly on developing competences by enhancing the AR process.

REFERENCES

Baskerville, R. L. & Wood-Harper, A. T. (1996). A critical perspective on action research as a method for information systems research. *Journal of Information Technology, 11*, 235-246.

Cassell, C., & Johnson, P. (2006). Action research: Explaining the diversity. *Human Relations, 59(6)*, 783-814.

Collis, J.; Hussey, R. (2005). *Pesquisa em administração: um guia prático para alunos de graduação e pós-graduação.* 2ed. Porto Alegre: Bookman. [*Research in Administration: A Practical Guide for Undergraduate and Graduate Students.* 2ed. Porto Alegre: Bookman.]

Dick, B. (1993). *You want to do action research thesis: how to conduct and report action research.* Retrieved September, 27, 2017, from http://www.aral.com.au/resources/arthesis.html.

East L., & Robinson J. (1994). Change in process: bringing about change in health care through action research. *Journal of Clinical Nursing, 3(1)*, 57-61.

Efron, S. E., & Ravid, R. (2013). *Action research in education: a practical guide.* New York: Guilford Press.

Elliot, John. (1994). Research on teachers' knowledge and action research. *Educational Action Research.* Vol. 2, No. 1.

Fraenkel, J. R., Wallen, N. E., & Hyun, H. H. (2016). *How to design and evaluate research in education.* Singapore: McGraw-Hill Education.

Franco, L.; & Meadows, M. (2007). Exploring new directions for research in problem structuring methods: on the role of cognitive style. *European Journal of Operational Research, 58*, 1621 -1629.

Freire, P. (1996). *Pedagogia da autonomia: saberes necessários à prática educativa.* 25.ed. São Paulo: Paz e Terra. [*Pedagogy of autonomy: knowledge necessary for educational practice.* 25 ed. São Paulo: Peace and Earth].

Greenbank, P. (2004). *Educational action research—has it a role to play in higher education?.* Retrieved August 29, 2017, from http://www. leeds.ac.uk/educol/documents/00003681.htm.

Hensen, K. T. (1996). Teachers as researchers. In J. Sikula (Ed.), *Handbook of research on teacher education* (4th ed., 53-66). New York: Macmillan.

Hine, G. (2013). *The importance of action research in teacher education programs.* Retrieved September 2, 2017, from http://www. academia.edu/4082600/The_Importance_of_Action_Research_in_Teac her_Education_Programs.

Kyro, P. (2006). Action research and networking benchmarking in developing Nordic statistics on woman entrepreneurship. *Benchmarking: An International Journal, 13* (1/2), 93 - 105.

Mckay, J., Marshall, P. (2001). The Dual Imperatives of Action Research. *Information Technology & People 14*, 46–59.

McNiff, J.; Whitehead, J. (2009). *Doing and writing action research.* Sage Publications.

Meyer, J. (2000). Evaluating action research. *Age and Ageing, 29*, 8-10.

Prasad, S., Rao, A., & Rehani, E. (2001). *Developing Hypothesis and Research Questions.* Retrieved September, 05, 2017 from http://www.public.asu.edu/~kroel/www500/hypothesis.pdf.

Rosenhead J. (2013). *Problem structuring methods*, S. I. Gass, M. C. Fu (Eds.), Encyclopedia of operations research and management science, Springer US, Boston, MA, 1162-1172.

Segal, S. U. (2009). *Action research in Mathematics in education: A study of Master's programs for teachers.* Retrieved September 12, 2017, from http://scholarworks.montana.edu/xmlui/bitstream/handle/1/2237/ SegalS0509.pdf?sequen ce=1.

Sparks, G. M., & Simmons, J. (1989). Inquiry-oriented staff development: Using research as a source of tools, not rules. In S. Caldwell (ed.), Staff development: *A handbook of effective practices*, Oxford, OH: National Staff Development Council, 126-139.

Vaughan, M., & Burnaford, G. (2015): Action research in graduate teacher education: a review of the literature 2000–2015, *Educational Action Research, 24* (2), 280 – 299. DOI: 10.1080/09650792.2015.1062408.

Schratz, M. (1993a). 'Researching while teaching: promoting reflective professionality in higher education,' *Educational Action Research*, Vol. 1, No. 1, pp. 11-133.

Street, A. F. (2003) 'Action Research'. In: V. Minichello, G. Sullivan, K. Greenwood and R. Axford (Eds.) *Handbook for Research Methods in Nursing and Health Sciences* (2nd ed.). Sydney: Pearson Education Australia P/L.

Tripp, D., (2005). Action research: a methodological introduction, *Educ. Pesqui.*, *31*(3), 443 - 466.

Ulvika, M., & Riese, H. (2016). Action research in pre-service teacher eudcation: A never-ending story promoting professional development. *Professional Development in Education*, 1-17. doi:10.1080/1941 5257. 2014.1003089.

Ventura, A., Dias, L., & Clímaco, J. (2014). On facilitating group decision making processes with VIP analysis. *Lecture Notes in Business Information Processing, 180,* LNBIP, 246-253.

Ventura, A. (2013). *Application of the action research method to the decision support process using the VIP Analysis System*, PhD Thesis, University of Coimbra, Retrieved September, 19, 2017 from http:// hdl.handle.net/10316/22052].

Zuber-Skerritt, O., & Fletcher, M. (2007). The quality of an action research thesis in social sciences. *Quality Assurance in Education, 15*, 4, 413-436.

In: (Participatory) Action Research   ISBN: 978-1-53613-041-6
Editors: J. Calder and J. Foletta   © 2018 Nova Science Publishers, Inc.

Chapter 8

TEACHER-CENTRED ACTION RESEARCH IN A REMOTE PARTICIPATORY ENVIRONMENT: A REFLECTION ON A CASE OF CHEMISTRY CURRICULUM INNOVATION IN A SWISS VOCATIONAL SCHOOL

*Ivano Laudonia[1,2] and Ingo Eilks[2,***

[1]Gewerbliche Berufsschule Chur (Vocational School),
Chur, Switzerland
[2]Institute for Science Education, University of Bremen,
Bremen, Germany

ABSTRACT

In 2002, Eilks and Ralle suggested a specific model of how to apply
participatory action research (PAR) for domain specific educational

---

* Corresponding Author Email: ingo.eilks@uni-bremen.de.

research and innovation. The model was described for the field of science education and was used in numerous projects and cases for evidence-based innovation of the science curriculum and its related media and pedagogy. The model bases on a close cooperation of a group of teachers with science educators from the university under involvement of graduate student teachers and PhD students in science education. However, it is not always possible to create a suitable environment on-site for such a research model if the practice field is remote to other potentially interested teachers and far away from a feasible academic institution fitting the research and innovation interest. This chapter describes such a case. It deals with research-based innovation of the pedagogy of chemistry teaching in vocational education in southern Switzerland. A teacher-driven approach for changes in teaching chemical bonding was chosen, inspired by the PAR model suggested by Eilks and Ralle. A remote access of the individual teacher researcher was established via email and Skype with an already existing PAR network of secondary chemistry teachers in the west of Germany. The network is coordinated and supported by an academic group experienced in PAR from northern Germany, namely from the University of Bremen. The chapter discusses the project and reflects on how the remote networking of the teacher action researcher with a PAR-driven community of practitioners and academic educational researchers helped strengthening the process of research and development and contributed to strengthen the teacher's continuous professional development.

Keywords: chemistry education, participatory action research, curriculum innovation, vocational school

1. INTRODUCTION AND BACKGROUND

The pedagogy of chemistry education has been described to suffer from problems that tend to impede motivation, interest and achievement of the students. For example, expository teaching dominates in many classrooms (Hohloch, Grove & Bretz, 2007); there is often a lack of close relation of instruction and theory to practical activities (Wright, 2008); and laboratory work often has low practical significance (Feyzioglu et al., 2011). Consequently, a lack of understanding is the result (Baddock & Bucat, 2008), students' motivation generally is not satisfactory (Stuckey et al., 2013), and together with lacks in the curriculum (Hofstein, Eilks &

Bybee, 2011) chemistry education becomes quite unpopular among many students (Osborne & Dillon, 2008). Concluding on this, modern books about the teaching of chemistry strongly suggest that student-active modes of learning need to be implemented more thoroughly (e.g., Eilks, Prins & Lazarowitz, 2013).

One reason for the persistence of a quite traditional pedagogy in chemistry education seems to be a lack of integration of science education research, curriculum design, and teaching practice in many countries (De Jong, 2000; Hohloch et al., 2007). This missing integration is caused by the "two communities problem" of researchers and practicing teachers (Huberman, 1991), or even "three communities problem" when involving the curriculum developers. This lack is suggested to be caused by missing cooperation and coordinated action of these three groups (De Jong, 2000, Eilks, 2014; Eilks & Markic, 2011). It might also be caused by differences in styles of thought and concluding misunderstandings and misinterpretations among the three groups (Stuckey, Heering, Mamlok-Naamen, Hofstein & Eilks, 2015).

In 2002, Eilks and Ralle suggested action research as a promising way to overcome the missing integration of science education research, curriculum development, and classroom practice. Based on the works of Whyte, Greenwood and Lazes (1989), they suggested cooperation and joint action of representatives from the different domains by action research for the field of chemistry education (see also Eilks, 2014; Mamlok-Naaman & Eilks, 2012). Tracing back to the works of Grundy (1982), their approach referred to three basic types of action research, namely technical, collaborative, and emancipatory action research (i.e., Eilks & Markic, 2011; Mamlok-Naaman & Eilks, 2012). In technical action research, the classroom is primarily a test-bed for theoretically based interventions. The practicing teachers primarily facilitate and support the process of evaluation and research. On the other end of the spectrum, emancipatory action research is driven and carried out by practicing teachers with only low support from outside the teacher's practice.

Between the two extremes of technical and emancipatory action research, Eilks and Ralle (2002) suggested to primarily invest into "practical", "interactive", collaborative, or "participatory" forms of action research. For the field of chemistry education, they suggested types of action research that are characterized by close cooperation and mutual understanding of teachers and accompanying researchers with both groups being equally important but following different roles (e.g., Eilks & Ralle, 2002). However, even single projects can merge the different forms or turn from one type to another. Eilks (2003) described a case in the field of science education that a project started unintentionally more or less technical, developed into a participatory mode, and in the end teachers took over a leading role in the action research process (see also Eilks & Markic, 2011).

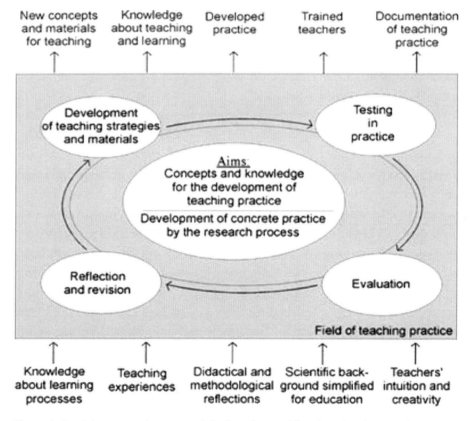

Figure 1. Participatory action research in domain-specific educational research according to Eilks and Ralle (2002).

In their suggestion from 2002, Eilks and Ralle outlined a specific form of participatory action research (PAR) as a suitable interpretation of action research for domain specific educational research integrated with curriculum development and practice improvement. This model directly addresses the mutual development of practice and research knowledge, as many forms of actions research do (Noffke & Somekh, 2009). Participatory action research, as suggested by Eilks and Ralle, describes a process of jointly developing, implementing, testing, evaluating, and reflecting innovations in the science classroom and at the same time being a process for leading to results of general interest to both the researcher and practitioner communities (Figure 1; Eilks, 2014; Eilks & Ralle & 2002).

Innovations and pedagogically relevant knowledge are developed by PAR via research activities in authentic practice, thus putting research into practice. At the same time, practically relevant knowledge is communicated back to theory (Eilks, 2014). This process is suggested to also reduce the time gap between generation of educational research knowledge and its application it in the classroom. It helps further to prevent theory from losing contact to pedagogical practice by keeping authenticity, feasibility, relevance, and worth of the results (Eilks & Ralle, 2002; Mamlok-Naaman & Eilks, 2012).

Starting PAR projects, as a joint project of practitioners and accompanying educators from the university, as suggested by Eilks and Ralle (2002), might be imposed by practical problems. Practitioners might not be able to find the right support for their research interest, e.g., not to find colleagues in the regional environment interested in a collaborative PAR project. Accompanying researchers might also not be available on-site near the regional field of classroom practice, as the field of practice might be remote from a feasible academic institution providing corresponding expertise for the research and innovation interest. Consequently, this paper describes a case of how to enable a practitioner to make use of the PAR model in domain-specific education by Eilks and Ralle (2002) if no network of teachers or support by a regional research institution is available.

In this chapter, an action research project is described and reflected that is teacher driven but remote supported by an existing PAR network. The practitioner and a science education researcher from a university with an existing PAR network in the corresponding field of interest are located at different sites, even in different countries, namely Switzerland and Germany. Communication and cooperation was conducted by synchronous and asynchronous communication tools, such as email, Dropbox and Skype. As the practical teaching and action research is conducted by one of the authors (I.L.) in his own classroom practice in southern Switzerland, the project is primarily teacher-centred. However, it is inspired by the PAR model suggested by Eilks and Ralle (2002). It is supported by both a domain-specific educational researcher (I.E.) and an already existing PAR group of roughly ten chemistry teachers from the west of Germany. The teacher communicated regularly with the PAR network that is coordinated and supported by an academic chemistry education research group having nearly 20 years of experience in PAR in science education (Eilks, 2014). The subject of the research is teaching chemical bonding in vocational chemistry education in Switzerland.

2. Innovating Vocational Chemistry Teaching on Bonding

The topic of this action research was innovating chemistry lesson on chemical bonding in vocational school chemistry teaching in Switzerland. Instead of expository teaching, a multimedia learning environment was developed to allow students to work in a more self-directed and autonomous as well as in a co-operative way. The whole lesson plan and the learning materials were originally designed by the teacher researcher regularly consulting the remote PAR network in Germany. Via Skype, the action research teacher was able to present his designs in the regular meetings of the PAR network about every four weeks. The PAR group who had chance to analyze the designs before the meetings, intensively discussed the design and materials and provided feedback, critique, and further ideas. Later re-designs were also discussed with the accompanying chemistry educator and members of the PAR network regularly. In essence, design, teaching, obtaining feedback, discussing it, and redesign followed the cyclical process shown in Figure 1.

The learning environment was designed inspired by the "Tour de Chemie" (Krause, Kienast, Witteck & Eilks, 2013) that was originally developed by the same PAR group in Germany. The "Tour de Chemie" is a set of multimedia-based learning steps with intermediate online self-assessments. After each phase of learning the students had to assess their knowledge in an online test. The online tests were solely designed for self-assessment in order to enable the students to control their learning achievement. Each online test consists of 10 to 20 tasks which are designed as single choice, multiple choice, and assignment tasks ("drag and drop"). If the test is passed with at least 80% achievement, the students are allowed to move on to the next phase; otherwise, the actual phase is to be repeated and to be assessed again. After two failures individual support is offered by the teacher (Figure 2).

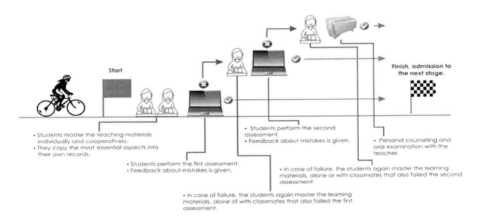

Figure 2. The idea of the "Tour de Chemie" (Krause et al., 2013).

Between the assessments, content is accessible and organized with the software PREZI (Figure 3) which allows for presentation of the content in a non-linear way to enable chances for dynamic navigation (Krause &

Eilks, 2014). The pedagogy to use the learning platform suggests that pupils are free to work alone, in dyads, or small groups of three to four (Krause et al., 2013). Within the learning environment, learning is stimulated at three levels: a) description of theory, b) experiments designed to demonstrate and exemplify the theoretical concepts, and c) online tests to provide feedback to the students about their progress on the different phases in the lesson plan.

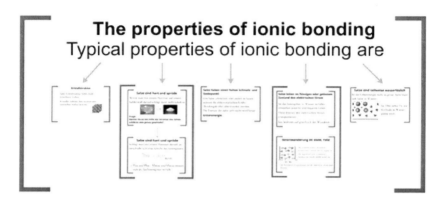

Figure 3. A view into the learning environment: Stage - The characteristics of ionic bonding.

The whole lesson plan lasts generally for seven weeks, with one or two lessons per week, depending on the performance of the students. The lesson plan is operated in steps divided by the assessments.

During the process of development, the vocational students were asked for feedback after each part of the lesson plan, using a Likert based questionnaire. In two consecutive years 2014 and 2015, 127 students from a vocational school in southern Switzerland participated, 68 in 2014 and 59 in 2015. Students were between 16 and 19 years old. Pupils provided feedback on two levels: Firstly, appraisals as well as comments about the learning material and structure, the PREZIs and the whole platform, were obtained using a questionnaire combining Likert scale items with two open questions. Secondly, two questionnaires referring to learning behavior and perceived learning climate were used (Bolte, 2004; Dilger, & Sloane, 2007).

The feedback given by the students via the questionnaires was used to evaluate motivation, acceptance, and learning effects, and – if necessary – to redesign parts of the curriculum (Figure 4). An example for redesigning the learning material in response to pupils' feedback refers to the overall structure: It became evident that the pupils preferred a finer modularization of the learning environment than originally provided. So the learning environment was restructured to form sub-units on ionic bonding, covalent bonding, and metallic bonding. After further feedback, five different PREZI environments were designed: (i) characteristics of ionic bonding, (ii) characteristics and nomenclature of salts, (iii) development of covalent bonding, (iv) characteristics of molecular substances with active forces (like van-der-Waals and dipole forces), and (v) metallic bonding and its characteristics.

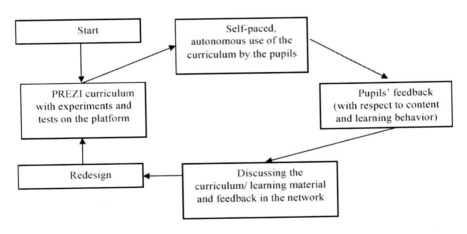

Figure 4. Course of the PAR project.

The integration of experiments into the learning environment was influenced by pupils' feedback too. A stronger relationship of the experiments to the pupils' everyday experience was pursued. For example, ionic bonding is exemplified by experiments for producing common salt crystals or for measuring the conductivity of salt solutions. For exemplifying the dipole bonding, experiments illustrating the dipole characteristics were further integrated, as well as dissolubility of common salt in water, organic solvents, and other liquids occurring in everyday life. Metallic bonding was illustrated by an additional experiment for producing sparklers.

3. REFLECTIONS ON THE ACTION RESEARCH PROCESS AND ITS NATURE

The action research process in this project can be described as basically teacher centered as the teacher conducted the lessons and the research as well individually and on his own responsibility. One teacher did the teaching, and collected and evaluated the data. However, the process was nevertheless near to the PAR model described by Eilks and Ralle (2002). The remote PAR group with its nearly 20-year long experience in similar projects had a strong influence on the project. Both, designing the learning environment along the idea of the "Tour de Chemie" as well as using PREZI to organize the content were innovations earlier developed within the remote PAR network in Germany. Corresponding technical and educational expertise became available to the action research teacher by being remotely integrated into the network.

The supportive PAR network of science teachers and academic science educators influenced the process at two levels:

- At the "content" level, the PAR group guided the teacher in terms of relevance, significance and comprehensibility of the content in the learning environment, e.g., which formulae, chemical reaction equations, composition of substances to be used and how the content and its presentation connected to practical activities is best to be organized and how to create a most promising mix of media types, like text and visualization.
- At the "process and interaction" level, the PAR group provided advice how the learning environment might best encourage autonomous learning and at the same time provide enough

guidance to allow also lower achievers to find a good way towards the content and to promote understanding.

For the action research teacher the integration into the existing PAR network with its rich expertise was a unique experience and supported both the development of the classroom practice as well as the intended continuous professional development of the teacher by the action research process. Reflections on the learning process by the action research teacher led to new professional insights into teaching, concerning

- structuring and sequencing of the learning environment,
- integrating experiments into a digital learning environment,
- providing higher significance of experiments by better connecting them to everyday experiences of the students,
- how to better assist and to consult students in organizing their own learning process and autonomous learning, and
- how to improve ways of cooperation and participation of the pupils.

The first three bullets of this list refer to content and structure. The last two bullets refer to structuring and to assist the learning process. Apparently, using the PAR network was more supportive with respect to content and structure than with respect to the process, because there was improvement with respect to content and structure from 2014 to 2015, but there was no change with respect to assisting the students in the learning process, to foster cooperation, etc. So the use of the PAR network might be considered to be partially successful in this case. However, it must be said that the PAR network is exclusively formed by teachers and science educators in general education. None of the teachers in the network had any practical experience in vocational education and maybe the differences in the pedagogy between general and vocational education might have limited the consultation in the process domain.

In his personal reflection, the teacher suggested for further developing his teaching by action research that it seems difficult to simultaneously make changes to content / structure on one hand, and to process on the other hand. These changes have to be carefully coordinated, and maybe it is the most promising way to do one step after the other, that is, to adjust structure and content first, and to take care of the process in a systematic manner in a second step. More generally, an explicit "roadmap" of when to implement which curricular aspect within an action research project seems sensible.

For the teacher, it is difficult to tell whether the inputs received from the PAR network might not have been optimal, or whether this was merely a problem of putting these inputs into practice. It was also not clear whether advice by a PAR network experienced in vocational education would have been more supportive. Unfortunately, such networks do not seem to exist in the domain of vocational chemistry education, at least for the cases of Switzerland and Germany. So a lesson from using a remote PAR network from general chemistry education might be that it is not enough to receive input just on a strategic, tactical, and design level, but also to discuss this input within the network at an operational level, discussing the practices and objectives generally operated in vocational education within the PAR network.

Overall satisfaction, cooperation and participation of the pupils in the lessons, and perceived practical relevance of topics did not improve significantly when comparing the lessons held in 2014 to 2015. Nevertheless, many students were happy about the changes and the more open pedagogy. However, feedback from other students indicated that changing a teaching method towards more autonomy is not always appreciated, as it might induce uncertainty. This is a big difference compared with corresponding studies in general chemistry teaching in Germany (e.g., Eilks, 2005; Krause et al., 2013, Witteck & Eilks, 2006). Further research is needed about whether innovations in vocational education should take the same road that is suggested from theory for general chemistry teaching.

Finally, it is suggested that the process of the teacher communicating with the PAR network, of receiving input from it, and of making this input operational might be conducted in a more systematic way. The process of when (and why) which kind of input is generated from the PAR network and how this input is put to operation in the remote classroom by the science teacher might be made more explicit and transparent. This might be an important task for a follow-up case.

CONCLUSION

This case describes a teacher-centered action research project to innovate vocational chemistry education in an environment where there was no chance to embed this research into an on-site participatory group of teachers or to get face-to-face support from an academic advisor. Nevertheless, an approach was chosen to make most use of the ideas of participatory action research as described by Eilks and Ralle (2002), an approach that seeks for close cooperation of groups of teachers with academic science educators. This was done by synchronous and asynchronous remote integration of the teacher into an experienced PAR group.

Although the process was not considered to be optimal following the participatory approach it enriched the research and development. Although not all aims were fully reached after the first two cycles of research and development, the feedback of the students in the open questions provided some indications for promising developments that should now be subject to further research and development in the next cycles. Further studies should also focus more thoroughly the fostering and hindering mechanisms that influence the remote cooperation of single teachers with remote networks based in PAR.

In what way ever the products and results will be considered, there is another aim of any action research that is to contribute to teachers' continuous professional development (Mamlok-Naaman & Eilks, 2012). Here it is clear that the support of the PAR network provided a unique learning experience for the teacher researcher. It provided a lot of access to knowledge and experience of the group in terms of curriculum development and teacher research. This rich base of information would have been neither available, since not all experience of the PAR network is documented in its publications, nor easily accessible, since it was communicated personally via email and Skype. Even if the results of the practice innovation seem to need further work the success in the teachers' professional development is obvious and is considered to be much higher than it would have been without the collaboration with the PAR network.

Concerning the theory of action research, in science education and beyond, there are several models that describe whether and how teachers are supported in networks and by academic advisors (e.g., Eilks, 2014). This case suggests that teacher-centered action research profits from the support of a network sharing similar interests too, even if the network is remote and even if collaboration is limited by technical channels of communication. However, since this is a very unique case on action research, it might contribute to identify the most promising processes of support and the most feasible tools and methods to be applied to make the teacher-centred approach a most participatory experience.

REFERENCES

Baddock, M., & Bucat, R. (2008). Effectiveness of a classroom chemistry demonstration using the cognitive conflict strategy. *International Journal of Science Education, 30*, 1115–1128.

Bolte, C. (2004). Qualitätsprüfung durch Analyse des motivationalen Lernklimas im eigenen Physik- und Chemieunterricht. [Quality assessment by analyzing the motivational learning climate in one's own physics and chemistry lesson]. In A. Pitton (ed.), *Chemie- und physikdidaktische Forschung und naturwissenschaftliche Bildung* (pp. 250-252). Münster: Lit (in German).

De Jong, O. (2000). Crossing the borders: chemical education research and teaching practice. *University Chemistry Education, 4*, 31-34.

Dilger, B., & Sloane, P. F. (2007). Das Wesentliche bleibt für das Auge verborgen, oder? Möglichkeiten zur Beobachtung und Beschreibung selbst regulierten Lernens [The essence keeps hidden for the eye – or? Possibilities of observation and description of self-regulated learning] *Berufs- und Wirtschaftspädagogik online*, Issue. 13. Available from www.bwpat.de/ausgabe13/dilger_sloane_bwpat13.shtml (in German).

Eilks, I. (2003). Co-operative curriculum development in a project of participatory action research within chemical education: Teachers' reflections. *Science Education International, 14* (4), 41-49.

Eilks, I. (2005). Experiences and reflections about teaching atomic structure in a jigsaw classroom in lower secondary school chemistry lessons. *Journal of Chemical Education, 82*, 313-320.

Eilks, I. (2014). Action research in science education – From general justifications towards a specific model in practice. In T. Stern, F. Rauch, A. Schuster & A. Townsend (eds.), *Action Research, innovation and change: International perspectives across disciplines* (pp. 156-176). London: Routledge.

Eilks, I., & Markic, S. (2011): Effects of a long-term participatory action research project on science teachers' professional development. *Eurasia Journal of Mathematics, Science & Technology Education, 7*, 149-160.

Eilks, I., Prins, G. T., & Lazarowitz, R. (2013). How to organize the classroom in a student-active mode. In I. Eilks & A. Hofstein (eds.), *Teaching chemistry – A study book* (pp. 183-212). Rotterdam: Sense.

Eilks, I., & Ralle, B. (2002). Participatory action research in chemical education. In B. Ralle & I. Eilks (eds.). *Research in chemical education - What does this mean?* (pp. 87-98). Aachen: Shaker.

Feyzioglu, B., Demirag, B., Ates, A., Cobanoglu, I., & Altun, E. (2011). Chemistry teachers' perceptions on laboratory applications: Izmir sample. *Educational Sciences: Theory and Practice, 11*, 1024–1029.

Grundy, S. (1982). Three modes of action research. *Curriculum Perspectives, 2* (3), 23-34.

Hofstein, A., Eilks, I., & Bybee, R. (2011). Societal issues and their importance for contemporary science education: a pedagogical justification and the state of the art in Israel, Germany and the USA. *International Journal of Science and Mathematics Education, 9*, 1459-1483.

Hohloch, J., Grove, N., & Bretz, S. L. (2007). Pre-service teacher as researcher: The value of inquiry in learning science. *Journal of Chemical Education, 84*, 1530-1534.

Huberman, M. (1991). Linking the practitioner and researcher communities for school improvement. *School Effectiveness and School Improvement, 4*, 1-16.

Krause, M., & Eilks, I. (2014). Innovating chemistry learning with PREZI. *Chemistry in Action*, 104 (Winter), 19-25.

Krause, M., Kienast, S., Witteck, T. & Eilks, I. (2013). On the development of a computer-based learning and assessment for the transition from lower to upper secondary chemistry education. *Chemistry Education Research and Practice, 14*, 345-353.

Mamlok-Naaman, R., & Eilks, I. (2012). Different types of action research to promote chemistry teachers' professional development - A joined theoretical reflection on two cases from Israel and Germany. *International Journal of Science and Mathematics Education, 10*, 581-610.

Noffke, S., Somekh, B. (2009). Action research. In S. Noffke, & B. Somekh (eds), *Handbook of action research* (pp. 89-96). New Delhi: Sage.

Osborne, J., & Dillon L. (2008). *Science education in Europe: Critical reflections*. London: Nuffield Foundation.

Stuckey, M., Heering, P., Mamlok-Naaman, R., Hofstein, A., & Eilks, I. (2015). The philosophy of Ludwik Fleck and its potential meaning for the teaching and learning of science. *Science & Education, 24*, 281-298.

Stuckey, M., Mamlok-Naaman, R., Hofstein, A., & Eilks, I. (2013). The meaning of, relevance' in science education and its implications for the science curriculum. *Studies in Science Education*, 49, 1-34.

Whyte, W. F., Greenwood, D. J., & Lazes, P. (1989). Participatory action research. *The American Behaviroral Scientist, 32*, 513-551.

Witteck, T., & Eilks, I. (2006). Max Sour Ltd. – Open experimentation and problem solving in a cooperative learning company. *School Science Review, 88* (323), 95-102.

Wright, L. J. (2008). Learning by doing: The objectification of knowledge across semiotic modalities in middle school chemistry lab activities. *Linguistics and Education, 19*, 225-243.

In: (Participatory) Action Research
Editors: J. Calder and J. Foletta

ISBN: 978-1-53613-041-6
© 2018 Nova Science Publishers, Inc.

Chapter 9

FROM GROUP DEVELOPMENT TO INTERVENTION: APPLYING PARTICIPATORY ACTION RESEARCH IN ITALY

Nadia Rania[1,*], PhD, Alessandra Brameri[2],
Laura Migliorini[1], PhD and Emanuela Gandolfo[3]
[1]Department of Education Sciences, University of Genoa, Genoa, Italy
[2]Psychologist and Psychotherapist of Social Services, Busalla, Italy
[3]Psychologist and Psychotherapist of Social Services,
Sant'Olcese and Serra Riccò, Italy

ABSTRACT

Since its origins, participatory action research has been characterized as a methodology that is able to promote change within the real world of everyday life.

---

* Corresponding Author Email: nadia.rania@unige.it.

Participatory action research, as Lewin understood it, is not academic research but instead is oriented toward modifying the "field" and the context through its knowledge; it is a co-generative process through which professional researchers and interested members of a local organization, community, or specially created organization collaborate to research, understand and resolve problems of mutual interest. Participatory action research is a social process in which professional knowledge, process skills, research skills and democratic values are the basis for co-created knowledge and social change. This methodology tries to transcend the difference between theory and practice in an attempt to activate a circular process between knowledge and the transformation of reality. In describing the structure of action research, it can first be asserted that it is not a linear methodology of research but instead a cyclical process that proceeds through greater levels of complexity and recursivity.

The aim of this chapter is to illustrate an application of participatory action research (PAR) conducted in Italy. The authors illustrate the three phases of a PAR project realized in fourteen small municipalities in a suburban area located in the hinterland of a medium-sized city in northwestern Italy to promote a change in students' feelings, perceptions and knowledge of well-being and, in particular, their relations regarding the use of new technologies.

Keywords: Participatory action research, Italy, group development

INTRODUCTION

Participatory action research (PAR) is research oriented toward modifying context through knowledge; it is a process through which researchers, practitioners and interested individuals in a community understand, confront and resolve problems that are part of their everyday life. PAR is characterized by shared power among partners over decisions in all phases of the research and action (Ozer et al. 2010) PAR involves people in communities and is based on the concept that people are experts on their own lives. The objective of PAR is to create a change in the context of people's lives and to stimulate in people critical reflection on problems and possible solutions through action (Denzin and Lincoln 2000). PAR was developed by Kurt Lewin (1946) with his experiences in the "field" and through his articles "Action Research and Minority Problems" (1946) and "Frontiers in Group Dynamics" (1947), in which he theorized that this methodology is able to promote change within the community. PAR includes participants, policymakers, and researchers in a co-learning process in which they learn from one another and from their own expertise. This methodology tries to activate a circular process between knowledge and the transformation of reality to promote a social change (Geenwood and Levin 1998). PAR represents a challenge: on the one hand, the processes of knowledge and thought, whose essential aim is to comprise, to explain and to give meaning, and, on the other hand, the action processes, that is, the practical activity, whose purposes are participation, transformation and change (Amerio, De Piccoli and Miglietta 2000). PAR is a cyclical process that proceeds through greater levels of complexity and recursivity; this characteristic is common to the method of qualitative research (Denzin and Lincolin 1994; Rania 2017). Moreover, as with all qualitative approaches, it emphasizes a deep understanding of the experiences and perspectives of the research participants (Karasz and Singelis 2009). As underlined by Rania (2017) in the international context, there is an increasingly strong need to give more space to qualitative research and to PAR to address emerging issues in contexts and in the community to confront new challenges such as multicultural contexts or the impact of new technologies. Under PAR, there are several methodologies that can be used to confront the new challenges of the society; in particular, the photovoice technique has recently been used to study the intercultural relations (Rania, Migliorini, Cardinali and Rebora 2015; Rania, Migliorini, Rebora and Cardinali 2015; Rania, Migliorini, Rebora and Cardinali 2014) or to promote social change in youths (Phillips, Berg, Rodriguez et al. 2010; Foster-Fishman, Law, Lichty et al. 2010).

Participation, which is a key aspect of PAR, is a positive experience for both people and institutions, as highlighted by community psychology and the literature regarding the community development (Montero 2011; Natale, Di Martino, Procentese and Arcidiacono 2016). Participation is the basis of the process to promote the social change and to improve the needs of the community and increase the quality of life of its members (Kagan, Burton, Duckett, Lawthom and Siddiquee 2011). Furthermore, the PAR is a methodology that permits linking of the participation processes and the social policy and it can reduce the differences of power within the relationship between the researcher and participants because participants are included in the research process (Migliorini and Rania 2017).

PAR includes three main moments: the planning, the execution and the research on the action's outcomes. Planning begins from a general idea that develops into the goal. In this phase, there is an accurate analysis of the situation that follows the elaboration of an action plan to obtain the desired results. The next phase comprises the execution of the plan, which is defined as the action taken to produce change. This phase is followed by an appraisal of what was realized and the new situation that, according to Kurt Lewin (1935), responds to various functions: an appraisal of action, establishing how much the execution corresponded to the expectations; the possibility of adding new intuitions about the validity or ineffectiveness of the action's techniques; and the eventual modification of the plan, realized in a circular process. Therefore, PAR is an approach to working with people who emphasizes the active participation of researchers and participants in the planning, implementation, and dissemination of research. In the present chapter, the authors illustrate the three phases of a PAR project realized in fourteen small municipalities in a suburban area located in the hinterland of a medium-sized city in northwestern Italy to promote a change in students' feelings, perception and knowledge of well-being and, in particular, their relations regarding the use of new technologies. This project adopted a participatory action research design. The authors used PAR and illustrate the partnership process and how the data were used to inform the intervention implementation procedures. The role of PAR working at the community level is highlighted.

PLANNING AND DEVELOPMENT OF THE PARTICIPATORY ACTION RESEARCH GROUP

The purpose of the present section is to illustrate the project planning related to a group of professionals who address youth welfare to promote the psychological well-being related to the use of new technologies in this target group. The group consists of a multi-professional team composed of social workers and psychologists.

The group's mission is to prevent and promote well-being in the territory. It is within this group that the reflection of this PAR project, called "Consciously Digital", was born.

Group discussions between professionals have developed within monthly meetings.

The group has represented a fertile laboratory of multidisciplinary experiences that, through a process of brainstorming, have created ideas and interest lines that have converged in defining a shared methodology of analysis and intervention.

Setting

The territory where the group works consists of fourteen small municipalities in a suburban area located in the hinterland of a medium-sized city in northwestern Italy that includes a total of 115.952 people over an area of 346.3 square kilometers and an average population density of 334 inhabitants per square kilometer.

The youth population (below 18 years of age) corresponds to 7.134 individuals.

Beginning: Perception of the Problem

In the social planning intervention, the need analysis represents the first step of the process. During its monthly discussion meetings, the work group felt the need to capture data related to the use of technological tools by adolescents and their families. This emerging issue is a relevant topic because, through some local institutions, the group became aware of cyberbullying cases that were brought forward by adolescents or by the families themselves.

Constitution of the Group and Definition of Goals

Through cultural initiatives and the promotion of a network that involved professionals from various areas, the group stimulated the attention of citizens on the themes of this PAR project, "Consciously digital", to promote insights and best practices. To that end, the group has involved health professionals, social workers and teachers who, due to their proximity to the young generation, feel the potential and the vulnerability that the adolescents carry. In this case, pediatricians and several local social agencies were involved, including the school and the afternoon educational centers that indicated and discussed with the group the emergence of situations of cyberbullying and the improper and dangerous use of the Internet and new technologies among the youth population.

Initially, the psychosocial operators felt the need to investigate and learn about the diffusion of the phenomenon in the territory to offer various technical and cognitive tools and interventions.

In light of these considerations, others involved in the group also included the Postal and Communications Police, the local University, which has supported the project from the scientific perspective, and local associations that have financially supported the project. It is also important to note that this PAR project, "Consciously digital", was approved by the Ministry of the Interior and is sponsored by the local Order of Psychologists.

The specific objectives of the group developed under the PAR approach are as follows:

- fostering the experience of teamwork as an incubator of ideas, in which individuals are holders of a value that must subsequently be exported outside the group;
- soliciting the direct experience of the group as a container of expectations, worries, and anxieties related to the task. Therefore, the awareness of the emotional aspects of the group as a container of emotional feelings that the learning and planning process convey was promoted. Doing so allowed us to gain experience in how teamwork is essential to address complex situations or issues. Therefore, this experience was closely connected to the development of a network, the objective of whose realization would be to become the common working methodology;
- identifying the necessary partners for the creation of the network who, based on their skills, could contribute to the realization of the different phases of the project;
- consolidating a working practice in the network to disseminate and sensitize the community and the different institutions.
- Furthermore, some objectives of the PAR project, "Consciously digital" are developed:
- acquiring epidemiological data on the knowledge of young adolescents and their families regarding the use of the Internet and new technologies and the well-being of adolescent related thereto, with a focus on cyberbullying and other misuses of the Internet;
- promoting intergenerational dialogue through training adolescents and their parents in new technologies in parallel to prevent adolescents from being the only individuals confronting this new challenge and to allow parents to become familiar with these new languages.

Group Training

After outlining the common critical issues and problems that the participants experience every day to confront the object of this PAR project, the group focuses on the sharing of objectives and strategies to achieve them. In this phase, the cooperative climate represents the dimension that helps in researching shared solutions and overcoming personal positions that are contrary to or distant from those held by others. Through the involvement in the individuation of the problematic situations and in the elaboration of the solution hypothesis, the participants proceed along their plan of change, increasing their ability to produce new knowledge and to develop innovative modalities of group living through the formulation of a different perspective regarding the context (Floris 2001). This flow of information and ideas, bound up with experiential activity, is conducive to implementing the acquisition of knowledge and the development of competences for personal and professional gain (Migliorini, Rania and Cardinali 2008).

In this phase, which we can define as the consolidation of the group's life, according to Lewin (1947), mental life and social relationships are exposed to intrinsic forces in the vital space. During this phase of training and the sharing of objectives, the group consolidates and defines the working methods.

Lewin highlights the role of the discussion phase from the first moment of group development. This process offers a chance to confront critical issues and to try participation instruments – based on a cooperative group approach – to respond to problematic situations in an adaptive manner.

In the performing phase (Tuckman 1965), in a game of exchanges addressed to the negotiation and the transformation of the same group, as soon as described, the feedback that every social and education worker will carry to the group is very significant. The researcher also has an important role; he has the task of offering filters to observe aspects that were not previously paid attention to. Thus, the classic dichotomy between expert and apprentice is transcended to state that both bring knowledge and experiences and are able to manipulate the cognitive aspects and operative instruments.

Appraisal

This phase represents the end and the beginning of participatory action research; that is, it is the point of articulation that defines the conclusion of an action cycle and the start of a new cycle planned based on the conclusions drawn from the previous verification. It represents a central part of the program because it is conducive to verifying the participants' satisfaction, estimating the extent to which the action plan has been consistent with the initial expectations and, eventually, trying to understand why goals have not been achieved.

In this case, the group has achieved its own identity and has identified common goals and common methodological lines. Therefore, the group has proceeded to action, developing the following phase of the research.

EXECUTION OF THE ACTION RESEARCH

The project involved approximately 850 adolescents, their parents and education professionals who, in various ways, are in contact with the new generations and the emerging issues that affect them.

The project took three years and has developed based on several dimensions:

1. phase of project sharing with local stakeholders: After the development of the working group, the group itself shared the project with teachers from different schools located in the territory through explanatory and operational meetings for the implementation of the activities planned during the training phase of the working group. The project was presented to parents by teachers through brochures and specific meetings; then, the students were informed by teachers and parents.

2. Laboratory-operative phase: This phase is divided into two different moments consisting of training sessions held by the Postal and Communications Police and an association in the

territory that addresses promoting the spread of IT tools through correct literacy.

The training sessions with the Postal and Communications Police, structured in lectures on the prevention of and on combatting cybercrime, are addressed to students and, separately, parents, teachers and educators; the meetings have actively involved the operators of the group. Specifically, the subject of these lessons has been risk analysis and the promotion of safety during navigation, with particular attention to the development of greater knowledge and awareness of crimes that one might suffer in regard to certain superficial links kept in the network. Attention has been focused on promotion and awareness raising not only in boys but also in parents, helping them avoid neglecting the power of technology and the consequences of a different use thereof and overcome their resistance from not belonging to the generation of digital natives. From the beginning, the interest of the group was aimed at providing greater protection to children and the parent-child relationship in the face of this new historic challenge that they must also view as emotionally connected in this field.

The training sessions with associations were structured through practical exercises in a computer classroom and were aimed at groups of students who were selected on the basis of their expressed interest or as a result of reports by teachers in the face of critical issues experienced in the network by the adolescents themselves. The technique used in the practical exercises was created along the lines of a particular martial arts technique that corresponds to the time of concentration and attention, "zanshin", the vigilance that protects a person against any external aggression. In the cyber environment, it refers to digital aggression management to create a virtuous circle of effective behaviors and correct information on network security to be shared with one's teammates following the peer education approach. The laboratories assisted the teachers and psychologists of the group.

3. Investigation phase: This phase consisted of the collection of information through a questionnaire. The questionnaire was co-constructed by the group during the training phase in which it discussed methodologies. The choice of the questionnaire was linked to the desire to gather information on the issue, reaching the largest number of adolescents and parents to ultimately obtain a picture of the perception of the phenomenon and the use of technologies. Listening to the different actors present in the territory, the psychologists in the group proposed a first draft of the questionnaire that focused on psychosocial aspects of their competence, including items aimed at acquiring descriptive data on adolescent habits and the level of sharing their knowledge and habits with adult references both within and outside the family. Therefore, two separate questionnaires, one for adolescents and another for parents, which have common parts, were designed.
   The local University has identified and discussed in the group the psychological constructs implicated and the areas to be investigated: the technological knowledge, bullying and cyberbullying behavior, well-being, self-esteem, loneliness, perceived support, educational parenting styles, parent-child communication and the school climate. Informed consent was obtained from the families and adolescents, the group collected the data, and the University conducted the data analysis.

THE ACTION'S OUTCOMES

The project results were presented to the citizens in a final event in which all actors involved shared the implemented activities. It was a meeting in which they discussed the results, the objectives achieved and the critical issues encountered.

The meeting was divided into several stages: the interventions of the working group alternating with recreational moments organized by students who had enrolled in the musical course of the schools involved in the project.

The number of parents present was below the expectations of the working group. Moreover, the working group noted that parental attention was mainly focused on the musical presentation of the students rather than the presentation, sharing and participatory reflection of the results in the different phases of the project in which they had been involved, directly or indirectly, through the active participation of their children.

The evaluation of the project as a whole led the working group to promote the project on social networks by opening a group to continuously inform about the events organized by the group and for the sharing of informational material that would be considered useful for the adolescents and families. During the development of the project, the working group, in listening to the different actors involved, decided to organize places of listening and sharing among students led by two psychologists in the working group. Therefore, the working group has introduced workshop moments, psychologically oriented, following the requests of some students who have found the courage to ask educators to share their concerns about relationship dynamics related to bullying and cyberbullying experiences. The parents have also turned to the restricted working group of psychologists to understand the reasons that prompted their children to share their bold images on the network and to find the educational tools to intervene.

CONCLUSION

From our perspective, there is no clear line between the development phase of the working group, the execution phase of the action research and the phase outcome of the action research itself. In the recursive process that is realized, various phases are occasionally implemented for the co-construction of a knowledge that would make it possible to better develop the subsequent steps and simultaneously make it possible to consolidate the working group and also share, in addition to the methodologies, the results that simultaneously become a source of new ideas and new procedures and choices of action to be activated.

This project illustrates how PAR can be used to co-construct an intervention through collaboration among a multi-professional team composed of social workers, psychologists, educators, teachers, university-based research staff, and associations in the territory. The group initially focused on partnering and better understanding the perspective of key stakeholders in the community to focus the initial challenge to confront the issue of new technologies and the well-being of adolescents. As the partnership unfolded, the group integrated scientific methods through reflexive discussion with the community, realizing a project that was practical, effective and responsive to the needs of the adolescents and to understanding the phenomenon being studied.

All actors involved were actively engaged in the implementation of the project, the data collection, the data interpretation process and the practice recommendations. Based on PAR methods, this project is characterized by the fact that a multi-professional community team, associations in the territory, researchers and stakeholders have worked together to co-generate knowledge and the joint implementation of the findings. As stated by Lewin (1946), action research applies theory to practice and learns from the process to improve theory. Furthermore, other relevant aspects are part of participatory action research, such as the potential benefits related to the dimension of psychological empowerment (Ozer and Douglas 2016). The perceptions of control and efficacy can be enhanced by involving communities in a participatory approach.

REFERENCES

Amerio, P., De Piccoli, N. and Miglietta, A. (2000). La ricerca azione come articolazione di teoria e pratica, in Amerio P. [Action research as an articulation of theory and practice, in Amerio P.] (2000). *Psicologia di comunità*. Bologna: Il Mulino.

Denzin, N. K. and Lincolin, Y. S. (1994). *Handbook of Qualitative Research*. Thousand Oacks: Sage.

Denzin, N. K. and Lincoln, Y. S. (2000) "The discipline and practice of qualitative research", in N. K., Denzin, and Y. S. Lincoln (Eds.) *The handbook of qualitative research* (4). Thousand Oaks, CA: Sage Publications.

Floris, F. (2001). Dalla progettazione dialogica alla ricerca-azione. [From dialogical design to action research.] *Animazione Sociale*, 5, 29-34.

Foster-Fishman, P. G., Law, K. M., Lichty, L. F. et al. (2010). Youth ReACT for Social Change: a method for youth participatory action research. *Am. J. Community Psychol.,* 46: 67. doi:10.1007/s10464-010-9316-y.

Greenwood, D. D. J. and Levin, M. (1998). *Introduction to Action Research: social research for social change*. London: Sage Publications.

Kagan, C., Burton, M., Duckett, P., Lawthom, R., and Siddiquee, A. (2011). *Critical Community Psychology* (1st ed.). West Sussex, UK: Wiley-Blackwell.

Lewin, K. (1947). "Frontiers in group dynamics. I. Concept, method and reality in social science; social equilibria", *Human Relations,* vol. 1, pp. 5-40.

Lewin, K. (1935). *A dynamic theory of personality*. New York: McGra-Hill.

Lewin, K. (1946). "Action-Research and minority problems", *Journal of Social issue*, 2(4), pp. 34-46.

Migliorini, L. and Rania, N. (2017). A qualitative method to "make visible" the world of intercultural relationships: the photovoice in social psychology. *Qualitative Research in Psychology,* vol.14, n. 2, pp. 131-145 http://dx.doi.org/ 10.1080/14780887.2016.1263698.

Migliorini, L., Rania, N. and Cardinali, P. (2008). Action Research and Group Development. *Gestalt Theory. An International Multidisciplinary Journal*, vol. 30, n. 4, pp. 461-471, ISSN: 0170-057X.

Montero, M. (2011). "A Critical Look at Critical Community Psychology", *Social and Personality Psychology Compass*, vol. 5, no.12, pp. 950-959. DOI: 10.1111/j.1751-9004.2011.00403.x.

Natale, A. Di Martino, S., Procentese, F. and Arcidiacono, C. (2016). Degrowth and critical community psychology: Contributions towards individual and social well-being. *Futures,* vol. 78-79, pp. 47–56.

Ozer, E. J. and Douglas, L. (2013). The Impact of Participatory Research on Urban Teens: An Experimental Evaluation. *Am. J. Community Psychol.,* 51: 66-75 doi:10.1007/s10464-012-9546-2.

Ozer, E.J. Ritterman, M. L. and Wanis, M. G. (2010). Participatory Action Research (PAR) in Middle School: Opportunities, Constraints, and Key Processes. *Am. J. Community Psychol.,* 46:152–166. doi 10.1007/s10464-010-9335-8.

Phillips, E. N., Berg, M. J., Rodriguez, C. et al. (2010). A Case Study of Participatory Action Research in a Public New England Middle School: Empowerment, Constraints and Challenges. *Am. J. Community Psychol.,* 46: 179. doi:10.1007/s10464-010-9336-7.

Rania, N. (2017). "Studying Migration from Different Perspectives and with Different Techniques" In Nadia Rania e Laura Migliorini (ed.) *Intercultural Relations and Migration Processes.* Hauppauge NY: Nova Publisher.

Rania, N., L. Migliorini, P. Cardinali and S. Rebora. (2015). "Giving a face to immigration and integration processes: the use of Photovoice with Italian young adults". *The Qualitative Report 20*(6): 780-798. Retrieved from: http://www.nova.edu/ssss/QR/ QR20/6/ rania4.pdf.

Rania, N., L. Migliorini, S. Rebora and P. Cardinali. (2014). "Enhancing critical dialogue about intercultural integration: The Photovoice technique". *International Journal Intercultural Relations, 41:* 17-31. doi.10.1016/j.ijintrel.2014.06.006.

Rania, N., L. Migliorini, S. Rebora and P. Cardinali. (2015). "Photovoice and interpretation of pictures in a group discussion: A community psychology approach". *Qualitative Research in Psychology, 12:* 382-396. doi:10.1080/14780887.2015.1019597.

Tuckman, B. W. (1965): Developmental sequence in small groups. *Psychological Bulletin,* 63, 384-399.

ABOUT THE AUTHORS

Nadia Rania obtained her Master degree in Educational Sciences, at the University of Genoa (Italy) and then her PhD in Research Methods in Human Sciences at the University of Genoa (Italy). She is Assistant Professor in Social Psychology since 2005 at the Department of Education Sciences where she taught Social Psychology, Psychology of Groups and Community, Qualitative methods and now she teaches Methods and Techniques of Group Intervention. Furthermore, she teaches in College PhD. in Migration and Intercultural Processes, University of Genoa (Italy) from 2006 to present. She is coordinator of the PhD in Migrations and intercultural processes (XXVIII cycle).

She is the author of several articles of migration issues, her main topics of interest and research include: family relationships; gender family relationship; migration patterns and processes of acculturation; well-being and quality of life in adolescence; women, work and family; quality of life and well-being; routine and ritual in life cycle in native and migration people, intercultural processes and migrations. The scientific production includes over 50 works, including books and articles on national and international journals and she is reviewer for national and international journals.

Alessandra Brameri obtained her Master degree in Psychology at the University of Padua (Italy) and she has specialized in individual and couple Psychotherapy at the University of Genoa (Italy) in 1993 where she taught psycho-diagnostic and clinical neuropsychology at the Department of forensic medicine and work -Section medical and general psychology. Currently she deals with social psychology at social services to the family of some towns in Liguria. She carries out supervision and training in educational services and is Honorary Advisor at the Court of appeal of the

Tribunale di Genova (Italy) for the section for minors. She also work as a psychotherapist. The main topics of interest and research include: minors and the family, the couple, well-being and the quality of life in adolescence, the parent-child relationship, flimsy parenting, family custody, abuse and mistreatment, even in cyber environment, about which she wrote several publications in national journals.

Emanuela Gandolfo graduated in Psychology at the University of Padova (Italy) in 1989. She then took a master in Sexology at the University of Genoa (Italy) and specialized in Infant Observation according to the Tavistock method. In 1990 she started working at the David Chiossone Institute of Genoa, where for almost four years she followed a project on psychological distress prevention in unsighted children, inspired by Martha Harris work at the Tavistock Clinic of London, in partnership with the Italian National Research Center. In that period she collaborated with Gianna Gaslini Children's Hospital of Genoa, where she worked in several training programs for the hospital staff, in particular for the trauma resuscitation and premature birth units. She became psychotherapist and in 1996 started her own private activity, after seven years of therapy and work supervision with psychoanalysts from the Italian Psychoanalytic Society and the Italian Association of Children's Psychoanalytic Therapy. She has also worked for the public service. In 1992, in fact, she became counselor for the social services of Serra Riccò and Sant'Olcese, in Genoa province, where she still is in charge of children and teenagers distress prevention, with a particular focus on school and family assistance. During the nineties she also started her collaboration with the Civil and Juvenile Court of Genoa, where she still works as official counselor. She worked as psychology trainer for the Ministry of Justice and for many schools and social cooperatives, offering specific education to training staff of large consortiums. Along her professional career she has worked as counselor for many legal firms, contributing to the solutions of some nationally relevant cases: she was once appointed technical counselor by the Belarus ambassador to assist in a delicate matter involving a Belarusian minor. She also teaches at the course in forensic psychology at the University of Genoa.

Laura Migliorini obtained her PhD in Methodology of Research in Psychology on 1997. She was visiting graduate student, supervised by Prof. Barry Schneider, at The Ontario Institute for Studies in Education, Department of Applied Psychology, University of Toronto, Canada.. She is Researcher at the University of Genoa (Italy), Faculty of Educational Sciences, in Social Psychology since 1999. Associated Professor in Social Psychology at the University of Genoa since 2006, where she teaches Community Psychology Method and Technique and Family Relation Psychology. She is Member of the Professor Team relevant to PhD Cultural Migration. Prof. Laura Migliorini was responsible of several national and international founded research projects in the area of well-being and migration issue. She has published more than one seventy scientific papers, appeared in peer-reviewed journals, either international or national ones and four books. Her research interests are in the fields of social environmental psychology, community and intercultural psychology, acculturation and migration processes, family psychology, qualitative methods. She is a reviewer for national and international journals. She organized and was scientific member of national and international congress.

In: (Participatory) Action Research   ISBN: 978-1-53613-041-6
Editors: J. Calder and J. Foletta   © 2018 Nova Science Publishers, Inc.

Chapter 10

THE APPLICATION OF PARTICIPATORY ACTION RESEARCH TO ENHANCE THE HEALTH CARE OF THE WOOD-CARVING COMMUNITY

Susanha Yimyam[1,*] *and Avorn Opatpatanakit*[2]

[1]Head of Excellent Center in Nursing, Chiang Mai University (CMU),
Faculty of Nursing, Chiang Mai University, Chiang Mai, Thailand
[2]Vice President for Societal Engagement, Chiang Mai University
(CMU), Office of Societal Engagement at CMU, Chiang Mai, Thailand

ABSTRACT

The Khun-Kong community is famous for its woodcarving production, which contributes significantly to the local economy.

---

* Corresponding Author: Professor Dr. Susanha Yimyam, Faculty of Nursing, Chiang Mai University 110/406 Intrawarorose Street, Sriphum Sub-district, Meaung district, Chiang Mai, 50200 THAILAND, Phone: 66-089-7586796, Email: syimyam@gmail.com.

However, the work conditions and environment may be harmful and detrimental to the workers' health. This developmental research study, *'Enhancing the Health of the Wood-Carving Community,'* used community collaboration to engage with various sectors and groups. Action research is considered one of the most important strategies in confronting health problems and promoting community health. The purpose of this study was to build the self-care capacity among wood-carving workers and their community. The study was divided into two phases: a community and health impact assessment phase; and an implementation phase. Both qualitative and quantitative methods were used in *Phase One (community and health impact assessment)* to investigate the work conditions and the environments that may impact the health of wood-carving workers and their community. Community-based participatory research was used in *Phase Two (community implementation phase)* to develop a network of woodcarving workers to promote self-care, to enhance the capability for self-care among peer leaders of wood-carving workers, as well as to develop a self-care guidebook and media tools for a health promotion campaign.

This chapter focuses on *Phase Two* to draw linkages between the principles, approaches and applications of community-based participatory action research through this case study on health promotion among wood-carving workers. Participatory learning was used for peer leader training. Community participation aided the development a self-care network for a health promotion campaign as well as a self-care guidebook and media materials. The self-care network consisted of the research team, a community committee, and trained peer leaders. Quantitative data were analyzed using frequency, percentage and a t-test, whereas qualitative data were analyzed using content analysis. During *Phase Two* one guidebook and three types of media instruments, namely posters, VCD, and radio spots, were developed. These materials were examined by a group of workers for appropriateness for both content and presentation and were found to be satisfactory. After receiving training, peer leaders' knowledge and awareness of work-related health problems and preventive self-care increased significantly. Their skills and confidence in risk assessment and self-care instruction also improved. The self-care network identified new ways of thinking, problem solving, and sustainable self-care. Self-reliance was perceived as an important aspect of health care. Finally, workers' health status, perception of health risk and health behaviors also improved. In the community, skills in problem identification and problem solving were learned. Although this project was successful in increasing health awareness of the workers and the community, the long-term impact and sustainability of networking and activities need to be examined. Furthermore, co-operation with other relevant institutions or professions are suggested to produce and use the guidebook and media materials with other woodcarving workers to improve work conditions and the environment.

Keywords: self-care, wood-carving workers, participatory action research, community-based participatory research.

INTRODUCTION: UTILIZING PARTICIPATORY ACTION RESEARCH TO IMPROVE HEALTH CARE

The definition of participatory action research (PAR) will be discussed. This includes the concepts, principles, overall process of PAR, and its application, especially in the community development domain to create social actions. The application of community-based participatory research (CBPR) as an approach to public health is also highlighted.

Concepts and Principles of PAR

Historically, PAR developed through a need for an alternative research methodology to promote social action; Kurt-Lewin has described action research as *"a comparative research on the conditions and effects of various forms of social action and research leading to social action"* (Lewin, 1946, p. 203). The underlying concept of PAR is to empower the oppressed (Freire, 1970) or subordinates (Fals Borda, 1979; 1988) by creating social action (Lewin, 1946). The critical perspectives proposed by these prominent thinkers reflect the need for disadvantaged stakeholders to equally participate in social change processes.

During the past five decades, PAR has been recognized as a research methodology that encompasses empowerment, people-centered development, civic engagement, and sustainable development, (Cohen & Uphoff, 1979; International Bank for Reconstruction and Development [IBRD], 1980; Korten & Klauss, 1984; Oakley, 1987; Turton, 1987;

Korten, 1990; Chevalier & Buckles, 2013), critical education (Carr & Kemmis, 1986; Kemmis & McTaggart, 2000, McNiff, 2010), self-reflection and evaluation (Elliott, 1981; McKernan, 1996), organizational development (White, 1992), feminism and gender (Maguire, 2008), and public health (De Koning & Martin, 1996; Eisenberg, Baglia & Pynes, 2006; Hills, Mullett & Carroll, 2007; Minkler & Wallerstein, 2008; George, Vickers, Wilkes, & Barton, 2006).

These formulations of PAR have in common the principle that research, action, and reflection need to be done by the people, not on or for the people. This paper focuses on the development sphere, thus PAR is referred to as a research methodology that emphasizes collective inquiry, participatory action, and critical reflection.

The community development sphere usually involves three key stakeholders: academics; development agents, such as public organizations, non-governmental organizations (NGOs), or the private sector; and community members. Thus, PAR is referred to as a collective inquiry based on a systematic approach to participatory investigation through which academics normally have experiences in beginning with the problem statement, research questions, and data collection. The most important thing is that the research questions come through the identification of problems by the community and other stakeholders who are concerned with community issues.

Community members, who become community researchers, are encouraged to identify actions through the cultivation of a mindset encompassing *"think before you act"* and *"practical actions"*. Under this premise, all actions must be designed within the participatory approach and based on collected data in accordance with the research questions. This way of thinking becomes a core PAR principle in the development sphere. As such, PAR is a powerful research methodology due to the multifaceted expertise and contributions by academics, development agencies, and community researchers.

What differentiates PAR from mainstream research is the participation of key stakeholders in the decision-making process as part of the core research team, which results in participatory actions being done in a collective manner. Accordingly, a series of participatory actions throughout the overall process could enable stakeholders to find effective solutions to solve problems, for social action and social justice. This collective inquiry and the "*think before you act*" and "*practical action*" worldview are key components that help create a successful project.

Overall Process of PAR

PAR is a cycle that includes a spiral progression of steps, each of which is composed of overlapping processes of planning, action, observation and reflection. This results in fact-finding, evaluating the results of actions taken, and learning outcomes. The overall PAR process includes: 1) formation of a core research team; 2) identification of research questions; 3) development of a research design for an appropriate action plan based on information gained from collecting data; 4) building a common understanding between the core research team and stakeholders; 5) management and re-planning; 6) utilization of situated practical knowledge derived from the critical reflection of the core research team and stakeholders; 7) evaluation of output, outcome and impact; and, 8) reflection of lessons learned. This process is depicted in Figure 1.

Throughout the research process, the core research team engages in planning, action, observation and reflection at every stage of the cycle. As a result, PAR empowers the core research team and increases their participation in the decision-making process of community development. At its heart, PAR is participatory, collective, and a self-reflective inquiry of core researchers and stakeholders whose undertaking could allow a deeper understanding and improvement upon the practices in which they participate and the situations in which they find themselves. In this regard, PAR helps to increase understanding, engagement, and empowerment of the core research team as change agents who could facilitate other stakeholders.

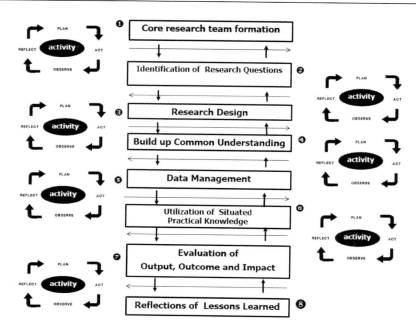

Figure 1. Participatory Action Research Process.

Definition and Concepts of Community-Based Participatory Research (CBPR)

To better understand the complicated health impacts and implementation of community health initiatives, it is a necessary to develop health care campaigns and provisions that are more *participatory* and that respond more holistically to the complexity of the needs which people may experience. Community-based participatory research is based on these concepts and the principles of participatory action research. As a result, CBPR is a process that can assist in achieving the goals of community health care.

CBPR integrates education and social action to improve health and reduce health disparities. CBPR is an approach to research that focuses on relationships between academic and community partners, with principles of co-learning, mutual benefits, and long-term commitment and incorporates community theories, participation, and practices into the research efforts (Wallerstein & Duran, 2006). As an approach to research for community empowerment, CBPR emphasizes participation and action as a means of better understanding the context so as to identify meaningful changes that will improve the community. Reason and Bradbury describe CBPR as "*communities of inquiry and action evolve and address questions and issues that are significant for those who participate as co-researchers*" (Reason & Bradbury, 2008, p. 1). Throughout the CBPR process, researchers or practitioners can make a concrete effort to integrate three basic aspects of societal engagement: participation (life in society and health care), action (engagement with local experience and wisdom), and research (soundness in thought and the growth of situated practical knowledge) (adapted from Chevalier & Buckles, 2013).

For health care service, the community typically includes the clients and target groups of service delivery. Health care service should maximize the benefits to vulnerable individuals, groups and communities targeted by the intervention. CBPR conceptualizes the participation of persons/populations affected by the problem and other target groups of intervention as important for philosophical reasons (respect, voice, rights), to ensure that the most responsive strategies are developed and to achieve the best possible outcomes.

Furthermore, CBPR in the health care context is practical. There are a variety of factors that contribute to a particular health problem, such as sexual and reproductive health, occupational health, women's health, etc. Responding in a way that improves the situation of health care service users often requires support or change from a variety of health agencies. The involvement of a diversity of stakeholders who may have a wide range of values, institutional locations, and organizational interests, means that CBPR in health services will need to have a practical as well as inclusive character.

In CBPR projects, the core research team from the community fully participates in all aspects of the research process such as identifying the problems, research gaps, and research questions; collecting data; designing the action plan, implementation, and critical reflection for re-planning and follow-up actions; and, evaluating the outcome and impacts. Community can be defined as a geographic community, a community of individuals with a common problem or issue, or a community of individuals with a common interest or goal. CBPR encourages the collaboration of community members and outside facilitators and partners from any area of expertise. All groups involved should be fully committed to a partnership of equals and produce outcomes usable to the community (Edwards, Lund, Mitchell, & Andersson, 2008).

APPLICATION OF PARTICIPATORY ACTION RESEARCH TO IMPROVE HEALTH

Background

Wood-carving is different from other types of sculptures as its core method involves removal of material to create a desired shape and design. Wood-carving expresses the beauty and neatness of the Thai culture. Wood-carving has strong cultural significance and was named one of the ten most important crafts in Thailand and is one of many protected occupations under Thai law. Wood-carving is a rural art form generally seen in the Northern Thailand. Sculptures include local animals such as elephants to represent their home environment. The art of wood carving has been passed down from generation to generation and the Thais' skill and artistry can be seen throughout history: Buddha images, graceful temple doors, church buildings, neatly carved fruit, with some works being displayed at the National Museum (Yimyam, Tiansawad, Wittayasakphan, & Jirapattarapimol, 2004; Yimyam & Jirapattarapimol, 2007).

Wood-carving involves five steps: designing the pattern, selecting the wood, copying the pattern onto the wood, carving, and decorating. There are two types of wood decoration. The first focuses on the wood texture. Since the natural texture of the wood is so beautiful, carvers use gouges to reflect the various textures of the different woods. Varnish rather than paint is used to showcase the wood grain, and is polished with a soft cloth so that the wax can seep into the wood. The second focuses on the overall composition of the wood pieces, the pattern, and decorative materials such as cut glass, leather, rope, cloth, among others. Painting may also be used. Woodwork also includes the replication of ancient pieces using antiquing methods. Examples include Buddha images, dancing puppets, angels, giants, and others. Since wood-carving has become very popular, wood carvers must buy wood for their work which makes the price more expensive (Yimyam, Tiansawad, Wittayasakphan, & Jirapattarapimol, 2004; Yimyam & Jirapattarapimol, 2007).

Wood-carving is one of the most popular types of informal work, especially in the Khun-Kong community in Northern Thailand, which is famous for its production. Almost all of the people in this community work in wood-carving and they are known for producing antiqued teak pieces. This community has been supported by the Thai government's *One Tambon One Product [OTOP]* and *tourist village* programs. Khun-Kong has received both national and international recognition for its rapid economic growth. This attention and the economic contribution of woodcarving communities highlighted the importance of protecting the health and well-being of the woodcarvers and their community (Yimyam, Tiansawad, Wittayasakphan, & Jirapattarapimol, 2004; Yimyam & Jirapattarapimol, 2007).

Phase One was a situational analysis of the community. A health impact assessment examined work conditions, health status, and self-care among 202 woodcarving workers (both male and female). We discovered that during the woodcarving process, most males were involved in the carving or made wooden figures, while most females did the decorating and assembling. Many workers were aware of the risk factors and health problems associated with their work, particularly from adopting poor physical positions for long periods of time, contact with dust and chemicals, and physical risks from working with machines. The most frequently reported conditions were physical aches and pains, especially backaches (77%). This was followed by respiratory diseases, such as asthma (21%), gastric ulcers (19%), poor eye health and eyesight (18%), skin problems (14%), and accidents (7%). If the condition was considered minor, workers treated them through self-medication. With serious illnesses that were beyond their ability to manage, workers would primarily go to health stations followed by private clinics. Most workers were satisfied with the quality and standard of services. They also believed that both private and governmental health providers offered more or less similar services. However, workers needed additional health services. They identified a need for medical treatment, followed by health promotion and advice. Every worker was enrolled in the national universal healthcare scheme and was generally satisfied with services received. Two-thirds of the workers were able to claim benefits through the national health coverage, though those seeking care at private clinics were responsible for their own medical bills (Yimyam, Tiansawad, Wittayasakphan, & Jirapattarapimol, 2004).

Communication of health information was mostly done via village loudspeakers and through personal communication with health officials, village health volunteers, and community leaders. Health care in these communities has been conducted through network coordination. Health officials and health volunteers play leading roles in setting up health clubs and funds. However, none of these clubs deal directly with health care for woodcarving workers. Entrepreneurs have set up a Ban Tawai wood carving handicraft group and members include shop owners from the Song Fang Khlong Handicraft Center. While the group mainly focuses on marketing, there is also emphasis on self-care and they sponsor group activities like exercising. Unfortunately, self-care activities are not held regularly. Many workers integrated self-care into their lifestyles; they are concerned about having balanced meals, recreation, sleep, social contacts, acquiring health services, and avoiding addictive substances (Yimyam, Tiansawad, Wittayasakphan, & Jirapattarapimol, 2004).

Representatives from two villages in the project area joined a community forum to learn about workplace protections. Though they were familiar with the many ways to protect their health, they seldom practiced these behaviors, especially the wearing of protective devices. There were many factors involved in this decision, such as inconvenience. It is possible that they did not perceive serious health risks at work and were not aware of potential fatalities or disability that could result from their work (reducing compliance/participation in self-protective care). The following suggestions from the community forum were identified: 1) set up a working group responsible for campaigning for the care of and solutions to health problems at work; 2) develop protective devices suitable with the work style that were convenient to use; 3) encourage entrepreneurs to persuade workers to use the protective devices; 4) campaign and distribute self-care information via village loudspeakers; 5) put up signs and billboards in community centers to provide self-care information; and, 6) develop and distribute posters about self-care at work to be put up in work places. From the forum and meetings, researchers concluded that the primary guidelines in self-care enhancement among woodcarving workers should be as follows: 1) campaigning to raise awareness among workers regarding health problems and self-care importance; 2) encouragement in the setting up of working groups responsible for the planning and campaigning for continual care and solutions to health problems; 3) emphasizing collaboration between workers and entrepreneurs; 4) encouragement of entrepreneurs' role in the provision of environment viable for workers' self-care; 5) identification of a workplace model; 6) equipping of health officials and village health volunteers with the necessary knowledge to enable them to provide advice and support for self-care among workers; 7) development of more effective, convenient, and easy to use protective devices; and 8) campaign and distribution of self-care information through village loudspeaker (Yimyam, Tiansawad, Wittayasakphan, & Jirapattarapimol, 2004).

The research team was composed of academic staff, health providers, community leaders, and relevant leaders from the government office (GO) and non-government organizations (NGOs). With our different disciplinary, professional and academic issues in health care and social welfare, and mass communication, a model for enhancing the health care of the woodcarving community was developed in the *Phase Two* of implementation stage. The model was based on the results and recommendations from *Phase One*. The implementation phase was carried out by focusing on the community participation action research approach, a main strategy for conducting all the activities, to improve the health of the wood-carving workers and their community (Yimyam, & Tiansawad, & Senaratana, 2008). The activities were designed as a response to the results of the combined qualitative and quantitative study on work conditions, health status and self-care behaviors of wood-carving workers and the community forum in *Phase One* (Yimyam, Tiansawad, & Senaratana, 2006; Yimyam, Tiansawad, & Senaratana, 2008).

Using Community Participatory Action Research

In the implementation phase, PAR was conducted to build capacity for self-care among wood-carving workers and the people of the Khun Kong community, Hang Dong, Chiang Mai, Thailand.

Conceptual Framework for Implementation Phase of this Project

A conceptual framework for the implementation phase of the project is presented in *Figure 2*. The project consisted of three steps including: 1) preparation, 2) implementation, and 3) evaluation and summary of lessons learned. During preparation, participatory action research was used for two main strategies: 1) developing a network of woodcarving workers for self-care and 2) developing a guidebook for self-care and media for a health promotion campaign for woodcarving workers. During implementation, the researchers, with cooperation from the health promotion committees, developed strategies for enhancing the health promotion capabilities of peer leaders. The research team (researchers, health promotion committee and peer leaders) implemented the health promotion campaigns. These activities included: 1) risk assessment and instruction of workers on self-care; 2) motto contest for use in the health promotion campaigns; 3) dissemination of health information through the local radio broadcast; 4) health promotion campaigns; 5) development of a healthy workplace; 6) dissemination of health information; 7) a poster contest among students in Bann Ton Keaw school; 8) a physical exercise contest among students in Bann Ton Keaw school; and, 9) a bicycling promotion campaign (Yimyam, Tiansawad, & Senaratana, 2006; Yimyam, Tiansawad, & Senaratana, 2008).

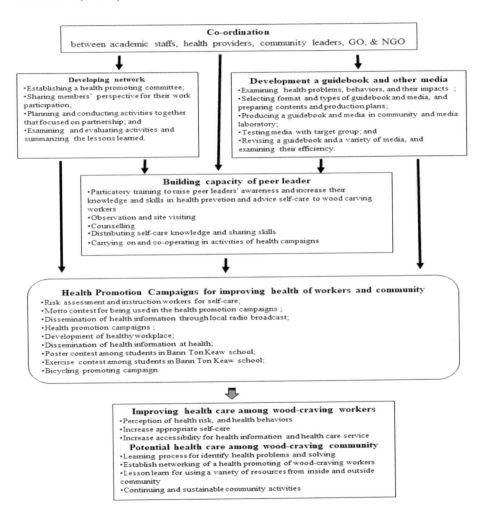

Figure 2. Conceptual framework for enhancing health care of woodcarving community.

In each activity, participatory evaluation was conducted by observation of working behaviors and interviews with 211 woodcarving workers and two focus group discussions with 39 health promotion committee members. An additional focus group discussion was done with 30 peer leaders. Finally, in the evaluation and summary of the lessons learned, the ultimate outcomes included workers' health status, perceptions of health risk, and health behaviors as well as potential community health care among this community. In the implementation step, the researchers with cooperation from the health promotion committees, developed another strategy for the enhancing capability of peer leaders in the health care of the wood-carving workers.

Preparation

Developing a Worker Network

Several strategies were used to develop a network including (Yimyam, Tiansawad, & Senaratana, 2006; Yimyam, Tiansawad, & Senaratana, 2008):

1. Establishment of a health promotion committee. Selection criteria for the health promotion committee was developed based on recommendations from the community forum in *Phase One (community and health impact assessment)* and included representatives from a variety of groups in each village. As a result there were two health promotion committees from two woodcarving villages. After two meetings between researchers and the committees, functional roles and responsibilities, management and process for evaluation their activities were identified.
2. Sharing members' perspective for their work participation. Throughout the project, monthly meetings were conducted for planning, reflection, joint observation and the evaluation of health promotion activities of the project.

3. Conducting activities that focused on partnership. After each meeting, activities were assigned to people responsible for the implementation and process of management as well as criteria of the evaluation process.
4. Examining and evaluating the activities and summarizing the lessons learned.

Developing a Guidebook and Other Media

The development of media health promotion materials and a guidebook for self-care also involved community participation. This process consisted of: 1) the examination of health problems and behaviors, the social and cultural context of the community, and communication channels within the community; 2) selection of the format and types of guidebook and media materials as well as the preparation of the content and production plans; 3) production of guidebook and media materials in the community and a media laboratory; 4) testing and examination of the effectiveness of the media materials with a target group; and, 5) revision of the guidebook and a variety of media materials (Yimyam, Tiansawad, & Senaratana, 2006; Yimyam, Tiansawad, & Senaratana, 2008):

The content for the guidebook was based on literature reviews and findings in *Phase One*. This consisted of three parts: 1) working conditions, health behaviors and impact assessment; 2) physical examination and job analysis for safety; and 3) explanations and suggestions for self-care.

A variety of informational and educational materials in this project were developed with the cooperation of the faculty, staff, and students of the Faculty of Nursing and Faculty of Mass Communication at Chiang Mai University as well as local health care providers and health promotion committees. These included (Yimyam, Tiansawad, & Senaratana, 2006; Yimyam, Tiansawad, & Senaratana, 2008):

1. Two posters designed to demonstrate proper working postures and stretching exercises.

2. A VCD designed to present information about work-related health problems and prevention.

3. Radio spot announcements, total of six short dialogs entitled: *1) Risk Behaviors at Work; 2) Responsibility to the Community; 3) Suggestions for Health Care; 4) Self-Care Before It's Too Late; 5) How to Care for your Beloved; and, 6) Using a "Green Brand" Process for Production.*

4. Dissemination of health information through local radio broadcasts. Peer leaders talked about health problems and self-care behaviors via local broadcasts. Each broadcast lasted about five minutes. A total of 45 broadcasts were made.

Implementation Steps

Building Capacity of Peer Leaders

In order to build the capacity of peer leaders, participatory learning/training was used to raise peer leaders' awareness and increase their knowledge and skills in prevention of work-related health problems, risk assessment, and advice for self-care to wood-carving workers. Quota sampling was used to recruit 30 participants from local community health care volunteers, youth, and school students in the community. Teaching methods included lecture, case studies, reflection, group discussion, role-playing, practice of risk assessment, the use of protective equipment, and field practice of risk assessment and instruction for self-care with wood-carving workers. Pretest and posttests (immediately and three months later) of knowledge were compared. Observations and focus group discussions were employed during and after the workshop for evaluation of their attitude and skills (Yimyam, Tiansawad, & Senaratana, 2006; Yimyam, Tiansawad, & Senaratana, 2008).

Developing Health Promotion Campaign Activities

The research team (researchers, health promotion committee and peer leaders) launched health promotion campaign activities and activities for improving the health of workers and the community. These activities included: 1) risk assessment and self-care instructions for workers, 2) motto contest for use in the health promotion campaigns, 3) dissemination of health information through local radio broadcasts, 4) health promotion campaigns, 5) development of a healthy workplace, 6) dissemination of health information at health, 7) poster contest for students at the Bann Ton Keaw School, 8) physical exercise contest among students at the Bann Ton Keaw School, and, 9) a bicycling promoting campaign (Yimyam, Tiansawad, & Senaratana, 2006; Yimyam, Tiansawad, & Senaratana, 2008).

Evaluation

This step involved data collection for project evaluation, a community forum to present a summary of the project, and transformational lessons learned from this project (Yimyam, Tiansawad, & Senaratana, 2006; Yimyam, Tiansawad, & Senaratana, 2008).

Data Collection for Project Evaluation

In each activity, participatory evaluation was conducted through observation of work behaviors and through interviews with 211 wood-carving workers about health protection behaviors. Two focus group discussions with 39 health promotion committees, one focus group discussion with 30 peer leaders as well as in-depth interviews with local health providers were held. Participants were asked about the health risks and health problems of wood-carving workers and their community, and accessibility to informational health and health care service.

Community Forum

A community forum presented a summary of the project outcomes and transformational lessons learned. One hundred forty-eight participants attended the forum including the research team, woodcarving worker representatives, stakeholders (particularly woodcarving entrepreneurs), both formal and informal community leaders such as representatives from local administrative organizations, teachers and students, youths, housewives and the elderly, community health care volunteers, health personnel, and relevant members from GO and NGOs. The aims of this forum were to present the initial results of the project for participants to confirm and clarify data as well as to discuss lessons learned from a variety of participant perspectives. The discussion also involved lessons learned from the process of community participatory action research for solving other problems of the community and application of the methods and media from this project in order to extend to other woodcarving villages.

Finally, the results of the final outcomes including workers' health status, perception of health risk, and health behaviors as well as potential community for health care were evaluated and analyzed. Qualitative data were analyzed using a content analysis whereas quantitative data were analyzed using descriptive statistics, a t-test and Chi-square (Yimyam, Tiansawad, & Senaratana, 2006; Yimyam, Tiansawad, & Senaratana, 2008).

RESULTS AND DISCUSSION

The ultimate outcomes of this project were the improvement of health care among woodcarving workers and potential health care among the woodcarving community.

IMPROVING HEALTH CARE AMONG WOOD-CARVING WORKERS

The direct ultimate outcome of this project was the improvement of health care among wood-carving workers including the health status and health behaviors, perception of health risk and health behaviors; increased appropriate self-care; and, increased accessibility for health information and health care service.

Health Status and Health Behaviors

It was hard to determine improvement in health outcomes due to the short two-year project time span (one year for health impact assessment and another year for implementation). Moreover, data were not always collected from the same participants (about 70% overlap). Due to the timescale of the project, some workers had changed their jobs and/or moved to other villages or provinces. However, the findings revealed that comparison between their health status and health behaviors prior to and after implementation suggested a trend of improvement in health behaviors as shown in *Table 1*

**Table 1. Health status and illness of the samples
before and after implementation**

Health status and illness	Before implementation (n = 202)		After implementation (n = 211)	
	n	**%**	**n**	**%**
Healthy	**54**	**26.7**	**58**	**27.8**
Some illness	**148**	**73.3**	**153**	**72.5**
• Backache	142	70.3	134	63.5
• Upper Respiratory Infection, Asthma	44	21.8	36	17.1
• Gastric ulcer	30	14.9	24	11.8
• Eyes and eyesight problems	26	12.9	23	10.3
• Skin problems	20	9.9	16	7.6
• Accidents	13	6.4	16	7.6

These findings correspond with the comparison data on the health report from Khun Kung Health Station between the year before and after implementation of this project in *Table 2*.

This is consistent with data from health personnel of the Khun Kong Health station, who was also one of the members of the health promotion committee. The reports revealed that all top five illnesses dropped, which included every body system (Yimyam, Tiansawad, & Senaratana, 2006; Yimyam, Tiansawad, & Senaratana, 2008).

Table 2. A comparison of the five top illnesses in Khun Kong in the year before and after implementation

No.	Abnormal/diseases of body systems	Before implementation (N_1 = 4,942)		After implementation (N_2 = 4,829)	
		n	Cases per 1000	n	Cases per 1000
1	Respiratory system	2,297	464.79	1,804	373.58
2	Circulatory system	1,161	234.93	1,106	229.03
3	Muscular and skeletal system	1,000	202.35	972	201.28
4	Endocrine glands and Metabolism	919	185.96	791	163.80
5	Digestive system	906	183.33	661	136.88

Source: Annual health reports of Khun Kong Health station in years 2004 and 2005

Perception of Health Risk

One participant provided additional information that:

"Today's people know that there are many health risks from their wood-carving work such as accidents, dust, and chemicals during painting or the paint removal process... So, they have to have self-care in terms of prevention and care of their own health."

Improvement of Health Behaviors

The workers should improve their protective and preventive behaviors including using the correct body postures at work, utilization of health protective equipment/tools during working, adjusting work conditions as well as rearranging for a healthy workplace. These may help to decrease health risks and risky behaviors. Their health behaviors changed in positive ways. A peer leader told us that:

"... Nowadays, the woodcarver works better and in a correct manner during work... For example, my mum does wood decorating. In the past, she stayed in the same posture through her working day, and did not change her position while working. She complained a lot about backache. Later, she started changing her posture while working. Her back pain got better. She does not get it as not so often as before. . ."

A youth described that:

"... Most workers seldom use their mask while they are working. They would use it only when painting gold. After participating in the health campaign, they are more aware of the health risks from dust and chemical hazards; therefore, they tend to wear the mask while working, particularly during the process of decorating and gold painting. This resulted in better health, improved respiratory symptoms and asthma symptoms which are gone, now she seldom goes to see the doctor."

Increase Appropriate Self-Care

The data from the group discussion among the health promotion committee confirmed that after implementation, wood-carving workers were healthier than before and were eager and interested in taking care of their health. A committee member said:

"In my opinion, this project could help the wood-carvers to learn about self-care practices to use while working and in life in order to have better health"

Increase of Accessibility to Health Information and Care Services

To increase accessibility of health information and care services, the guidebook and three types of media materials were developed for a health promotion campaign including posters, a VCD, and radio spots. After production, the guidebook and media materials were reviewed by a group of wood-carving workers. The overall response was that they found the content and presentation of the media materials satisfactory.

A Guidebook for Self-Care

The guidebook content included health status and risk assessment and instructions for self-care.

Posters

Two posters were designed to demonstrate proper working postures and stretching exercises.

VCD for Health Promotion Campaign

A "taking care of your health" VCD was designed to present information about work-related health problems and prevention. The VCD was a short documentary with health information and knowledge about health risks and problems relevant to the working process; self-care and health protection/prevention from accidents or chemicals; correct posture; and exercises for stretching the body during work. This VCD was shown at a local health promotion station in the waiting room. The workers appeared to find the video fascinating as the issues were relevant to their situation and health concerns. Moreover, the actors and actresses featured in the VCD were their fellow wood-carving workers. One of the workers said:

> "It is interesting since it is about the health problems from our daily work life. If we learned this and follow the suggestions from the VCDs, it would be easy for us to prevent them".

Spot Announcements

Radio spot announcements included six short dialogs entitled: 1) *Risk Behaviors During Work*; 2) *Responsibility to the Community*; 3) *Suggestions for Health Care*; 4) *Self-Care Before It's Too Late*; 5) *How to Care for your Beloved*; and, 6) *Using a "Green Brand" Process for Production.*

Health Articles for Presentations via Local Community Radio

The researchers and the local community radio committee selected health promotion articles from various sources. There were 37 topics including physical, mental, social, and spiritual health issues. In total, 45 sessions were presented through local community radio to promote self-care in the community; each session lasted 5 minutes. The contents were adjusted for format and style and written in lay language. In addition, the sessions were designed to motivate the audience to participate by sharing their comments and suggestions via phone. This included articles on leading a healthier lifestyle through eating, exercise, and relaxation, as well as answering questions relevant to health issues. The health article presentations were appreciated and very popular. A peer worker radio DJ (disc jockey) explained that:

> "Previously, presentations via local community radio used to be about general issues, but nowadays I include self-care at work via announcements and spots that we learned from the project. The response from the audience is very good; people phoned to ask for more information about these issues. I think people are now aware and are taking responsibility for their health".

POTENTIAL HEALTH CARE AMONG WOOD-CARVING COMMUNITY

The indirect ultimate outcome of this project was the potential to improve health care among the wood-carving community including learning the process for identifying and solving health problems, building a network of health promoting wood-carving workers, developing peer leaders to encourage self-care among workers, and determining lessons learned from using a variety of resources from inside and outside the community. Additionally, they wanted to build continuing and sustainable community activities.

Learning Process for Community Health Assessment and Identifying Problems and Solving

Through community-based participatory action research, people in the community were involved at an early phase of the project. Along with the research team, they learned how to assess community health, find out about health risks, and identify health problems. After the project, they gained confidence to develop their own activities for community health promotion. A local village leader said:

"Though participating in this project, I had the chance to survey wood-carving workers in my community. So, I learned that our workers have a lot of health risks and problems. I also learned and gained a better understanding of how to improve our health. . . I think it is a very good project and should be continued and I will make this part of the action plan for the community".

The community network also recognized the importance of environmental and health issues; this began a social movement among people in this community. In the future, they plan to contact the Tourism Authority of Thailand (TAT) to request funding to support projects in community health, waste product management (problem-solving garbage), and landscape improvement of shopping centers in the community.

Lessons Learned about Teamwork among Multi-Sectors/ Multi-Organizations

There were several people from different organizations and sectors involved in this project. They reported that they learned how to improve their routine work. As the director of Khun Kong Health Promotion Station said:

"... Most people from this community were wood-carvers. Therefore, health risks and problems relevant to their work were the most common concern. This project was very practical and useful. Its benefits were not only for wood-carvers, but also for all people in our community. As health care providers we learned about occupational health; however, we have also learned many techniques and processes for problem solving such as how to effectively set up a community health network, build the capacity of peers as well as health campaigns. Furthermore, this project is flexible and allows us to integrate health with our duties and responsibilities. It helps in terms of networking and building the capacity of peer leaders in a variety of groups in our community".

Participation in Self-Care Health Campaign Activities

The results found that the health care for wood carvers was formed through the two village committees for health promotion among woodcarvers. These committees were comprised of woodcarving workers, entrepreneurs, community leaders, community health care volunteers, health personnel, representatives from local administrative organizations, teachers and students, youth, housewives, and the elderly. The committees were responsible for planning and conducting health campaigns to solve work-related health problems and the promotion of workers' health and community health. They set up several activities for health promotion campaigns at the workplace, school, and health care facilities. Each activity was successful at meeting its goals, and every committee cooperated and participated in the activities. They reported that they learned how to work together as a team. As one village headman said:

"As a member of the village health promotion committee, I learned how to develop a health campaign. It is very good and benefits the health of people in our community. I think we would continue and expand to other villages. Health should be the responsibility of everyone not only health personnel. You cannot buy your health but you could live a healthy life".

Health Promotion in the Local School

Director of Ton-Keaw school told about his experience with the project:

> "At first glance, based on the project title, I did not think the project was relevant to our school. Health issues should be the business of health personnel. After I was invited to be a member of the health promotion committee, I learned a lot. We integrated information from the project into our teaching about school health. By participating in this project, the teachers and students engaged in some activities about health concerns and health campaigns in terms of self-care for themselves as well as community health. Finally, our school was recognized as a gold-level health promotion school."

Lesson Learned for Using a Variety of Resources

Through reflection in community forums, participants learned how to plan and solve problems in the community together as a team by using several resources from both outside and inside their community.

Health information and knowledge could be widely distributed and transferred through local broadcast radio and local broadcast towers as well as through peer leaders who were trained in self-care related to health risks and health problems in their community. They could be enabled to become exchange people in health issues in terms of knowledge and skill. A peer leader who was a volunteer DJ explained how he applied his knowledge as a DJ:

> "…After the training program, I had a better understanding of how media is important for health information and health campaigns. As a peer leader, I brought my health knowledge and communication skill into my responsibility as a DJ. I have some sessions to talk about our health relevant to our daily work. At first, it was boring, however some audience members phoned in to discuss these issues since it interests them and concerns the community. I also do spot announcements for this project. In

my opinion, it is a very good idea to bring health knowledge into spot announcements because it focuses on important knowledge and presents it in a more relaxed way and allows it to be integrated into the daily lives of our communities".

Continuing and Sustainable Community Activities

All activities were interesting to participants. They suggested continuing these health campaigns. Representatives from the workplace, local health care facilities and the local government planned to include some activities in the community action plans. In addition, network members and researchers have learned lessons that allowed them to adjust their perspectives. This included the process of systematic community problem-solving and sustainable self-reliance, and mutually beneficial team work with multi-disciplinary and multi-sectors/organizations through sharing their knowledge and learning together as well as understanding and consideration of the potential of each member of the network. These are essential for development and the sustainability of the network.

To continue sustainable self-care among woodcarvers and to ensure community health, issues on occupational health and self-care for wood-carving workers are included in the yearly plan of the local administrative organizations and health stations.

Potential Peer Leaders to Encourage Self-Care among Workers

After the participatory learning workshop, peer leaders' knowledge and awareness of health problems and self-care to prevent work-related health problems increased significantly at a level of .05. Their skills and confidence for risk assessment and instruction for self-care also improved. They joined the networking committee in several health promotion activities. Furthermore, some peer leaders applied their knowledge and experiences from training and site visits to solve the health risks and problems in their everyday working life.

As one of them said,

> "At present, I discussed with my sister a plan to set up a small room for collecting dust that will connect to the carving room. This room will have an industrial mist fan to suck up the dust on the floor. Then, it will be easy to clean the room."

Moreover, some of them could create new innovations based on local wisdom such as making a face shield from old plastic to prevent pieces of wood from flying into their face during carving.

CONCLUSION

This project showed that community-based participatory research was an excellent method for successfully enhancing health care in the woodcarving community through the application of three main strategies: 1) developing a network of woodcarving workers for self-care; 2) enhancing the capability for self-care among peer leaders of woodcarving workers; and 3) developing a guidebook for self-care and media for health promotion campaign among woodcarving workers.

After participating in the project, the project network (the village committee for health promotion, peer leaders, and researchers) learned new ways of thinking and problem-solving and ways to sustain self-care among wood carvers. Self-reliance was perceived as an important aspect of health care. Learning together was found to be the most important element for the network development. Understanding each other and recognizing the potential of team members was necessary to develop and sustain a network. Consultation meetings, workshops, participatory learning and reflection of lessons learned were helpful in sharing perspectives among the members of each team.

All of the activities were interesting to participants and they were successful in their goals. All network members actively participated in all activities. Most participants suggested continuing activities, and some of these activities were put into the yearly plan of local administrative organizations and health stations.

Finally, ultimate outcomes such as workers' health status, the perception of health risk, and health behaviors were improved. Lessons learned from this project included the problem identification process and community potential in problem solving, which is essential for promoting self-care and community strength. Although this project was successful in increasing health awareness of workers and the community, the long-term impacts and sustainability of networking and subsequent activities needs to be examined. Furthermore, co-operation with other relevant institutions or professions are suggested in order to produce and use guidebook and media materials with other wood-carving workers and to improve work conditions and the environment.

Implications of this Project

1. Wood-carving workers and entrepreneurs should bring the knowledge that they gained from the health care providers and peer leaders as well as from a guidebook for self-care and media material to continue promoting their self-care behaviors as well as protecting and preventing their health from work-related risk factors.

2. The community should bring the process learned in this project to identify and solve other health problems and assist in the solution of community-based issues by focusing on self-reliance, using a variety of resources from inside and outside the community.

3. Health care providers and relevant organizations should expand this project into other woodcarving communities.

4. Researchers and academic staff should apply these project strategies and research methods to conduct participatory action research in different areas. Through participation, they have a better understanding of how to establish a network of people and

stakeholders in the community for successfully conducting CBPR. After finishing this project our research team conducted four other research projects using CBPR with three main strategies.

5. Academic staff should take the lessons learned from this project and integrate them in their teaching and training of students. For example, a professor (first author) who teaches research to graduate students used this project as an example in her lecture on applying PAR to health problems and/or health concerns. Students practiced some aspects of the research processes in the community, such as data collection, conducting community forums, etc. Other academic staff from the Faculty of Mass Communication had students participate in developing media in the community such as the posters, spot announcements, and the VCD. PAR can be used as a method to introduce and engage students in the research process.

6. Health administrators and health policy makers should bring the lessons learned from this project to launch policies for promoting self-care behavior among people of working age. In addition, they should coordinate with multidisciplinary experts to improve health policy for work conditions and create healthy workplaces. This project was discussed at the National Health Assembly in 2011 and was voted as one of the top five examples of local empowerment and healthy public policy. It was selected as a site visit for the Asia and Pacific Regional Conference on Health Impact Assessment.

REFERENCES

Carr, W. & Kemmis, S. (1986). *Becoming critical: Education, knowledge and action research.* Victoria: Deakin University.

Chevalier, J. M. & Buckles, D. J (2013). *Participatory action research: Theory and methods for engaged inquiry.* Abingdon (UK): Routledge.

Cohen, J. & Uphoff, N. (1979). *Feasibility and Application of Rural Development Participation: State of the Art Paper.* New York: University of Cornell.

De Koning, K. & Martin, M. (1996). *Participatory research in health: Issues and experiences.* London: Zed Books.

Edwards, K., Lund, C., Mitchell, S. & Andersson, N. (2008). Trust the process: Community based researcher partnerships. *Pimatisiwin: A Journal of Aboriginal and Indigenous Community Health*, 6(2), 187-199.

Eisenberg, E. M., Baglia, J. & Pynes, J. E. (2006). Transforming emergency medicine through narrative: Qualitative action research at a community hospital. *Health Communication*, 19(3), 197–208.

Elliott, J. (1981). *Action research: Framework for self evalution in schools.* TIQL working paper No. 1. Cambridge Institution of Education.

Fals Borda, O. (1979). Investigating reality in order to transform it: The Colombian experience. *Dialectical Anthropology*, 4, 33–55.

Fals Borda, O. (1988). *Knowledge and people's power.* New Delhi: Indian Social Institute.

Freire, P. (1970). *Pedagogy of the Oppressed.* New York, Continuum.

George, A., Vickers, M. H., Wilkes, L. M. & Barton, B. (2006). Working and caring for a child with chronic illness: careerist concerns and stressful choices. *Proceedings of the 14th Annual International Conference 2006 of the Association on Employment Practices and Principles.*

Hills, M., Mullett, J. & Carroll, S. (2007) Community-based participatory research: Transforming multi-disciplinary practice in primary health care. *Pan American Journal of Public Health*, 21 (2-3), 125-35.

IBRD [International Bank for Reconstruction and Development]. (1980). Thailand: *Toward a strategy of full participation.* Washington D.C.: World Bank.

Kemmis, S. & McTaggart, R. (2000). Participatory action research. In K. N. Denzin & Y. S. Lincoln (eds.), *Handbook of qualitative research.* London: Sage.

Korten, D. C. & Klauss, R. (1984). *People centered development: Contributions toward theory and planning frameworks*. West Hartford: Kumarian Press.

Korten, D. (1990). *Getting to the 21st century: Voluntary action and the global agenda*. West Hartford: Kumarian Press.

Lewin, K. (1946). Action research and minority problems. In G. Lewin (Ed.), *Resolving social conflicts: Selected papers on group dynamics*, (pp. 201–216). New York: Harper and Row.

Maguire, P. (2008). *Doing Participatory Research: Feminist Approach*. Amherst: University of Massachusetts.

McKernan, J. (1996). *Curriculum action research: A handbook of methods and resources for the reflective practitioner*. New York: St. Martin's.

McNiff, J. (2010). *Action research for professional development: Concise advice for new and experienced action researchers*. Poole, Dorset: September Books.

Minkler, M. & Wallerstein, N. (2008). *Community-Based Participatory Research for Health: From Process to Outcomes*. San Francisco, CA: Jossey Bass.

Oakley, P. (1987). State or process, means or end? The concept of participation in rural development, Reading Rural Development Communications, *Bulletin 21*, Berkshire: Reading University.

Reason, P. & Bradbury, H. (2008). *The SAGE handbook of action research: Participative inquiry and practice*. London: Sage.

Todhunter, C. (2001). "Undertaking Action Research: Negotiating the Road Ahead", *Social Research Update*, Issue 34.

Turton, A. (1987). *Production, power and participation in rural Thailand: Experiences of poor farmers' groups* (Report No. 86.11). Geneva: UNRISD.

Wallerstein, N. & Duran, B. (2006). Using community-based participatory research to address health disparities. *Health. Promotion Practice*, *7*(3), 312-23.

Wang, Caroline C. (1999). Photo voice: a participatory action research strategy applied to women's health. *Journal of Women's Health*, *8*(2), 185-192.

White, L. P. & Phodeback, M. J. (1992). Ethical Dilemmas in Organization Development: A Cross-Cultural Analysis. *Journal of Business Ethics, 11*(9), 663–670.

Yimyam, S., Tiansawad, S., Wittayasakphan, J. & Jirapattarapimol, B. (2004). Enhancing Self-Care Among Woodcarving Workers: A case study of woodcarving Phase I (work conditions & health). *Technical report, unpublished document.* Chiang Mai: Faculty of Nursing, Chiang Mai University.

Yimyam, S., Tiansawad, S. & Senaratana, W. (2006). Enhancing Self-care of Wood Carving Workers: Community Participation. *Technical report, unpublished document.* Chiang Mai: Faculty of Nursing, Chiang Mai University.

Yimyam, S. & Jirapattarapimol, B. (2007). Work conditions and health promotion among woodcarving workers. *Thai Journal of Nursing Council, 22* (4), 79-100. [in Thai].

Yimyam, S., Tiansawad, S. & Senaratana, W. (2008). Enhancing Self-care of Wood Carving Workers: Community Participation. *Area Based Development Research Journal, 1*(2), 17-30.

INDEX

A

access, xiii, 79, 98, 103, 109, 150, 157, 160, 165, 169, 216, 227
accountability, 137, 142
acculturation, 248, 250
acquisition of knowledge, 240
action research, v, vi, vii, ix, x, xi, xii, xiii, xiv, 52, 80, 83, 84, 86, 87, 89, 90, 91, 92, 97, 103, 108, 110, 111, 112, 113, 116, 117, 118, 126, 127, 128, 129, 130, 131, 132, 136, 145, 146, 147, 148, 151, 152, 153, 157, 158, 164, 165, 166, 167, 170, 171, 172, 173, 175, 178, 191, 192, 193, 194, 195, 197, 198, 199, 200, 201, 202, 203, 204, 209, 210, 211, 212, 213, 215, 216, 217, 218, 219, 220, 224, 225, 227, 228, 229, 230, 231, 233, 234, 236, 241, 244, 245, 246, 252, 253, 256, 262, 268, 274, 279, 280, 281, 282
Activists, 128, 146
activity analysis, 154, 155, 172
adolescents, 82, 84, 238, 239, 241, 242, 243, 244, 245
American Educational Research Association, 88, 115, 118

analytic rationality, 128
Appadurai, A., 136, 145
art, ix, 53, 79, 83, 87, 90, 91, 95, 103, 104, 105, 106, 107, 109, 110, 111, 112, 113, 115, 119, 120, 204, 230, 258, 281
assessment, viii, xii, xiv, 43, 49, 70, 75, 102, 116, 171, 178, 181, 183, 187, 188, 192, 194, 197, 210, 221, 228, 230, 252, 266
asynchronous communication, 220
attitudes, 112, 155, 156
authenticity, 113, 208, 209, 219
autonomy, 186, 211, 226
awareness, viii, xv, 86, 106, 129, 158, 160, 182, 239, 242, 252, 261, 266, 277, 279

B

barriers, x, 4, 90, 107, 110
base, 8, 12, 45, 166, 227, 253
behaviors, xv, 60, 87, 91, 242, 252, 260, 262, 264, 265, 266, 267, 268, 269, 270, 279
benefits, viii, 1, 4, 11, 17, 24, 48, 55, 62, 64, 68, 106, 112, 165, 179, 201, 204, 256, 257, 260, 275
bias, 97, 99, 103, 122

Blumenreich, Megan, 78
Bobbitt, F., 154, 155, 171
bonding, viii, xiii, 216, 220, 222, 223
brainstorming, 70, 205, 237
Brazil, 137, 142, 150, 197
Bruner, Jerome, 60
bullying, 243, 244

C

campaigns, 256, 262, 267, 275, 276, 277
candidates, x, 126, 127, 130
Caro-Bruce, Cathy, 79
case study, viii, xiv, 138, 180, 183, 195,
    252, 283
causal relationship, 199
challenges, xii, 17, 75, 87, 94, 95, 96, 106,
    108, 111, 116, 130, 132, 134, 135, 144,
    165, 197, 201, 235
checklists, 70, 71, 72, 73, 74, 75, 80, 204,
    205
chemical, viii, xiii, 216, 220, 224, 228, 229,
    271
chemistry education, 216, 217, 218, 220,
    226, 227, 228, 230
children, 5, 7, 21, 32, 45, 47, 53, 55, 58, 59,
    65, 68, 69, 70, 71, 72, 75, 77, 80, 84, 85,
    86, 155, 166, 172, 187, 242, 244, 249
circulation, 12, 77, 130
citizens, 13, 14, 238, 243
citizenship, 10, 136, 172
classroom artifacts, 19, 20, 23
classroom environment, 7, 75
classroom teacher, 9, 66, 76, 107
climate, 83, 222, 228, 240
collaboration, xiv, 61, 105, 107, 116, 132,
    141, 142, 149, 165, 178, 183, 184, 189,
    192, 228, 245, 249, 252, 258, 261
collaborative working environment, 180,
    189, 191
college students, 96, 103

communication, 243, 265, 276
community development, 236, 253, 254,
    255
community innovators lab, 137, 141, 142,
    145, 149
community participation, xv, 252, 262, 265,
    283
community psychology, 236, 247
community service, 194
community-based participatory research,
    xiv, 252, 253, 256, 278, 281, 282
complexity, viii, xiv, 171, 234, 235, 256
composition, 189, 192, 224, 259
comprehension, 62, 84
compulsory education, viii, xii, 178, 182
computer, 112, 115, 116, 117, 230, 242
conception, 128, 185
conceptualization, xi, 151, 153, 157, 158,
    161, 170
confidentiality, 2, 63, 206
conflict, x, 90, 97, 99, 103, 108, 109, 110,
    111, 117, 228
conflict resolution, 109
confrontation, 182, 184
consciousness, 146, 208
consolidation, 171, 240
construction, ix, 57, 159, 184, 185, 198, 244
consulting, 200, 207, 220
content analysis, xv, 252, 268
context-specific knowledge, 128, 202
contextualization, 159, 172
continuous professional development, viii,
    xiii, 216, 225, 227
conversations, 12, 16, 19, 20, 21, 22, 36, 47,
    59, 60, 64, 65, 66, 70, 71, 77, 79, 82, 84,
    96, 106, 108, 137
cooperation, xiii, 165, 216, 217, 218, 220,
    225, 226, 227, 262, 264, 265
cooperative learning, 61, 231
coordination, 186, 260
creativity, 66, 107, 204, 205, 210

critical friends, 24, 84, 179, 183, 189, 194, 195
critical incidents, xii, 178, 189
critical PAR, 136
critical theory, 127
critical thinking, xii, 197
culture, 2, 43, 98, 120, 121, 122, 123, 153, 162, 163, 171, 258
culture media, 122
curricula, 4, 6, 15, 17, 48, 49, 94, 155, 156, 160, 161, 163, 172, 192
curricular materials, 156
curriculum contextualization, 159
curriculum design, 175, 217
curriculum development, 155, 156, 182, 217, 219, 227, 229
curriculum innovation, vi, 174, 215, 216
curriculum justification, 153
curriculum relevance, v, vii, xi, 151, 152, 153, 154, 155, 156, 157, 158, 159, 160, 161, 162, 163, 164, 165, 166, 167, 169, 170, 172, 173
curriculum studies, vii, xi, 151, 153, 154, 157, 158, 161, 170, 172, 175
cyberbullying, 238, 239, 243, 244
cycles, xii, 128, 139, 167, 197, 200, 202, 203, 208, 209, 210, 227
cyclical process, viii, xiv, 207, 221, 234, 235

deconstruction, 180, 192
democracy, 10, 52, 53, 83, 122, 128, 136
democratic capacity, 130, 136, 142, 143, 146
democratization, 136, 189, 192
Department of Education, 5, 53, 120, 177, 248
depth, 20, 27, 93, 133, 139, 140, 179, 267
Dewey, John, 9, 55, 60, 127, 128
dialogue, v, 17, 45, 57, 59, 60, 62, 64, 65, 70, 72, 74, 75, 99, 109, 122, 129, 130, 239, 247
dilemmas, 135, 137, 140, 179, 189, 190, 192
discussion groups, 58, 84, 183, 184, 189
discussions, vii, ix, x, xi, 3, 8, 9, 10, 15, 22, 39, 54, 57, 58, 59, 60, 61, 62, 64, 65, 66, 68, 70, 71, 72, 73, 74, 75, 76, 77, 81, 84, 96, 97, 99, 100, 101, 102, 103, 105, 108, 109, 126, 131, 132, 133, 137, 138, 139, 140, 143, 152, 153, 170, 179, 182, 183, 184, 185, 187, 189, 190, 207, 237, 240, 245, 247, 264, 266, 267, 268, 271
diversity, 61, 80, 88, 92, 94, 136, 159, 163, 211, 257
DJ (disc jockey), 273, 276
documentation, 7, 19, 20, 21, 47, 50, 132, 182, 184
drawing, 133, 135, 137

D

data analysis, 23, 65, 82, 96, 97, 133, 134, 170, 181, 190, 243
data collection, 21, 33, 49, 62, 64, 65, 96, 97, 99, 104, 134, 137, 138, 141, 165, 205, 206, 207, 210, 245, 254, 267, 280
data gathering, 133, 181, 190
DCI, 99, 100, 101, 102
decision makers, 200
decision-making process, 254, 255

E

educational experience, 105, 155
educational institutions, 144, 201, 210
educational materials, 265
educational objective, 156
educational process, 185, 198
educational research, viii, xii, 112, 131, 216, 218, 219, 220
educational services, 248
educational settings, 93, 110, 131, 204

educational system, 93, 178
educators, xiii, 2, 6, 7, 8, 9, 10, 11, 13, 14, 15, 16, 17, 18, 27, 46, 48, 49, 50, 61, 75, 78, 79, 80, 83, 92, 94, 95, 104, 110, 111, 122, 131, 147, 166, 200, 216, 219, 224, 225, 227, 242, 244, 245
eight year study, 156, 172
elaboration, 150, 182, 236, 240
elementary school, xi, 5, 8, 88, 152, 167
empower, 59, 77, 80, 136, 253
empowerment, v, ix, 57, 67, 80, 83, 91, 109, 129, 200, 245, 247, 253, 255, 257, 280
engagement, v, vii, ix, 87, 89, 90, 91, 95, 97, 99, 103, 106, 107, 109, 110, 120, 130, 132, 137, 138, 148, 149, 157, 165, 251, 253, 255, 257
engineering, vii, ix, 89, 90, 91, 95, 100, 111, 115, 116, 117
engineering education, 90, 115, 116
entrepreneurs, 261, 267, 275, 279
environment, xiii, xiv, xv, 7, 43, 61, 66, 75, 76, 84, 93, 104, 110, 115, 136, 180, 184, 186, 189, 191, 199, 202, 208, 216, 219, 220, 221, 222, 223, 224, 225, 227, 242, 249, 252, 253, 258, 261, 279
environmental sustainability, 149
ethical dilemmas, 135, 137, 140, 283
ethics, 132, 134, 141, 145, 283
everyday life, xiii, 16, 224, 233, 234
evidence, xi, xiii, 17, 47, 48, 59, 64, 67, 72, 74, 94, 109, 152, 182, 216
evolution, ix, 25, 90, 91, 111, 153
exclusion, 92, 112, 190
execution, vii, ix, 57, 236, 244
exercis(es), 30, 128, 136, 138, 242, 265, 272, 273
expertise, 130, 136, 219, 224, 225, 235, 254, 258
exposure, 4, 13, 110, 140
extrinsic motivation, 169, 173

F

facilitators, 99, 100, 166, 258
families, 5, 63, 80, 86, 169, 238, 239, 243, 244
feelings, xiv, 7, 20, 23, 62, 64, 108, 234, 236, 239
flexibility, 183, 186, 187, 189, 192
foundations, 13, 52, 122, 135, 182, 187
Franklin, Benjamin, 92
Freire, Paulo, 128, 129

G

general education, 112, 225
general systems thinking, 127
generalizability, 138, 144
geographical education, 153
geography, 31, 32, 153, 160, 173
Germany, xiii, 83, 215, 216, 220, 221, 224, 226, 230
grades, 2, 9, 54, 58, 70, 86, 161
graduate education, 139, 140, 144
graduate students, x, 90, 126, 127, 131, 143, 144, 280
group development, vi, 233, 234, 240, 246
growth, vii, ix, 1, 10, 17, 20, 23, 29, 30, 33, 37, 41, 44, 48, 49, 69, 73, 77, 86, 107, 208, 247, 257
guidance, 182, 202, 205, 225
guidelines, 70, 133, 185, 186, 187, 206, 261

H

Harvard Law School, 149
health care, xii, xv, 197, 202, 211, 252, 256, 257, 260, 261, 263, 264, 265, 266, 267, 268, 273, 275, 277, 278, 279, 281
health impact assessment, xiv, 252, 259, 264, 269, 280

health information, 260, 262, 266, 267, 269, 271, 272, 276

health problems, xiv, xv, 252, 259, 261, 265, 266, 267, 272, 273, 274, 275, 276, 277, 279, 280

health promotion, xiv, 252, 260, 262, 264, 265, 266, 267, 269, 271, 272, 273, 274, 275, 276, 277, 278, 283

health risks, 261, 267, 270, 271, 272, 274, 275, 276, 278

health services, 257, 260

health status, xv, 252, 259, 262, 264, 268, 269, 272, 279

higher education, vi, viii, xii, 122, 146, 148, 159, 177, 178, 193, 194, 195, 197, 198, 200, 201, 203, 210, 211, 213

history, 8, 9, 12, 14, 46, 47, 48, 50, 53, 54, 66, 79, 82, 91, 92, 95, 122, 127, 136, 153, 154, 161, 182, 188, 258

hypothesis, 102, 157, 204, 212, 240

I

identification, xv, 154, 182, 184, 252, 254, 255, 261, 279

images, 104, 106, 107, 109, 244, 258, 259

immersion, 90, 100, 109, 110

impact assessment, xiv, 252, 259, 264, 265, 269

improvements, xi, xii, 38, 70, 77, 97, 152, 170, 178, 183, 186, 191, 192, 199

individuals, 2, 80, 108, 136, 159, 234, 237, 239, 257, 258

informal education, 90, 98, 100, 103, 118

initial training, 179, 185, 192

innovation, xii, 137, 149, 177, 178, 183, 184, 190, 197, 216, 219, 228, 229

inquiry, 10, 52, 53, 86, 87, 88, 98, 128, 129, 135, 136, 141, 142, 143, 145, 146, 147, 158, 172, 180, 193, 195, 202, 212, 230, 254, 255, 257, 280, 282

institutions, xv, 145, 236, 238, 239, 252, 279

integration, ix, 90, 91, 95, 103, 104, 105, 106, 107, 108, 109, 110, 113, 180, 217, 223, 225, 227, 247

International Bank for Reconstruction and Development, 253, 281

intervention, 109, 131, 136, 180, 188, 207, 208, 209, 210, 236, 237, 245, 257

interviews, 19, 20, 21, 22, 167, 168, 169, 170, 183, 207, 264, 267

issues, x, xi, xii, 11, 61, 62, 70, 80, 84, 88, 111, 112, 116, 126, 131, 133, 137, 138, 141, 145, 152, 153, 157, 161, 165, 178, 180, 183, 188, 189, 192, 202, 230, 235, 239, 240, 241, 242, 243, 248, 254, 257, 261, 272, 273, 274, 276, 277, 279

J

journals, 20, 21, 23, 28, 29, 32, 55, 62, 63, 64, 65, 66, 67, 68, 69, 70, 71, 72, 73, 83, 84, 85, 110, 111, 112, 115, 122, 123, 145, 147, 148, 171, 172, 173, 175, 193, 194, 195, 211, 212, 228, 229, 230, 246, 247, 248, 249, 250, 281, 282, 283

justification, 153, 166, 230

K

K-12 STEM, 90, 97, 103

K-12 STEM education, 90

K-20, v, vii, ix, 89, 90, 95, 109, 110, 117

K-20 education, 90, 110, 117

Klehr, Mary, 79

knowledge, ix, xii, xiii, xv, 12, 25, 43, 45, 50, 63, 70, 75, 77, 86, 90, 94, 97, 98, 105, 107, 110, 112, 128, 129, 130, 132, 133, 134, 135, 136, 137, 138, 139, 142, 143, 144, 145, 146, 147, 148, 149, 154, 155, 157, 158, 159, 160, 162, 163, 165,

166, 177, 183, 191,192, 195, 198, 199, 200, 201, 202, 204, 207, 209, 211, 219, 221, 227, 231, 234, 236, 239, 240, 242, 243, 244, 245, 252, 255, 257, 261, 266, 272, 276, 277, 279, 280, 281

L

lack of confidence, 29
leadership, 13, 172, 198, 201
learners, 48, 50, 58, 82, 84, 156, 159, 160, 179, 184, 195
learning environment, 7, 115, 175, 220, 221, 222, 223, 224, 225
learning outcomes, 255
learning process, 14, 19, 46, 93, 204, 209, 225, 235
lesson plan, 220, 222
Lesson Study, xii, 177, 178, 193, 194, 195
Likert scale, 222
literacy, 2, 61, 62, 86, 242
literature circles, v, vii, ix, 57, 58, 59, 60, 61, 62, 63, 64, 65, 66, 67, 68, 69, 70, 71, 72, 73, 74, 75, 76, 77, 78, 80, 81, 82, 83, 84, 85, 86
lived experience, 128, 136
local government, 277
logical reasoning, 160

M

magnet schools, 5
management, 199, 212, 242, 255, 264, 265, 274
materials, xv, 61, 62, 105, 170, 205, 220, 252, 259, 265, 271, 279
mathematical achievement, 15
mathematical knowledge, 12, 50
mathematical literacy, 2
mathematical methods, 3

mathematics education, xi, 3, 8, 9, 10, 11, 12, 15, 16, 17, 50, 53, 54, 55, 152, 153, 230
meaningfulness, 162, 163, 164
media, xiii, xiv, xv, 121, 122, 147, 216, 224, 252, 262, 265, 268, 271, 276, 278, 279, 280
medical, 202, 248, 260
memories, viii, xii, 178, 182, 184, 188
mentor, 79, 96
mentoring, 82, 96
methodology, viii, x, xiii, 78, 87, 90, 97, 112, 199, 200, 201, 205, 233, 235, 236, 237, 239, 253, 254
migration, 248, 250
misconceptions, 65
mission, 94, 237
mixed team, 179, 180, 181, 183, 189, 190, 191, 192
models, 100, 129, 178, 179, 182, 228
modules, 135, 136, 140
monopoly, 146, 147
motivation, 162, 163, 164, 169, 173, 201, 210, 216, 223
multimedia, 220, 221
mutuality, 173, 175

N

narrative, 20, 122, 133, 138, 184, 199, 281
narrative analysis, 138
National Assessment of Educational Progress (NAEP), 12
National Council of Teachers of Mathematics (NCTM), 3, 10, 11
National Research Council, 13, 54
negotiation, 132, 148, 189, 240
network, xiii, xiv, 79, 174, 216, 219, 220, 224, 225, 226, 227, 228, 238, 239, 242, 244, 252, 260, 262, 264, 273, 274, 275, 277, 278, 279

network members, 277, 278
networking, viii, xiii, xv, 212, 216, 252, 275, 277, 279
NGOs, 149, 254, 261, 268
NGSS, x, 90, 94, 98, 99, 100, 101, 102, 103, 112

O

observations, 8, 19, 20, 99, 100, 205, 207
obstacles, 17, 47, 165, 190, 192
occupational health, 257, 275, 277
opportunities, 2, 16, 32, 61, 91, 104, 105, 109, 139, 171, 192, 200
organizational development, 254
organize, 24, 224, 229, 244
outreach, 116, 117
overlap, 9, 269
ownership, 61, 62, 83, 134, 166

P

parent-child relationship, 242, 249
parenting, 243, 249
parents, 5, 11, 15, 80, 97, 239, 241, 242, 243, 244
Parrell, Sara, 79
participants, xi, 6, 17, 18, 20, 22, 62, 91, 95, 96, 98, 99, 100, 102, 104, 106, 107, 108, 109, 152, 166, 167, 179, 201, 206, 207, 209, 235, 236, 239, 241, 266, 267, 269, 276, 277, 278
participatory action research, v, vi, vii, x, xii, xiii, xiv, 111, 125, 126, 127, 129, 132, 136, 137, 145, 146, 147, 172, 177, 178, 194, 215, 216, 218, 219, 227, 229, 231, 233, 234, 236, 237, 241, 245, 246, 247, 251, 252, 253, 256, 258, 262, 268, 274, 279, 280, 281, 282
pedagogical relationship, 179, 180, 184

pedagogy, x, xiii, 9, 50, 87, 93, 111, 122, 126, 127, 129, 131, 132, 134, 143, 144, 145, 146, 171, 211, 216, 217, 222, 225, 226, 281
peer leader, xiv, 252, 262, 264, 266, 267, 270, 273, 275, 276, 277, 278, 279
photovoice, 87, 235, 246, 247
physical exercise, 263, 267
physics, 92, 93, 115, 228
platform, 50, 104, 222
policy, 80, 130, 134, 148, 149, 150, 280
policy makers, 80, 235, 280
Portugal, xi, 151, 152, 167, 174
posters, xv, 252, 261, 265, 271, 272, 280
practical knowledge, 207, 255, 257
practical wisdom, 128
practice, x, xii, xiii, xiv, 3, 7, 12, 17, 18, 47, 52, 55, 68, 74, 78, 79, 82, 83, 86, 107, 111, 112, 117, 126, 127, 128, 129, 131, 135, 136, 137, 139, 140, 142, 143, 144, 145, 146, 147, 148, 156, 157, 159, 165, 173, 174, 177, 179, 180, 181, 182, 183, 184, 185, 186, 187, 190, 191, 192, 193, 194, 197, 198, 199, 200, 202, 204, 205, 209, 211, 216, 217, 219, 220, 225, 226, 228, 229, 230, 234, 239, 245, 246, 260, 266, 280, 281, 282
practicum, viii, xii, 178, 182, 184
preparation, 13, 262, 265
prevention, 242, 249, 266, 270, 272
principles, viii, xiv, 54, 61, 131, 135, 136, 140, 143, 144, 174, 252, 253, 256
problem solving, vii, ix, xv, 1, 7, 26, 30, 31, 32, 33, 35, 36, 37, 38, 39, 40, 41, 42, 43, 44, 45, 49, 106, 107, 157, 160, 231, 252, 275, 279
professional careers, 143, 144
professional development, viii, xiii, 2, 5, 76, 78, 87, 111, 116, 117, 140, 166, 178, 179, 192, 193, 194, 200, 201, 213, 216, 225, 227, 229, 230, 282
professional teacher, 179

project, vii, viii, ix, xi, xii, xiii, xiv, xv, 1, 2, 3, 17, 28, 31, 32, 45, 60, 64, 69, 75, 76, 77, 78, 79, 90, 91, 93, 95, 96, 97, 98, 99, 100, 102, 103, 104, 105, 106, 107, 108, 109, 110, 112, 130, 133, 137, 138, 141, 142, 152, 153, 157, 158, 164, 166, 167, 170, 172, 173, 175, 177, 178, 183, 184, 190, 194, 207, 210, 216, 218, 219, 220, 223, 224, 226, 227, 229, 234, 236, 237, 238, 239, 240, 241, 243, 244, 245, 249, 252, 255, 260, 262, 264, 265, 267, 268, 269, 271, 273, 274, 275, 276, 278, 279, 280
promotion campaigns, 262, 267, 275
protection, 242, 267, 272
psychological distress, 249
psychological processes, 85
psychological well-being, 237
psychology, 84, 248, 249, 250
public health, 253, 254
public schools, 92, 93
public science project, 132, 133, 137, 147

Q

qualitative research, x, 20, 52, 113, 126, 127, 133, 144, 193, 235, 245, 246, 247, 281
quality of life, 236, 248
quantitative methods, xiv, 133, 138, 252
quantitative research, x, 125, 126
questioning, 98, 179, 183
questionnaire, 222, 243

R

radio, xv, 252, 262, 266, 267, 271, 273, 276
radio spots, xv, 252, 271
rationality, 128, 129
reading, vii, ix, 23, 44, 57, 58, 60, 61, 62, 63, 67, 69, 77, 81, 82, 83, 84, 85

reality, xiv, 159, 234, 235, 246, 281
reasoning, 17, 32, 40, 41, 42, 43, 44, 45, 46
reasoning skills, 40
recognition, 132, 136, 259
recommendations, 13, 205, 245, 261, 264
reconstruction, 155, 156, 183
reconstruction of knowledge, 183
reflective practice, 127, 139, 145
reform mathematics, v, vii, viii, 1, 2, 3, 4, 8, 9, 12, 15, 16, 17, 18, 19, 20, 21, 22, 24, 25, 29, 30, 32, 33, 40, 46, 47, 48, 49, 50, 55
Reggio-inspired, 6, 7, 19, 47, 49, 55
relevance, vii, xi, 134, 151, 152, 153, 154, 155, 156, 157, 158, 159, 160, 161, 162, 163, 164, 165, 166, 167, 169, 170, 171, 172, 173, 179, 187, 208, 219, 224, 226, 230
research design, 18, 133, 134, 141, 255
research findings, x, 125, 126, 134, 137, 139, 166
research methods, x, 125, 126, 127, 133, 138, 144, 198, 199, 204, 207, 213, 248, 279
researcher, v, viii, xiii, 18, 19, 20, 22, 23, 50, 66, 89, 90, 91, 95, 97, 99, 108, 111, 122, 135, 142, 166, 172, 179, 182, 184, 185, 191, 193, 194, 195, 198, 199, 201, 202, 206, 208, 216, 219, 220, 227, 230, 236, 240, 250, 281
researcher engagement, 90
resistance, 165, 242
resolution, 128, 148
resource management, 149
resources, 16, 17, 75, 78, 204, 205, 211, 273, 276, 279
response, 10, 22, 37, 68, 100, 104, 106, 223, 262, 272, 273
restoration, 97, 99, 101, 102
risk assessment, xv, 252, 262, 266, 267, 272, 277
routines, 27, 46, 153, 167

S

Schön, Donald, 127
school climate, 243
school experiences, 184
school improvement, 230
school learning, 157
schooling, 18, 104
Schwab, J., 157, 173
science education, vii, ix, xi, xiii, 90, 91, 92,
    93, 94, 95, 98, 100, 103, 110, 112, 116,
    117, 119, 143, 152, 153, 160, 161, 164,
    170, 173, 215, 216, 217, 218, 220, 228,
    229, 230
science education research, 217, 220
scientific knowledge, ix, 90, 110, 128, 136,
    154
scientific method, 128, 135, 245
scientific understanding, 127
scope, x, 125, 126, 139, 206
secondary education, 54
secondary schools, 112, 160
secondary teachers, 103
self-care, xiv, 252, 253, 259, 260, 261, 262,
    265, 266, 267, 269, 270, 271, 272, 273,
    275, 276, 277, 278, 279, 280, 283
self-reflection, 49, 254
self-reliance, xv, 252, 277, 278, 279
seminars, 183, 185, 205, 206, 207, 210
social change, xiii, 111, 128, 130, 135, 137,
    139, 144, 146, 160, 234, 235, 236, 246,
    253
social class, 155, 157
social construct, 98, 121
social justice, 80, 87, 88, 91, 109, 136, 137,
    166, 255
social movements, 129, 157
social psychology, 246, 248
social workers, 237, 238, 245

society, ix, 1, 8, 13, 14, 16, 17, 25, 27, 32,
    50, 85, 93, 94, 95, 113, 128, 153, 155,
    160, 164, 171, 182, 198, 235, 257
solution, 15, 44, 204, 205, 206, 207, 208,
    240, 279
specialists, 9, 17, 156
specific knowledge, 128, 202
Spencer, J., 154, 171, 173
spot announcements, 266, 272, 276, 280
standardized testing, 75
statistics, 102, 212, 268
STEM, v, vii, ix, 89, 90, 91, 95, 98, 104,
    110, 112, 113, 115, 117, 119
STEM integration, 90, 95, 110, 119
structure, viii, xiv, 6, 13, 84, 100, 105, 131,
    135, 143, 202, 203, 204, 222, 223, 225,
    226, 229, 234
student autonomy, 186
student creativity, 66
student development, 50
student participation, viii, xii, 178, 186, 192
student teacher, xiii, 216
style, 61, 107, 199, 217, 261, 273
sustainability, viii, xv, 252, 277, 279
sustainable community, 273, 277
sustainable development, 253
sustainable self-care, xv, 252, 277
Switzerland, xiii, 215, 216, 220, 222, 226

T

teacher journal, 21, 23, 64
teacher research, viii, ix, xiii, 1, 2, 18, 19,
    45, 50, 53, 54, 57, 76, 77, 78, 79, 80, 82,
    86, 87, 195, 216, 220, 227
teacher training, 184, 201, 210
teachers, xi, xii, xiii, 2, 7, 11, 13, 15, 16, 17,
    19, 25, 32, 46, 47, 48, 50, 58, 60, 61, 76,
    77, 79, 80, 93, 99, 103, 104, 105, 106,
    107, 111, 112, 115, 116, 117, 121, 131,
    139, 152, 157, 158, 165, 166, 167, 171,

178, 179, 180, 182, 183, 185, 186, 187, 188, 194,195, 197, 198, 200, 201, 202, 203, 204, 205, 208, 210, 211, 212, 216, 217, 218, 219, 220, 224, 225, 227, 228, 229, 230, 238, 241, 242, 245, 268, 275, 276

team interactions, 104

team members, 167, 169, 278

teams, 157, 165, 179, 183, 189, 191, 192

techniques, 3, 5, 59, 64, 69, 74, 113, 115, 133, 134, 135, 165, 180, 183, 206, 236, 275

technologies, xiv, 234, 235, 236, 237, 238, 239, 243, 245

tension(s), 21, 108, 109, 135, 139, 140, 155, 164, 165

territory, 237, 238, 241, 242, 243, 245

testing, 6, 171, 199, 207, 219, 265

textbook, 9, 12, 15, 123, 93

Thailand, 251, 258, 259, 262, 274, 281, 282

theories of practice, 127, 139, 140, 142, 144

thoughts, 7, 20, 21, 22, 24, 32, 98, 106

training, xv, 46, 92, 133, 179, 180, 182, 183, 185, 187, 188, 191, 192, 210, 239, 240, 241, 242, 243, 248, 249, 252, 266, 276, 278, 280

transformation, xiv, 53, 129, 131, 184, 192, 208, 234, 235, 240

types of action research, 217, 218, 230

U

undergraduate education, 2

United States (USA), 4, 10, 17, 53, 54, 55, 58, 88, 92, 127, 141, 142, 156, 157, 230

university teaching, 178, 191

urban, 2, 4, 86, 118, 127, 130, 134, 141, 150

V

variables, 157, 159, 162, 199, 206, 208

VCD, xv, 252, 266, 271, 272, 280

videotapes, 71, 72, 73, 76

virtual documentation, 182

vision, 8, 12, 14, 19, 46, 157, 185, 188, 189

vocational education, xiii, 165, 172, 216, 225, 226

vocational education and training, 172

vocational school, vi, 215, 216, 220, 222

Vygotsky, Lev, 60, 84, 85, 98, 113

W

well-being, xiv, 234, 236, 237, 239, 243, 245, 247, 248, 250, 259

wood-carving workers, viii, xiv, 252, 253, 262, 264, 266, 267, 268, 271, 272, 273, 274, 277, 279

workers, viii, xiv, xv, 252, 253, 259, 260, 261, 262, 264, 266, 267, 268, 269, 270, 271, 272, 273, 274, 275, 277, 278, 279, 283

workplace, 16, 17, 260, 263, 267, 270, 275, 277

Y

young adults, 247

young people, 137, 173

Z

Zeichner, Ken, 79

zone of proximal development, 61

zoology, 92